A
Year
Full
of
Pots

BLOOMSBURY PUBLISHING
Bloomsbury Publishing Plc
50 Bedford Square, London, WC1B 3DP, UK
29 Earlsfort Terrace, Dublin 2, Ireland

BLOOMSBURY, BLOOMSBURY PUBLISHING and the Diana logo
are trademarks of Bloomsbury Publishing Plc

First published in Great Britain 2024

A catalogue record for this book is available from the British Library

Library of Congress Cataloguing-in-Publication data has been applied for

ISBN: HB: 978-1-5266-6747-2
eBook: 978-1-5266-6746-5

10 9 8 7 6 5 4 3 2 1

Project Editor: Zena Alkayat
Designer: Glenn Howard
Photographer: Jonathan Buckley
Illustrator: Esther Palmer
Botanical proofreader: Jamie Compton
Proofreader: Claudia Connal
Indexer: Hilary Bird

Printed in China by Toppan Leefung Printing Ltd

MIX
Paper | Supporting
responsible forestry
FSC® C104723

To find out more about our authors and books visit
www.bloomsbury.com and sign up for our newsletters

Cover A classic Boiled-sweet
Brilliant (see p28) tulip collection,
including the pink 'Mariette',
orange, scented 'Ballerina',
'Sarah Raven' and 'Unique de
France', in long tom pots along
the path in the Perennial
Cutting Garden.

A
Year
Full
of
Pots

Container flowers
for all seasons

Sarah
Raven

BLOOMSBURY PUBLISHING
LONDON · OXFORD · NEW YORK · NEW DELHI · SYDNEY

Photographs by
Jonathan Buckley

6   *Introduction*
Adding colour, form and an essential
flourish with pots

14   *Designing Pots*
Simple rules for outstanding combinations

46   *January & February*
Early container colour and new year cheer

58   *Primulas*
66   *Hyacinths*
80   *Practical: planning quantities;*
        sowing sweet peas

88   *March*
The month of transformation

96   *Early tulips*
104   *Narcissi*
118   *Pot toppers*
124   *Practical: sowing for pots;*
        pricking out

132   *April*
A colour crescendo from bulb lasagnes

140   *Main season tulips*
170   *Practical: planting hardy annuals;*
        taking dahlia cuttings

178   *May*
The return of the tender perennials

188   *Violas*
196   *Practical: dismantling pots;*
        preparing for planting

204   *June*
An early summer show and flowers
for the vase

214   *Nemesias*
224   *Practical: creating plant supports;*
        making pot fertiliser

230 July
The pot garden becomes a jungle

240   *Pelargoniums*
256   *Petunias*
264   *Practical: watering; feeding pots*

270 August
An extravaganza of flowering pot plants

276   *Drought-tolerant plants*
282   *Shade-tolerant plants*
288   *Dahlias*
308   *Practical: creating bulb designs;*
      taking tender perennial cuttings

312 September
Our tender perennial climbers reach their peak

318   *Scented plants*
328   *Annual climbers*
340   *Practical: sowing pot toppers;*
      forcing bulbs

346 October
Grouping pots for an autumn show

354   *Salvias*
364   *Long and late performers*
372   *Plants for pollinators*
378   *Practical: planting bulbs;*
      adding pot toppers

382 November & December
Hardy flowering plants take centre stage

392   *Amaryllis*
398   *Practical: planting bulb lasagnes;*
      forcing paperwhite narcissi

406 Index
414 Acknowledgements

From left to right *Narcissus* 'Minnow', *N.* 'Prinses Amalia' and *Muscari armeniacum* 'Siberian Tiger'; tulips 'Orange Princess', 'Antraciet', 'Black Hero' and 'Royal Acres' with *Erysimum* 'Sugar Rush Purple Bicolour'; *Nemesia* 'Sunsatia Plus Papaya', *Calibrachoa* Superbells Unique 'Tropical Sunrise' and *N.* 'Framboise'; *Dahlia* 'Mystic Dreamer', *Scabiosa incisa* 'Kudo Pink' and *Verbena peruviana* 'Endurascape White Blush'.

Introduction

Pots are essential to the character of every part of the garden at my home, Perch Hill. Get the pots right and the garden will take on an ebullient, cheerful energy of its own. Perch Hill would lose something absolutely vital without them and that's true of any garden, large or small, sunny or shady, paved or lawned. They are the bubbles in the glass of champagne, the cherries on the cake, the grace notes of a composition. They are the essential flourish in the creation of a beautiful garden.

With pots, there is one cast iron rule: more is more. I follow that rule to the letter. I've just had a walk round the garden and counted 382 of them. Forty-eight whoppers, all about 60cm (2ft) tall and wide, including six large water troughs, 160 medium-sized containers, an average of 50cm x 40cm (20in x 16in) and a bevy of small pots, 15cm (6in) high or less. I'm not saying that as a boast but, having tended thousands of pots over the course of two decades, I have learnt what works and what doesn't. I now know which plants are the outstanding performers, looking good for longest without needing much primping, and also how best to combine plants. And one of the central gardening passions of our head gardener, Josie Lewis, is creating exciting and beautiful pot combinations that work brilliantly together. That's what you'll find in this book.

I moved from London to Perch Hill in East Sussex in May 1994 with my husband, Adam Nicolson, who is a writer. Our eldest daughter was then 10 months old. I was still in the final stages of training to be a doctor, working pretty ruinous hours. As a contrast to the white-coat life of the hospital ward, the garden became my haven and creative space. By 1996, my second daughter was born and I put medicine on hold. I started growing cut flowers and, after a year or two, I also began writing and then teaching about what I had learnt. I made a garden and built the foundation of the online nursery, as well as the garden school that now occupies one of the farm buildings here. The garden has continued to expand to 1½ acres and, with it, our team of gardeners – and we all sow, grow and assess plants as we go.

Over the last few decades, we've trialled and tested several thousand different container plants for our online nursery and have gradually identified many great performers. We've also worked out design rules for planting combinations and we've experimented with a range of composts, as well as feeding and watering regimes, so I can give you tried and tested advice on all of these practical things.

Pots are absolutely everywhere in our garden. We have an area on the north side of the house known as the Dutch Yard devoted to pots of all shapes and sizes. We have pots lining our paths in both cutting gardens as well as the Oast Garden.

Previous page Feeding a huge pot full of two matching argyranthemums, 'Grandaisy Red' and 'Madeira Red'.
Below and opposite Traditional dolly tubs filled with tulips in spring, and dahlias (including 'Dalaya Devi') with half-hardy annuals (such as *Cuphea* 'Torpedo') in summer.
Next page The Oast Garden at its spring peak with tulips a go go in lots of pots and repurposed water troughs. Tulips in containers are a key player in achieving an abundant look and feel in the garden.

The steps and doors on both sides of the barn are laden with pots, and we have tables and plant theatres (shelves carrying pots in layers) packed with containers on our terrace and also in shade by our back door.

We crowd together pots at all the gates and entrances to give a sense of anticipation – a need to find a way through. This technique applies as much to small city yards as it does to large rural gardens and it's one we stick to in our Dutch Yard, which has a slightly urban feel. In spring, I love having a range of pots of all sizes filled with the same family of plants, starting with crocuses and irises and then moving to narcissi or tulips as the weeks go by. In summer, we then fill the whole bricked space with combinations of dahlias in large pots, with clutches of smaller pots filled with equally long performers such as gerberas, verbenas and nemesias (to create a lower storey) and tender perennial climbers (for good vertical shapes and interesting silhouettes).

I'm a great believer in having a few rules to steer the planning of what to sow, grow or buy, and to help get one's combinations spot on. We bear these in mind when we do our pot plan for summer and autumn in the quiet months at the start of the year, and then again in September at the start of bulb-planting time.

To make life easier, we have some low-maintenance perennial pots planted with things like agapanthus, phygelius and the more compact varieties of honeysuckle, buddleja and hydrangea. But on the whole, we change our pot contents and designs twice a year.

I'll give you recipes to copy – and spur you on to invent your own – so you can have pots packed with colour, drama and brilliance all through the year. Having spectacular pots at Perch Hill is one of our central garden themes and I hope, with this month-by-month guide, I'll show you enough good combinations, and how we made them, to inspire you to make pots that you will love month after month.

Designing Pots

Carefully choosing which plants to grow is the enjoyable starting point of any good pot design. We have various rules of thumb at Perch Hill that we keep in mind as we put together the planting schemes for our pots.

The first thing we think about is the flowering period of each plant. If it's a mix of flower colour that we're aiming for, we need to make sure the plants perform at the same time. There is no point planting sweet peas to climb up a frame above a clump of dahlias: the sweet peas will be looking ropey by the time the dahlias hit their stride. Instead of sweet peas, you'll need a late-season tender perennial climber such as thunbergia, ipomoea or rhodochiton. These, each combined with dahlias, create a series of pairings we use successfully here all the time.

This consideration of timing is important with spring bulbs, too. If you're designing great colour combinations, then you need to make sure the bulbs are all in flower concurrently, so checking each plant's peak flowering moment is key.

Occasionally, particularly in spring, we deliberately do the opposite: we choose bulb varieties that flower one after another, performing in succession to give us a long-flowering season. We struck upon a good design to achieve this longevity in a spot we describe as our calm colour area, which sits around the lawn on the north side of the barn. All the plants in this part of the garden are white or very soft pink mixed with silver and green. The pot design was a lasagne (the bulbs layered, one on top of the other) and included an exceptionally early tulip called 'Ice Stick', followed by the early to mid-season tulip 'Purissima',

Previous page *Dahlia* 'Molly Raven', *Hibiscus acetosella* 'Mahogany Splendor' and *Rhodochiton atrosanguineus*; these plants are chosen because they flower together and each fulfil different roles: the dahlia is the Thriller, the hibiscus is the Pillar and Filler, and the rhodochiton is a Pillar as well as a Spiller (see p43).

Opposite A collection of pots from March to May with a succession of flowers in soft, cool shades to enhance the calm feeling around our lawn. First comes *Tulipa* 'Ice Stick', then *T.* 'Purissima' and, finally for May, *T.* 'Angélique' with *Narcissus* 'Xit'. These bulbs are planted together in a bulb lasagne (see p399).

and concluded with tulip 'Angélique' and the strongly scented daffodil 'Xit', which both flower late. With all four planted in a series of dolly tubs and old farm troughs, we had pots that looked good from the start of March to the middle of May – a good ten-week season. That was a success!

Beyond timing, it's also important to know that what you're planting together is compatible in a pot, in that one doesn't behave like a thug and push out the others. We find this can be a problem in our pot trials, as we don't necessarily know how the plants are going to behave. We had this issue when we trialled the super vigorous *Petunia* 'Tidal Wave Red Velour' (a massive favourite of mine), as it choked the more delicate things we tried to combine it with. *Anagallis monellii*, *Cosmos atrosanguineus* and any of the compact, annual cosmos didn't stand a chance – the petunia just carpeted them over. Our carefully considered colour combinations evolved quickly into monoplant, monochrome pots, and that was a disappointment. Finally, we found that dahlias can hold their own with this petunia (pictured on p23).

The most crucial design point for me is colour. Colour has always been key in the garden here with calm colours as important as the strong oranges, scarlets and crimsons. I love colour and firmly believe that all hues and tones can be beautiful depending on how they're combined. But, to make a success of a wide range of shades – particularly for pots, as the plants are packed in cheek by jowl – it's useful to have a set of rules.

The same goes for the forms and habits of the plants you combine. The larger the pots become, the more important it is to think about how the plants mix together, with elements for contrast so that the pots are not just a low mound with nothing to draw the eye. Instead, you could include a plant that naturally grows up, another down and something airy in between. To get form spot on, it's useful to follow some design principles.

The following pages are, in a nutshell, my go-to rules and tips for all of these aspects of pot design. With these up your sleeve, creating great pots should be a breeze. Use them as a basis and experiment with them as much as you can. The more pots you put together, the more you'll see that these rules really work, so much so that you can start to break them a bit. Spring, summer, autumn or winter, you'll see pots following these principles at Perch Hill, tried and tested for three decades.

Top *Tulipa* 'Sarah Raven' has great shape and colour, so works perfectly en masse in a pot on its own. It's perennial too – lift the bulbs and plant them in the garden after flowering.
Bottom *Pelargonium* 'Pink Aurore' in a repurposed water trough. Deadheaded every couple of weeks, this flowers well all through summer. It's so showy, it needs nothing with it.

Colour

When it comes to colour, the key is to avoid the liquorice all-sorts look, with yellow, pink, white, blue, black and orange all thrown in together resulting in pots competing with each other. That's too busy – and noisy – and easily ends up looking a mess. A bit of rigour here helps with decision-making and, ultimately, pot-design success.

Option 1: A single plant in a single pot or multiple pots

One type of plant in one pot can be wonderful: a clump of gaura, the compact *Euphorbia hypericifolia* 'Diamond Frost', or the ever-flowering *Erigeron karvinskianus*. We use these in small and medium pots repeating through the garden – in lines down paths, sitting on tables or steps, all gently echoing one another. And we do this quite a bit with tulips, massing just one variety in a large pot on its own. Particularly if we choose a showy form, such as the lacquer-red 'Pretty Woman' or my namesake, 'Sarah Raven' – it can deliver a real punch if the pot is placed at a prominent corner or somewhere that leads the eye to a view.

Similarly, in the summer and autumn, having a mass of one pelargonium we know flowers for ages (such as 'Shrubland Rose', 'Pink Aurore' or 'Aurora') in a giant pot on a central table can look marvellous. Or one dahlia. I love the gargantuan pot we place at the entrance to the Oast Garden, which we fill with three tubers of *Dahlia* 'Black Jack' growing on their own (pictured on p414). Standing over 3m (10ft) tall, including its pot, this dahlia looks fantastic, with its classy, ebony-washed stems and leaves, and huge, almost black flowers from late summer until the first frost. The scale and drama give it an Alice in Wonderland feel, and is just what we want as a sentry post guarding the jungle-like Oast Garden.

Option 2: Multiple plants in a single colour in multiple pots

We also make families of pots each containing a different plant, but all in a matching colour. Much like option 1, this is simple but striking, but takes it one step up in terms of showiness.

We've had many examples of this over the years. One of my a favourites is a group of pots that create a purple corner as you come into the Dutch Yard. There's *Angelonia angustifolia* 'Archangel Dark Rose' in a zinc container beside a huge pot containing *Cleome* 'Señorita Rosalita' and *Dahlia* 'Abigail', and in a smaller planter, the velvety *Nemesia* 'Lady Lisa'. They all produce purple flowers in a similar tone and, between them, look good from May until the end of October, their vibrant colours glowing amid the deep green rosemary that is planted all around them in that corner.

Bear in mind, green doesn't really count as a garden colour. We are sort of blind to it, like the white of a page. That's not *always* true, but you can assume the darker greens are largely neutral, acting as background, so with the purple of these plants, you're adding just one colour.

Below *Petunia* 'Tidal Wave Silver' billows out of one pot and pretty perfectly matches the flower colour of *Phlox* '21st Century Blue Star' below it.
Opposite *Cleome* 'Señorita Rosalita' and *Dahlia* 'Abigail' in the top pot, with *Nemesia* 'Lady Lisa' and *Angelonia angustifolia* 'Archangel Dark Rose' in the pots below.

Option 3: Multiple plants in a single colour in a single pot

Opposite This is the White Pot Collection: it includes *Cosmos bipinnatus* 'Sonata White' with matching *Phlox* '21st Century White' and *Osteospermum* 'Akila White Purple Eye'.

Below left *Dahlia* 'Dalaya Devi' and *Petunia* 'Tidal Wave Red Velour' matching perfectly in the same container. Both are strong growers so they are compatible.

Below right *Phlox* '21st Century Blue', *Heliotropium arborescens* 'Marine' and *Lavandula dentata* in a purple pot combination.

When I first started creating large numbers of pot combinations, I tended to stick with multiple plants in the same colour. I started with a White Pot Collection, which I put together over a decade ago for the online nursery and I still love: a compact *Cosmos bipinnatus* 'Sonata White', *Osteospermum* 'Akila White Purple Eye' and *Phlox* '21st Century White'. There's just enough contrast from the osteospermum's purple eye to make the trio sing.

I'm also particularly keen on a crimson-themed design we plant most years that includes just two plants, *Dahlia* 'Dalaya Devi' and *Petunia* 'Tidal Wave Red Velour'. This pairing is a huge success, between them flowering from May or June until the end of October. They are a rich colour duo with texture to match.

During summer and autumn, you'll see lots of pots using this single-colour, multiple-plant recipe at Perch Hill. It's a really safe option: simply choose your favourite colour for a certain spot in the garden and really go for it. If the growth rates of the plants are compatible, you can't go wrong.

Option 4: Multiple plants in multiple colours in a single pot

Below I love this tulip collection, the epitome of palette 2, Boiled-sweet Brilliant (see p28). It's in the Oast Garden at Perch Hill and features tulips 'Muriel' as the Bride, 'Nightrider' as the Bridesmaid and 'Orange Favourite' as the all-important colour contrasting Gatecrasher (see p38).
Opposite A beautiful soft mix of tulips around the lawn. These are Double Lates, which are very long-flowering, and include 'White Touch' (Bride), 'Danceline' (Bridesmaid) and the famous 'La Belle Epoque' (a gentle Gatecrasher) together with *Heuchera sanguinea* 'Splendens'.

This option – where we combine colours in pots and across pots – is where I really hit my stride. I love the flamboyance this can give you. It's like a really good vase of flowers, but rather than lasting a week, it lasts for more like 12 or even 16 weeks, if you get the plants right.

To help us get these mixes spot on – so they are colourful and joyful, not a random, felt-tip-pen-set jamboree – I have devised four colour palettes of compatible colours that I know work well together and look beautiful. Each of these groups give a slightly different feel. Do you want your pots to seem velvety and enveloping (palette 1)? Or stand alone, crisp and smart (palette 4)? Do you fancy pots that excite and pull you in (palette 2) or ones that are calming and in what I call cashmere jersey colours (palette 3)? Palettes 1 and 3 are earthy, with a certain muddiness to them, which I think feels rich. Palette 2 and 4 have a greater clarity and radiance. You'll have your favourites.

Palette 1: Dark and Rich

This palette is my first love. A rich family of colours: conker brown, nearly black, copper, gold, vermilion (or red-orange), olive green, deep purple, indigo and, above all, crimson. They suck up the light. I think of them as the velvet colours you want to wrap yourself in. These are all earthy colours and very saturated. I used to group palettes 1 and 2 together, calling them Rich and Brilliant, but have come to see them as two similar but distinct families – this one earthy yet refined, the next one more vibrant and luminous.

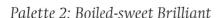

Palette 2: Boiled-sweet Brilliant

Next come the brilliant colours:
blackcurrant, raspberry, strawberry,
orange, lemon, lime and cobalt blue. These,
to me, are translucent, like stained glass.
They are joyful and light on their feet,
but we need to take care not to get carried
away. This palette can quickly descend into
what looks like a pre-schooler's painting.

To avoid too much razzmatazz, select
just a couple of colours and stick to them.
The first colour should dominate and
the second should be used sparingly, as a
sprinkling, filling no more than a third of
the overall design. We often have a mass
of orange flowers here, with a smattering
of blackcurrant. Orange is also great with
cobalt, as is raspberry or fuchsia with lime.

Palette 3: Soft and Warm

The third family of colours have plenty of white in them, so that orange, brown, gold or crimson become peach, milky coffee, ivory, apricot (with more yellow in it than peach), faded coral and muted, smoky pink. This palette is fashionable at the moment, with a vintage, 1970s air.

I think of these as cashmere jersey colours, lovely to wear and work with, but you don't want too much of a good thing – you wouldn't wear cashmere top-to-toe. This palette benefits from a splash of copper or bronze, or a bit of sobriety from crimson or mahogany from palette 1. This stops the colour combinations becoming too cloying.

Palette 4: Soft and Cool

Finally, there's the cool lot, where mauves, soft blues, blue-pinks, primrose yellows and off-whites continue getting paler until you reach the purest bright white flower. For me, the perfect real life version of the white end of this palette is the White Garden at Sissinghurst Castle in June, when clouds of white flowers in full bloom are joined by bold, silver leaves from plants like cardoons and the giant thistle, *Onopordum acanthium*.

This is what I think of as the chicest palette, very crisp and smart, like well-pressed clothes and elegant stilettos.

Mixing Palettes

Top left Tulips 'Sarah Raven'
together with 'Lasting Love' from
palette 1 and 'Ballerina' from
palette 2 to brighten and sharpen
the combination.
Top right Tulips 'Ballerina',
'Mariette' and 'Unique de France'
from palette 2 calmed by 'Sarah
Raven' from palette 1.
Bottom left Tulips 'Copper Image',
'Apricot Foxx' and 'Apricot Copex'
from palette 3, with 'Ridgedale'
from palette 1 stopping the
combination from being too sweet.
Bottom right White tulips
'Purissima' and 'Exotic Emperor'
from palette 4 are brought to even
greater life by *Cerinthe major*
'Purpurascens', whose purple
flowers belong in palette 2, while its
soft and cool leaves live in palette 4.

If you want to be safe, you can stick with one palette – the colours will always be compatible. But we sometimes borrow one colour from a different family to refine and open up our combinations. Some borrowed colours work well, but others truly don't.

There's no (or very little) white in the colours grouped in the first two palettes, but plenty in the other two. Many of the same colours in palettes 1 and 2 are the basis of palettes 3 and 4, but they are softer versions, with pastel shades that reduce the colour intensity. So there are opportunities to play around with combinations, and that's just what we do at Perch Hill.

1 Dark and Rich

These rich colours all look wonderful together but can benefit from a splash of a single colour from palette 2. If I'm using lots of plants with flowers and leaves of mahogany and crimson, I'll often use gold (from the same palette) to brighten it, or take orange or lime from palette 2 and use it as a light dusting.

All importantly, though, this borrowed colour should not take over – it shouldn't total more than a third of the overall flower colour, or even just a quarter. Think of it like a squeeze of lemon over smoked salmon, the citrus sharpener lifting and setting off any richness. Using a boiled-sweet colour in this way prevents this dark palette from becoming too sombre.

2 Boiled-sweet Brilliant

Borrowing a little mahogany, bronze or crimson from palette 1 is good for a dash of sobriety when planting pots in palette 2 – the dark shades calm down the zingy citrus colours in a good way. Again, don't use too much as it will make the combination heavy. We find crimson and nearly black useful in our pot combinations, and you'll see plenty of examples of that throughout the book.

3 Soft and Warm

The colours in this family are quite earthy and organic at one end with milky coffee a good example, moving to a bit sweety-sweet with the peaches and apricots. Neither looks good with the clear brilliants of palette 2 or the sharp cool shades of palette 4. But they are lovely with crimson, bronze or copper from palette 1, which are also earthy. These will add depth and cut through what can be a cloying sugariness. You'll see this mix put to use in lots of our tulip collections.

4 Soft and Cool

This is the trickiest palette to mix successfully with the others and I think, in the end, it is really best kept on its own. The whites can mix with the warmer ivories in palette 3, as well as the clear purples from palette 2, but they don't bring the house down.

Mixing Colours

When mixing colours, even within one palette, it's useful
to have a hierarchy to work out how to best combine plants.

First, select your Bride, the star of the show, the attention
seeker. A classic for spring would be a showy tulip, something
with peony-like flowers from the Double Early or Double Late
groups. For summer, it might be a dahlia or a pelargonium.

Once you have the Bride, it's easy to choose the next
ingredient, which is what I call the Bridesmaid, as it's the
same colour as the Bride, but smaller and less conspicuous.
It backs up the Bride, but does not compete with her. If you've
got an impressive tulip for your spring pot, then partner it
with a smaller-flowered tulip, a narcissus or maybe a scented
wallflower. In summer, this could well be a grass such as
Panicum capillare 'Sparkling Fountain', a rudbeckia or a
zinnia – all lovely, but a little less noisy than the dahlia Bride.
I recommend filling about three quarters of the pot, with
these two, using equal amounts of both.

Finally, it's the all-important Gatecrasher. This provides a colour contrast, which brings the whole pot to life. Without the Gatecrasher, things can look a little boring, but when they're there, you know you've got a party. For spring, you could stick with a contrasting-coloured tulip or a seed-grown annual like cerinthe, which if sown early will flower at tulip time. For summer, this might be another more delicate dahlia or an osteospermum, petunia or tumbling calibrachoa. But this Gatecrasher mustn't be allowed to dominate – don't let it fill more than a third or even just a quarter of the pot.

You may know straight away which palette you prefer and how you're going to mix it. But if not, there are ways to try out colour combinations without having all the plants to hand.

Using colour swatches from a paint shop is useful. I also find coloured candles or skeins of wool excellent (which is apparently what Van Gogh used when working out his palettes) as they give you a flower-like density of colour, which is more like the end result than small paper swatches. So set yourself up with one or the other and have a play with the colours until you work out which combinations are right for you.

Once you've chosen your palette (or two), the 'best of' selections in this book will set you on the right track for beautiful pot designs.

Where to Place Your Pots

The colours you choose will be led by personal preference and the feel you're after, but the position of the pots should influence your choices too. The backdrop, the setting, the things already planted in the location, as well as what makes up the ground and walls, all have an impact on how the colours will be seen.

As I've already said, we have pale plants including whites around our lawn. It's important to us that this area is calm and quiet throughout the year and the colours used in the pots need to reflect this. The pale colours in palettes 3 and 4 are also super useful in the darker parts of a garden. That's where we have many of our ivory, white, cream and pale yellow plants, brightening gloomy corners. You can have a scattering of another colour (such as purple or blue), but the overall effect

needs to be white. We use white or very pale-coloured flowers in all our areas of dappled shade, be it in spring with very pale narcissus (such as 'Thalia', 'Xit' and 'Silver Chimes') or equally pale tulips (such as 'Exotic Emperor' and 'Purissima'), or in summer and autumn with pastel-coloured foxgloves or the tobacco plants, *Nicotiana sylvestris* 'Only the Lonely' and *N. alata* 'Grandiflora'. And finally, the cool pale pinks, whites and mauves of palette 4 are used in the Farmhouse Garden. This space leads out to a view of the fields and woods beyond the house and we want it to blend in with that landscape – cool, calm colours seem to achieve this best.

The strong, bright colours of palettes 1 and 2 are collected in the Oast Garden, as we want this space to be exciting and stimulating. And we usually go for brights down the central path in the Perennial Cutting Garden. This is the entrance people come through when they arrive to look round the garden and we want them to be wowed by this first view. We tend to have rich shades in our Dutch Yard, with a few brilliants scattered through for contrast. The colours of palette 1 with some daubs of palette 2 go well with the red brick and, even though some parts of this area are shaded for a few hours a day, I want it to feel enveloping. I love including a crimson-flowered pot (pictured on p256), but it's worth noting that it is carefully positioned to stand out from a sea of bright green *Amelanchier* × *lamarckii* 'Robin Hill' leaves. Rich, dark colours need a well-lit spot, otherwise they become invisible as the light fades and then create a black hole. The acidity of the green acts as a good backdrop, highlighting almost every petal of the crimson flowers – you *really* see them.

In the spring, we have palette 1 in our Rose Garden, too. We go for the coppers and crimsons, selecting tulips in those colours as they look so marvellous with the matching rose foliage – a great range of rich hues when the rose leaves first emerge. Tulip 'Brown Sugar' looks splendid in a pot all on its own in showy harmony with its rose backdrop, and I love the copper and crimson-black mix of tulips 'Brownie', 'Request' and 'Queen of Night' for this spot too.

Form

Opposite *Dahlia* 'Totally Tangerine'
(Thriller) with *Salvia* 'Amistad'
(Pillar) and *Panicum* 'Frosted
Explosion' (Filler) in one of our
huge metal troughs. *Erigeron
karvinskianus* sits below.

As well as colour, the perfect pot combination relies on careful consideration of the form and habit of the plants, particularly important when a pot is large. As with colour, I have an easy recipe to follow, which uses three or four different ingredients, all serving different roles.

The first is what I refer to as the Thriller – the showiest plant which dominates the group. This overlaps with the Bride (see p38) and, in truth, in summer and autumn it is more often than not the same plant (namely a dahlia), but here the showiness is about scale and size rather than colour. Every pot will have one of these dominating plants. They're the focus, the head turner.

Then we select a Filler, which froths and fills the gaps. In spring this is often a wallflower, in summer and autumn it might be a snapdragon or one of our favourite pot grasses such as *Panicum* 'Frosted Explosion'. This Filler makes the pot feel full and abundant, with an airy aesthetic but no gaps.

For tabletop pots and real whopper containers, we also use a Spiller to break up the rim and sides of the pots. I love calibrachoas in this role, as well as trailing verbenas. Or for a huge pot, it could be one of the new tumbling buddlejas, such as 'Buzz Lavender'. These are key for softening the whole look and making the plants the point, rather than the pot.

Finally, for real showstoppers, we include a fourth and final ingredient to give height. This is the Pillar, and we often use a tender perennial climber supported on a hand-woven silver birch frame. The frames are essential to the practicality and design of our big pots, preventing the contents from collapsing and creating instant and beautiful architecture. The taller grasses, such as the perennial *Chasmanthium latifolium*, also serve the Pillar role well, as does the crimson-leaved *Hibiscus acetosella* 'Mahogany Splendor' (pictured on p14 and the bottom of p44). And for our large zinc water troughs we often use the famous *Salvia* 'Amistad' – staked and supported, this gives great height and, drought tolerant, it's surprisingly happy in a pot.

Above One of our living table
centrepieces. This one is a ribbed
metal container with *Glandularia*
'Aztec Silver Magic' (Thriller), *Isotoma*
axillaris 'Gemini Blue' (Filler) and
Helichrysum petiolare 'Silver' (Spiller).
Right A pot in the Dutch Yard with
Calceolaria 'Kentish Hero' (Thriller),
Cuphea subuligera (Filler), *Hibiscus*
acetosella 'Mahogany Splendor'
(Pillar) and *Calibrachoa* 'Double
Can-Can Wine Red' (Spiller).
Opposite One of our whopper
pots in the Oast Garden with
Dahlia 'Waltzing Mathilda' (Thriller),
Antirrhinum 'Orange Scarlet' and
A. 'Sonnet Burgundy' (both Fillers),
and *Lotus berthelotii* (Spiller).

January & February

Pots are crucial in the garden during the first months of the year because they allow us to bring spring forward. January can be a good month for hibernation and a reset after all the Christmas and new year razzmatazz, but by February most of us have had enough of hiding away, yet it's not quite possible to emerge into spring. That's where pots come in.

I passionately recommend collecting a jewel-like family of pots planted with early flowerers to create pools of colour and life on windowsills, doorsteps and outdoor tables. Gather up plant stands, if you have them, and position them near the house. Find some evergreen potted plants for structure (rosemary is ideal, or a compact pittosporum or even a bonsaied bay), then stud the group with brilliant-coloured flowers in their own containers.

We use pots in this way to bring life to the areas we use the most – all around the Dutch Yard and along all the paths from doorstep to workroom, doorstep to car and back door to hen run – so that however grim the weather, we pass these cheery messengers of spring several times a day. We also have a south-facing terrace along one side of our kitchen and French windows: I crowd all of the best-looking pots here to enjoy looking out at them every day. Once winter is over, we spread these pots around the garden.

Which are the must-have plants? I'm obsessed with primulas (that's primroses and polyanthus) for these early months. We have rows in the cutting garden for picking right the way from autumn through to the end of spring, with flowers coming thick and fast by the end of January. Because they're compact, they turn into perfect container plants. We lift and divide the plants after flowering and replant most back into the cutting garden, but a few are lifted before flowering, in autumn, and added to pots.

If you don't already have plants you can lift, they're easy to find online. I love the extremely hardy apricot to smoky pink *Primula* 'Stella Champagne'. It's one of my favourite things for our post-Christmas doorstep. I also love the airy nature of *P. malacoides* for greenhouse pots. This isn't hardy, but if you have somewhere frost-free, such as a cold greenhouse or conservatory, I could not recommend it more. Both polyanthus and primroses are guaranteed to be in flower now, and there are lots to choose from (see p59).

Mossy saxifrages are also reliable winter flowerers. I remember first seeing *Saxifraga* × *arendsii* filling a series of window boxes and pots around a terraced house in Brighton when I was visiting one new year. I was amazed by the cheery look of the plant en masse, just one variety, but probably 30 or more plants: simple, pretty and elegant, and in January.

Previous page A shallow bowl of *Crocus minimus* 'Spring Beauty', forced to flower a little early by growing in cold frame through the autumn and winter.

Below A huge and handsome stone trough at Hanham Court planted with snowdrops (the whopper, *Galanthus nivalis* 'S. Arnott') and *Cyclamen coum*.

Next page A good collection of spring pots on one of our plant theatres including *Primula* 'Ooh La La Pastel Pink', *Hyacinthus orientalis* 'Purple Sensation' and *Saxifraga* × *arendsii* 'Alpino Early Picotee'.

I've copied this many times since, massing pots together, both inside and out, when I want something lively for tables before spring arrives. Like primulas, saxifrage is easy to look after and doesn't bat an eye, whatever the weather. Another favourite, *S. × arendsii* 'Purple Carpet', is a stalwart, always emerging from a good canopy of snow looking perky.

Certain hellebores are excellent performers too. Most of the classic varieties flower a little later, but there is, of course, the Christmas rose (*Helleborus niger*). 'Potter's Wheel' is worth looking out for, with flowers substantially larger and more impressive than the straight *H. niger* species. But my favourites for pots are the slate-crimson *H. × ballardiae* 'Maestro' (which opens in November), joined by its brother, *H. × b.* 'Merlin', which starts to flower at the beginning of February, just as 'Maestro' becomes less prolific. If you have both, you've got the whole of winter covered.

These particular hellebores have handsome slate-coloured leaves, so are good elevated in pots rather than hidden down in a border. Add to these one or two more, such as *H. × ericsmithii* 'Shooting Star', *H.* 'Ivory Prince' and *H. × nigercors* 'Emma', and you have a shady pot 'glade' for your doorstep. I pot these hellebores up in the autumn and, once they've done their stuff, reinstate them into a shady area with moist soil in the garden, sometime in May. I don't pot up the same clump again for at least a couple of years; like forcing rhubarb, this tires the root. Don't leave them languishing in a pot through a hot, dry summer either. They'd really struggle.

With these hellebores mixed with primulas, your early doorstep pots can supply plentiful vases for inside too. Mature hellebore stems (where one flower is already at seedpod stage) make pretty good cut flowers. Cut the stems, score with a pin all the way down both sides of the stem and then sear the ends for ten seconds in just-boiled water. After searing, lay them flat in a sink of cold water and leave overnight. Don't cut the seared stem off when you arrange them.

Cyclamen coum and snowdrops are also brilliant pot fillers throughout February, both are happiest in dappled shade. This simple pairing reminds me of one of the most impressive winter containers I've ever seen, put together by the garden designers Julian and Isabel Bannerman in their old garden at Hanham Court in Gloucestershire.

They had a huge stone trough sitting at the base of an aged, craggy wisteria that tumbled over a stone wall and was covered in flower, and then leaf, from April onwards. Preceding this, the trough was full of a magnificent carpet of cyclamen, topped with the hanging white bells of one of the larger snowdrops, *Galanthus nivalis* 'S. Arnott'. The pair coincide in their winter flowering, first the beautiful cyclamen leaves (which come before the flowers) just beginning to shoot as the wisteria foliage dropped. Genius. This would be expensive to plant but would thrive for decades.

Also outside, flowering in the sun by the middle of February, are the miniature irises (*Iris histrioides* and *I. reticulata*). There are lots of beautiful, velvety varieties. My favourite is 'Purple Hill' for its delicious, soft, primrose-like perfume and an extraordinarily rich colour and texture. 'Harmony' is another winner. I have a new-found favourite soft blue iris, 'Alida', which seems to flower a couple of weeks earlier than the others. Their colour would be radiant at any time of year, but particularly in drear February. They sing out, even from a distant garden table – and that's where we often have our February irises, in pots in the middle of the Perennial Cutting Garden table, which we can see from our kitchen window despite it being 30 metres or so away.

We also use these reticulata irises as the top layer in almost all of our bulb lasagnes; I love the contrast once the tulip foliage starts to emerge below the iris flowers. The strong purple stripes on the early tulip 'Neper', for instance, matches iris 'Purple Hill' perfectly.

At this time of year, it's not just colour that's a joy, but scent too, somehow more so when garden pickings are so thin. We often have the strongly scented paperwhite narcissi we forced for Christmas flowering in the greenhouse in a pot or two. Close behind are the early *Narcissus* 'Grand Soleil d'Or' and the pretty orange-trumpeted *N*. 'Cragford'. I love the jasmine-like perfume of these two. Then there are hyacinths, the perfumed classics for January and February. We find these are much easier to bring into flower now, rather than for Christmas. Grown more slowly they form stronger, more anchored roots, so are less prone to toppling over.

We are lucky enough to have a greenhouse at Perch Hill and we use it to protect winter-flowering violas from the worst of the weather and to force a wide range of spring bulbs, which we use to jazz things up in the house and to flower early on our doorstep. A garden shed with a window, a cold frame, polytunnel or even just a cool room will do the job.

My favourite violas for very early in the year are 'Sorbet Phantom', with scented flowers in deep purple, and 'Tiger Eye Red', which has delicate flowers in the colours of the semi-precious stone. With a little protection, their flowers look good even in January and February. Having a bit of under-cover space allows you to cheat the seasons by at least three to four weeks.

For colour at this time of year, don't forget the early *Crocus tommasinianus*, *C. sieberi* subsp. *atticus* 'Firefly' (a new-found very early favourite), *C. minimus* 'Spring Beauty' (pictured on p46) and *C. chrysanthus* varieties, such as the white and purple 'Ladykiller' and the pure white 'Snow Bunting'. Add to that list the super early, pale blue *Scilla mischtschenkoana* and all snowdrops, including the lovely *Galanthus elwesii*. These all flower in the garden by mid- to late February, but grown in a cold frame or cold greenhouse, we can bring their flowering date forward by a month.

Below Pots of winter bulbs including *Iris reticulata* 'Alida' and 'Harmony' along with the early *Crocus sieberi* subsp. *atticus* 'Firefly'.

Next page Winter sunrise on a snowy day. We get snow pretty reliably once or twice a year at Perch Hill. Most of the pots are full of bulbs at this stage, all hardy enough to withstand the conditions. Many of these species hail from parts of the world where they could well be carpeted in snow for much longer than they are in Sussex.

We also have amaryllis for January and February, but inside only. A variety like the stylish *Hippeastrum* 'Green Magic' or spidery and elegant 'Emerald' seem to be reluctant to be forced for Christmas, but we can almost always have them in flower (using a bit of basal heat) about a month later, still a good couple of months before their natural flowering time. And I've recently fallen in love with a fully double, pale-coloured form called 'Nymph' (pictured on p392 and p397). This feels quite spring-like.

We also force pots of *Anemone coronaria* and, in a mild winter, Iceland poppies (*Papaver nudicaule*), plus the delicate snake's head fritillary (*Fritillaria meleagris*), which is perhaps the loveliest of them all. We force all these in our greenhouse, which makes good use of its downtime. I thoroughly recommend this, if you are lucky enough to have any under-glass space.

With this range of plants up your sleeve it feels as though a new season has begun well before it actually has. To me and, I know to many of us, that feels like a huge relief. But there's one more excellent reason to grow at least a few of these.

I made a BBC programme about pollinators some years ago called *Bees, Butterflies and Blooms*, and in its making I discovered that these late-winter flowerers are crucial to the survival of the buff-tailed bumblebee amongst other bees. At a moment when pollen and nectar can be scarce, these bee species, and particularly their queens, are starting to emerge hungry from hibernation. They're looking for a good source of pollen, for protein and nectar, for carbohydrate, which many of these flowers – the hellebores, irises, crocuses, snowdrops, cyclamens and hyacinths – will provide. It's not just humans who need early spring flowers.

If you support your taller-stemmed bulbs as they grow with nests of hazel catkins or pussy willow, just coming into flower (pictured on p76), these will add to the pollen and nectar count. Decorate with carpets of velvet bun moss, a scattering of dried oak or chestnut leaves and mini-alder catkins for good measure, and your bulb pots, trugs and bowls will do far more than look good.

So, in January and February, it's pots, pots and more pots, inside and out, for me.

Primulas

We have a small flock of rare breed hens at Perch Hill and every morning and evening I walk through the Cutting Garden to let them out or herd them back in. It's a walk I'll do at all times of year and in every weather, and I love it for making me notice what has opened or gone over.

It's this walk that reminded me what exceptional plants primroses and polyanthus truly are. Certain varieties resolutely come into flower in late autumn and carry on lightly all through winter to gather pace in a flowering flurry by the first weeks of spring. The only downside is that they are prone to vine weevil (see p225).

I have a long-held fondness for primulas, fostered by regular visits to an outstanding nursery of so-called Barnhaven primroses when I was a child. It was near my aunt's house in Westmorland (now Cumbria) and whenever we stayed with her in winter or spring, when the plants are at their floweriest best, we'd visit this specialist nursery. My parents rarely returned without a car boot full of some of the most exquisitely rich and beautiful flowers I'd ever seen. I remember thinking they looked like a carpet of velvet butterflies, and I loved them.

The Barnhaven primroses were bred in America from the early 1940s when the hybridiser, Florence Bellis, began developing the colours and characteristics of primroses. She produced doubles and singles, all perennial, mostly easy to look after and in a radiant colour range. The breeding didn't stop with Florence – there have been fantastic developments ever since.

The English writer Vita Sackville-West loved polyanthus for their textures, colours and forms, as well as their appearance so early in the year to cheer us gardeners along. Several forms have recently been reintroduced to the garden at Sissinghurst, the home she lived in from 1930. The flowers are now cut for mini-bottles and sherry glasses, just as she would have arranged them, and placed on her desk in the Tower and on the side tables in the Big Room, as the library is known, for visitors to admire.

Top Clumps of primroses that have been dug up from the garden borders and brought inside where they come into flower a few weeks early. I love their scent and delicate flowers. Bottom A window ledge filled with polyanthus and vases of early *Anemone coronaria* for my birthday in February.

At any other time of year, these miniature beauties might be overshadowed by other cut flowers, but they're perfect now.

The primroses – each stem topped by one individual, saucer-like flower – are the most delicate, but it's the polyanthus lot, which have a clutch of flowers on top of longer stems, that are the most impressive. With more and more showier, yet not gaudy, varieties coming onto the market, we decided the time was right to put them to the test. We did a trial of twelve of them a few years ago, planting them in early autumn. We then judged each one on its earliness and length of flowering, prettiness and drama, plus how it performed in pots and vases.

There were three winners: *Primula* 'Stella Champagne', *P.* 'Stella Lilac' and *P.* 'Stella Neon Violet'. And what we can now appreciate a few years on is their easy perennial nature. They sit in the shade of the annuals we grow for picking for most of spring and summer, but once the annuals are pulled out, it's their turn to shine again. Whether it's the dullest of days, or we've just had a hard frost, even if they've been buried in several inches of snow, I know these three will carry on flowering. Their hardiness never ceases to amaze me.

That's why every autumn we dig up a clump or two – or in summer we sow seeds or buy a few seedlings – to cram into pots for our doorstep and the table outside our kitchen window. And we often bring them inside for a quick spell as table centre pots. In the warmth of the house, they struggle after a while, so out they must go again.

My birthday is in February, and before I discovered these three supremos I would just head to the local garden centre and select whichever primulas looked loveliest on the day. Polyanthus make perfect table centrepieces in contrasting ceramic bowls as long as their roots are kept properly moist, and are much cheaper than British cut flowers at this time of year, with the advantage that, rather than ending up on the compost heap, they can be planted out into the garden.

Incidentally, they do also make great cut flowers: with their stem ends seared (dipped into just-boiled water for two or three seconds), they last seven to ten days in a vase. And as with all primulas, they can be used as an edible flower, scattered over winter puddings, risottos or salads.

They're the unsung queens of January and February, and invaluable for pots.

Best of the primulas

There are many different shapes, sizes and forms in the vast Primula *genus, which includes all the polyanthus and primrose forms.*

There are the simple and beautiful wild primroses, which I love potted up, three or five plants grouped together in a shallow table-centre pot, with moss and dried leaves added to make it more of a mini-landscape (pictured on p61). It's mainly the impressive, chandelier-like ones we grow for pots, rather than the more delicate single-flower forms. These flower from winter and through most of spring and, like all primulas, love a rich, moist, but well-drained soil with plenty of organic matter. *Primula auricula* varieties are also splendid (if a little fussier), but flower in April and May. I have included a few later-flowering varieties here, so you can see the incredible range of this underused family, perfect for winter and spring pots, large and small.

1 *Primula* Cowichan group
In this group of true Barnhaven primroses, 'Garnet' (pictured) is the plushest, ruby velvet and flowers in March and April. A reliable perennial which appears year on year without much lifting and dividing.

2 *P.* 'Francisca'
A unique vivid green polyanthus flowering in April and May. I love this both in terracotta pots and picked for a vase. We used to grow lots of 'Francisca', and I've made a note that we need to do so again. I miss her!

3 *P.* Gold-laced and Silver-laced group
Exotic and glamorous, the so-called laced groups are as they sound, featuring more intricate flowerheads. These flower from mid-March to mid-May with us in Sussex. They're not as vigorous as other forms here, with fewer flower spikes, but are still reliable perennials, thriving in dappled shade. The Silver-laced group has perfect eyeliner-thin silver rims around crimson-black petals with golden hearts. The Gold-laced group has similarly outlined petal rims, but the line matches the golden flower's centre. 'Elizabeth Killelay' is a double Gold-laced form and its flowers are like velvet pompoms, fit for the buttonhole of a king.

4 *P. malacoides*
Not enough of us grow this marvellous, winter-flowering species polyanthus, almost indistinguishable from its Chinese brother, *P. forbesii*. This is hugely popular as a winter houseplant in Japan,

but hardly grown here. Find a source of plants or seedlings and they'll give you a continuous supply of frothy, soft to deep pink flowers from Christmas until the middle of spring. They are the making of our winter greenhouse. Plant them up in terracotta pots and bring them inside in autumn (out of the frost) to flower now, from early in the new year. They are prolifically self-seeding, but not hardy, so need to be grown under glass.

5 *P*. 'Ooh La La Pastel Pink' This one (also pictured on p50) and 'Ooh La La Blood Orange' (pictured here, behind) are both hybrid forms from the species primula – they are later flowering and have larger flowerheads. They are a little less delicate looking than some others, but good value.

6 *P.* Stella series
A recently bred range of polyanthus that features long-stemmed, candelabra forms, with flowers that often start in autumn and continue right through spring with us in Sussex. Because the large flowers sit in an impressive cluster at the top of a decent length of stem, they are much more noticeable in a pot. 'Stella Champagne' (pictured) is a seed strain with a mix of colours, varying slightly from apricot to smoky pink. They have one downside: in a hot spring, a few plants can turn a little too ochre for me; they only retain the plum and pink shades when it's cool. 'Stella Lilac' (syn. 'Victoriana Lilac Lace') is not quite as rich and luscious as the Gold-laced group, but this comes into flower a good four months earlier and is *much* more

prolific. 'Stella Neon Violet' varies a little from purple velvet to a brighter purple-blue. Flowering a little later than 'Stella Champagne' and 'Stella Lilac', it continues to bloom as the tulips come into flower and it seems to be the most visited by pollinators. Finally, we found 'Stella Scarlet Pimpernel' can be a bit too brassy planted en masse in our large Danish pots, but it has its benefits: it's a brilliant early edible flower, a winter showstopper in small pots, and it looks bright and beautiful in a vase.

7 *P.* 'Strong Beer'
This is a double, dome-forming primrose and, as such, can get lost in a flower bed. Flowering from the start of February, it's ideal for pots. Massed together it looks like a velvet carpet.

8 *P. vulgaris* 'Avondale'
This is in the Kennedy Irish series and has a delicate flower in a lovely bright mauve. It is a strong grower and its early flowers make it ideal for doorstep or table pots from the end of February, or a month earlier if brought under cover in autumn. It makes a lovely cut flower.

Hyacinths

Opposite *Hyacinthus orientalis* 'Woodstock' is my long-standing favourite for pots.

Hyacinths are at their best in pots rather than in the ground. That's my view. They're too top-heavy and chunky for ground level, but gain a certain magnificence when planted in pots and raised up on walls, plant theatres and tables. Up close like this you see the colour variations in the flowers – and it lifts the scent nearer.

I remember seeing them planted for a trial and filling a whole field in East Anglia many years ago, and I saw them again in the living bulb museum Hortus Bulborum in the Netherlands. Their perfume was extraordinary, but both times it struck me how odd they looked with their huge flowers on short stems – it rather put me off. None of this applies if they're grown in pots both little (such as a single bulb forcer) or large. Planted this way, they look and smell marvellous.

I also feel hyacinths earn their keep even more if forced, which simply means growing them under glass indoors to bring them into flower earlier than they would naturally flower outdoors. If you leave them to flower in March and April without forcing, they're up against so many good flowerers that they are hardly exceptional. But there is a limited range of plants that shine in January and February. It is genuinely easy to force hyacinths this early if you start them off in September (see p343), and that is why *now* is the hyacinth's time to shine.

You may think a hyacinth is a hyacinth, but it turns out from a recent trial of 16 different varieties I saw at West Dean in Sussex, that this is not the case. The well-known hyacinths are the whites, pinks and blues, but there are yellows, so-called oranges (more pink flesh than orange) and purples. There are dumpy varieties that have overpacked florets on the stem, and there are airy ones, with elegant, well-spaced spires through which you can see the light. There are truly fragrant ones (the blues) and others with less intense perfume (the pinks). And there are earlies (ideal for forcing) and lates. They don't all come into flower at the same time, with some fully over as others are just emerging. After 30 years of experimenting, I have my firm favourites.

Designing Pots with Hyacinths

My all-round favourite garden hyacinth is *Hyacinthus orientalis* 'Anastasia', which looks like a cross between a bluebell and a garden hyacinth, but this looks oddly messy, even wimpy in a pot.

The chunky garden hybrids are better in pots. I tend to choose the single-flowered forms over doubles (though the latter can look impressive and glamorous in a vase), and I hugely rate the multifloras. These are more expensive, but with double-sized bulbs, they're worth it. The flower spikes are finer, more openly spaced and abundant, coming one after another in succession for almost twice the average length of flowering time.

My advice would be to pick a single colour and just one type per pot. That's playing it safe, but for pots it never fails. I think I will always count the beetroot-purple *H. orientalis* 'Woodstock' as my number one for this – though in winter I do love any of the whites. My parents had a large Edwardian wooden plant stand with a zinc inner that my mother had inherited from

Below The multiflora pink *Hyacinthus orientalis* 'Pink Festival' gives great value for money in a pot, with huge numbers of flowers over many weeks.

Opposite A table arrangement of *H. o.* 'Woodstock' with the matching striped foliage of *Tulipa* 'Queen Ingrid' in a shallow bowl with moss and dried leaves.

her mother. This was filled with forced white hyacinths every January and placed in our sitting room, the heating turned right down so they'd last. The planter was about to collapse in my mother's barn, so I asked if I could take it away and restore it and now, in winter, I also fill it with white hyacinths (pictured on p76). It sits in our greenhouse and perfumes the whole space. I occasionally lift it into the house for a fragrant fantasia for a few days, but the cool of the greenhouse keeps the plants flowering for a good six weeks, twice as long as with heating. It may seem extravagant, but I love it, and the bulbs then go out in the garden for future picking.

We have experimented with mixing hyacinth colours in one pot, and I think a few bulbs of perhaps three varieties from a single palette work well, but the palettes must be kept separate. If designing mixes, also make sure to check flowering times to avoid planting an early hyacinth (such as 'Delft Blue') with a late (such as 'Purple Star'). They won't look good at the same time.

Another thing we've played around with is mixing the dramatic hyacinth with an understorey of more delicate bulbs. The wood anemone *Anemone blanda* 'White Splendour' is easily

Below A zinc window box at Perch Hill with *Hyacinthus orientalis* 'L'Innocence', *Primula* 'Snow White' and *Anemone blanda* 'White Splendour'. This can be forced into flower in February in the greenhouse or will flower naturally in the garden by the middle of March.

forced to flower at the same time as *H. o.* 'L'Innocence' and you can add in a harmonious early-flowering polyanthus for lower-storey saucer-like flowers and elegant foliage. Then you've got a spectacular winter-to-spring window box.

Caring for Hyacinths

There are a few things worth knowing about when forcing and looking after potted hyacinths, particularly if they're coming inside for a spell.

Aim to plant them in October and select varieties with an early or mid-flowering season. These will be easier to force for January or February. And if you love hyacinths and fancy a succession to bring into the house or to have on the doorstep from Christmas until spring (for that you'll need to plant them in September, see p343), then select one or two from each flowering period.

With the extra warmth and less light that comes with growing them inside, they get top-heavy and floppy stemmed. Make a nest of twigs to support them and keep them elegantly upstanding.

This one is critical: don't water once they've come into growth. I had a bowl of hyacinths for scent on a table last January; I went away for a month and when I came back they were flowering marvellously, better than I'd ever seen. I think when you're looking at them sitting in the warmth, you think, poor flowers, they must need water. But they don't. In fact, watering encourages the tip of the flower to rot and for that rot to carry on down the stem. Once their flowers start erupting, stop watering.

Once in flower, keep your hyacinths out of the heat to prolong their season. A cool window ledge or conservatory is ideal. As they're going over, give them a potash feed (tomato or comfrey fertiliser). When they're done, lift the bulbs (leave the foliage if it's still green) and put them in crates to die down completely.

Then, come the following September, plant your forced bulbs from the previous year into the garden (they don't perform well if forced year after year). As with many bulbs, they can fail to flower the first year after forcing, but should start to bloom well the year after and will then carry on with finer, well-spaced flower spikes, which fit in the garden well.

Finally, whenever handling hyacinth bulbs, wear gloves. They're allergenic and make me very itchy.

Best of the hyacinths

To make the most of your hyacinths keep your palettes apart: the bright and rich shades separate from the pastel shades, both cool and warm. Here are the best varieties we've trialled over the years.

Flowering times

I've indicated the season of flowering for each hyacinth, and while there may only be two weeks between them, it's worth knowing about if you want to plan a succession.

Early: opening naturally in March outside and most easily forced for Christmas or January; these are quite rare.

Mid: opening naturally in March into April outside and, forced, they'll easily flower for February; most hyacinths are in this group.

Late: opening naturally from April into May. We find these are also pretty easy to force for February, but will certainly flower for March.

Bright and Rich

This palette is a combination of the Dark and Rich palette 1 and Boiled-sweet Brilliant palette 2 (see p26 and p28).

Purples

1 *Hyacinthus orientalis* 'Miss Saigon'
A bright, amethyst purple – like a Liberty bag. Shorter and stockier than the others here, which in a pot is quite handy. And it doesn't flop about. Mid.

2 *H. o.* 'Purple Sensation'
The latest to flower of the purples, about ten days after the rest. This does not age well – it goes a muddy colour as it dies – but it's a wonderful, rich purple while in flower. Late.

3 *H. o.* 'Woodstock'
A true beetroot colour, dark and intense. Its form is slender and delicate with a more naturalistic quality than most varieties. It ages well. A favourite. Mid.

Pinks

4 *H. o.* 'Eros'
A double in the same intense pink as 'Jan Bos' with lots of green to soften its brightness; it keeps its colour better, too. Flowers for ages in a pot and has an exceptional vase life of nearly two weeks, but the bulbs are expensive. Mid.

5 *H. o.* 'Jan Bos'
In a trial at West Dean by head gardener Tom Brown, this made it into the top ten. However, in a poll of the garden's visitors, it really divided opinion. Tom rates it

for being super bright with huge impact, but the colour is too strong for many people. I have grown this one in the garden at Perch Hill and rather love it, but for me it becomes too salmony as it fades. Mid.

6 *H. o.* 'Pink Festival'
This multiflora hyacinth may be too full-on pink for some, but I've been impressed. We had it in a large, shallow terracotta bulb pan in a dark corner of the school room and it looked good for well over a month. Then it came out into the light to be photographed and stayed in the cool greenhouse looking good for another four weeks. We left the bulbs in the pot and, the following year, they did the same again! Expensive bulbs, but worth it. Late.

Blues

7 *H. o.* 'Aida'
A standout for its rich, almost indigo colour, darker than any other widely available blue. Smaller flower spikes than most, but not bad for that. Mid.

8 *H. o.* 'Anastasia'
With delicate flower spikes and a soft blue colour, this is like a glorious and unusual bluebell. I adore this in the garden and also as a single stem (or arranged en masse) in a small vase, but they're a bit fleeting in a pot and look almost insubstantial. Mid.

9 *H. o.* 'Blue Star'
A bright mid-blue, lovely for its dark foliage as it emerges and the dark burgundy flush to its stem. This makes it outstanding amongst the blues. I also find its mid-tone versatile. It can fit in either palette here. Good for forcing. Early–mid.

10 *H. o.* 'Dark Dimension'
Impressive and unusual. You need to be a little careful with these nearly-black varieties – they need good light to not look too dark and gloomy. Mid.

11 *H. o.* 'Delft Blue'
Similar to 'Blue Star' in colour and also early, so ideal for forcing. Mid.

12 *H. o.* 'Peter Stuyvesant'
An old form that is still widely available. Tall and well packed with florets, but not overstuffed. A strong all-rounder with famously good scent. Late.

13 *H. o.* 'Purple Star'
With throats of blue and petal tips of purple, this is the purple-washed version of 'Blue Star' and is just as good. Late.

Soft and Cool

These are mainly from palette 4, with just a few from the Soft and Warm palette 3 (see p30 and p32).

Yellow

1 *Hyacinthus orientalis* 'City of Haarlem' Along with 'Yellowstone' (from which it is indistinguishable, in my view), this butter-yellow hyacinth is worth growing for its unusual colour. It also has excellent scent. Mid.

Whites

2 *H. o.* 'Carnegie' One of the best whites because it has an elegance to it, with tall spires and well-spaced florets. And it's a pure crisp white. Overall, I think better than the popular 'Aiolos' and even the widely available 'White Pearl', which are both very dense with florets, making them look a bit dumpy. Late.

3 *H. o.* 'L'Innocence' A classic white and a naturally early flowerer, this is most commonly used for forcing. I've grown this now for over 30 years and have never been disappointed. Mid.

4 *H. o.* 'Multiflora White' The most widely available multiflora. Each bulb is so huge it can fill the base of my palm. It crops lightly for twice as long as standard white varieties (such as 'Carnegie') and hence is popular for forcing. It flowers from early in the year until spring, so it is both an early and a mid-season hyacinth.

Blues

5 *H. o.* 'City of Bradford'
A sort of silvery-blue, this
is an old and traditional
hyacinth which I first
saw and loved at Hortus
Bulborum in the Netherlands.
It's now difficult to find. Late.

6 *H. o.* 'Sky Jacket'
Unusual for its soft and pale
colour compared with other
hyacinths, this one is good
mixed with darker blues. Mid.

Pinks

7 *H. o.* 'Annabelle'
A double in a soft to bright
pink with nice green
markings on the flowers
when they first emerge.
Like all doubles, this is more
expensive but very long-
flowering. Mid.

8 *H. o.* 'Anna Marie'
This emerges a traditional
pink to begin with, but turns
a soft apricot after about ten
days, when I find it a bit sickly
and too pink-flesh toned. It's
worth knowing that, along
with 'Delft Blue' and 'Purple
Sensation', this flowered two
weeks earlier than the rest
in the West Dean trial, so it's
good for forcing. Mid.

9 *H. o.* 'China Pink'
I love 'China Pink' for the
softness of its colour: a gentle,
shell blush. But it is a little
dumpy, with a lack of air
between the florets. Mid.

10 *H. o.* 'Splendid Cornelia'
With a pale blue throat to
each floret trumpet and pink
petal tip, this has an unusual
but beautiful coloured spire.
It's becoming difficult to
find. Mid.

January & February

There are very few practical tasks you need to do out in the garden at this time of year and, with the exception of one or two slow-growing plants, it's too early to start sowing as the temperatures and light levels are so low.

Cuttings taken last summer and autumn need checking, pinching out and perhaps potting on, but you can safely put the garden to the back of your mind and simply enjoy the occasional foray.

That's why it's the perfect time to plan and design your pots. Many of us leave this until May, when the frosts are over, and we find ourselves pushing a trolley down the garden centre aisles, choosing things that happen to be looking good that day. I urge you not to do this. Instead, use the early part of the year to plan your pots. Get creative and work out how you want them to look for summer and autumn. Put together exciting and beautiful recipes with thoughtfully chosen, guaranteed performers.

Find old catalogues and magazines, dig out garden notebooks and look through plant photos you may have taken at garden shows or visits. Select some favourite plants and cut out their pictures. Find yourself some nice, thick watercolour or cartridge paper, a bit of sticky tack and some coloured crayons or pens. Read the recipes and rules outlined in this book (see the design section that starts on p15), take inspiration from the 'best of' lists I've put together throughout this book, and then get drawing and sticking.

Once you've settled on some great combinations on paper, work out your shopping, sowing and planting lists and timings (see examples on p82) – then you're away!

Pot Design

I love planning which plants are going in which pots all around the garden. With our design rules (see p15) in mind, the fire roaring and everything I need laid out on the table, it's a pastime that's ideal for lifting the spirits in January and February.

We have black and white line drawings of the garden at Perch Hill, with the paths and bigger plants marked on, as well as the position and numbers of all the pots. I'd recommend making this sort of base garden plan, even if it's rough, as your first step.

I overlay the garden plan with tracing paper or baking parchment and mark everything out. Then I cut out round shapes representing each pot (particularly the whoppers). I tack these on and, in pencil, mark what's going in the pot, with photographs cut out from catalogues surrounding it if I need a reminder. I then hang this on the wall to live with, think about and check until I'm 100 per cent happy with each recipe – and where it is in the garden – before final sign-off. That then leads to a comprehensive month-by-month sowing, growing and buying list.

Making a plant list

Once you have worked out your designs, you can create a plant list of what you want and how many you'll need.

When working out how many plants to sow/buy of each, I always think it's best to halve the spacing distance you would give them in a garden (which is the spacing that is often recommended on the label).
Pots mean packed-in gardening, so you will need more plants and they will need more food and water as a result. For example, with most average-sized annual seedlings, you can plant nine, evenly spaced, into a 45cm (18in) pot. With pelargoniums, a guide would be one plant to a 30cm (12in) pot. And for a smaller perennials, like erigeron, three seedlings to a 30cm (12in) pot.

Once I have an idea of how many plants to each pot, I then create a chart outlining what I'm going to sow, buy or may already have cuttings of. Here is an example of two combinations I planned for the Oast Garden using our Bride, Bridesmaid, Gatecrasher and Pillar/Spiller system (see p38 and p43).

POT COMBO 1: SIX POTS

Type	Plant	Quantity		Month to plant
BRIDE/ THRILLER	*Dahlia* 'Dalaya Devi'	18 tubers (3 to a pot)		March
BRIDESMAID/ FILLER/PILLAR	*Petunia* 'Tidal Wave Red Velour'	12 seedlings (2 to a pot)		March
GATECRASHER/ PILLAR	*Thunbergia alata* 'African Sunset'	18 seedlings (3 to a pot)		March

POT COMBO 2: FOUR POTS

Type	Plant	Quantity		Month to sow/plant
BRIDE/ THRILLER	*Antirrhinum* Sonnet series	28 seedlings (7 to a pot)		February
BRIDESMAID/ FILLER/PILLAR	*Petunia* 'Tidal Wave Red Velour'	8 seedlings (2 to a pot)		March
SPILLER	*Ipomoea* 'SolarTower Black'	8 cuttings (2 to a pot)		Order Jan/Feb to arrive May

Sowing

As far as pots are concerned, there's very little that needs sowing this early in the year, but sweet peas, the climber cobaea and snapdragons are the exceptions. They are all excellent container plants that benefit from having that bit longer to get growing before the summer. Sowing them now gives them plenty of time to germinate and develop their roots to ensure the maximum length of flowering. In late February, we also sow a few hardy annuals for our June pots. I love linaria, gypsophila and heliopsis.

Here you'll find instructions on sowing sweet peas and cobaea. When planting these out in March and May (see p130 and p201), remember they are only suited to whopper pots, with a deep root run. We grow cobaea in repurposed animal water troughs, and they then tumble down from the balcony of the Oast House (pictured on p330).

Sowing sweet peas

To achieve the healthiest, most floriferous plants with good long stems, get going with your sweet pea sowing now.

We use root trainers, but you can use loo rolls, as both give a deep, narrow root run, just what sweet peas need. When the seed first germinates, it puts down one long root. This breaks off when it hits the air at the bottom of the pot, and like pinching out the tip, the root then throws out lots of side roots further up. When these reach the walls of the root trainer, they slot into a groove-like channel and are directed straight to the bottom of the pot. They then break off and produce their own side roots, so you get a virtuous circle of root development, with a root system forming very quickly. If you sow into a short, stumpy pot, the initial root will be shorter and will branch out less. Essentially, a longer root means more root branches, which equals a bigger plant!

- Sow one seed to a root trainer. If destined for the garden, we sometimes sow two seeds to each root trainer, but that will be too much for pot growing, where individual seed sowing is advisable. You don't need to soak the seeds; they will germinate in 10–14 days.
- Use a peat-free loamless compost with an open structure (such as a multipurpose potting compost). The plant roots need air, as well as moisture and nutrients.
- Dampen the surface of the compost and then push each seed in about 2.5cm (1in) below the surface. Water again.
- Label and put in a cold greenhouse or cold frame. Don't mollycoddle them – that's the most common mistake. No heat is needed. Heat can inhibit germination and, with it, you're likely to get more seed rot. So put the trays somewhere cold. They're frost tolerant to about −5°C (23°F). A bit of frost seems to do them good.
- Guard against mice. Mice love sweet pea seed and your whole crop may disappear in one go. If you have the trays in a cold greenhouse, put them on a sheet of wood or ply (not hardboard), and make sure that there's a good overhang from the side of the bench so that the mice can't climb up on to the plants. Or you can soak the seeds in liquid seaweed fertiliser overnight to make them unpalatable. That seems to work too.
- Check for germination every day. Don't water until you see seedlings appear.

- Once the seedlings come through, keep them cool at about 5°C (41°F). This promotes root growth, rather than stem growth. A cold greenhouse or cold frame is ideal. When I started growing sweet peas, I just used a couple of straw bales with a reclaimed window over the top.
- When there are three or four pairs of leaves, pinch out the leaders – just squeeze off the growing tip between your finger and thumb. This promotes vigorous side shoot formation, directing the energy of the plant toward growing out, not up.
- Every week, check your plants. Water them lightly if they are dry. If they have started to shoot again, pinch out any spindly tips. About a month from germination, check the bottom of the pot for white roots. As soon as roots are visible through the holes, pot the plants up. Don't let them get pot-bound, they will never be the same again. A slim, deep, 1litre-pot is ideal. Use a good compost and water them in.
- See p130 in March for planting out your sweet peas in pots.

Sowing Cobaea

Cobaea scandens (cup and saucer vine), needs to be sown early in the year. It won't flower until it reaches about 2m (6½ft). Sown late, it tends to reach this height just when we get our first hard frost of the autumn, meaning you'll never see flowers. Sown early, it will fill your autumn with cups and saucers.

- Each seed has a large surface area and is a round, wafer-thin saucer shape: sow vertically (any end up), not flat, into their own individual small pots (see p173).
- Put them in a propagator. They'll germinate, warm and moist, within 2–3 weeks.
- Once the seedlings start to grow, after about 3–4 weeks, they need a climbing frame to clamber over – don't leave them sprawling. Pot them on, and in their new pot, create a frame. We make ours from silver birch pea sticks, which we weave into mini, pot-sized teepees (see p202).

- Plant them out once the frosts are over, taking care to move them with their mini-climbing frame intact to their final position.

Sowing snapdragons and *Erigeron karvinskianus*

Start sowing these slow-growers under cover. We grow snapdragons as a half-hardy annual, but strictly speaking they're tender perennials. Snapdragons have a long growing season and can take up to 20 weeks from seed to flower. *Erigeron karvinskianus* – one of the all-time classic plants for a window box – is a perennial, so is also on a slower time frame than the annuals we sow in March, so it's good to sow it in February to give it a head start.

Get going with single-coloured snapdragon varieties such as *Antirrhinum majus* 'Liberty Classic Crimson' or 'Giant White'. Or try the newly bred varieties in the Chantilly series, which have a lovely fruity scent. There's also 'Appleblossom', which smells of cinnamon. Seeds sown now should flower from June. I love a richly coloured mix, jammed together in a large pot, just as you might mix them in a vase.

Both snapdragons and erigeron have tiny seed, so are too fiddly to sow into guttering or Jiffy-7 pellets. You have to sow them into a seed tray (see p86). The seedlings should appear within 10–14 days from sowing, but can take up to three weeks, so don't lose heart. In a month or so from sowing, the seedlings will need pricking out (see p128).

Below Sowing seeds into a seed tray and using the underside of a second seed tray to create slight indentations in the compost, which is helpful for sowing in lines.

Sowing into seed trays

- Fill the tray with soil-based, peat-free compost, breaking up any lumps as you go.
- Instead of a tamping board, we use a clean, empty seed tray to gently press down the compost. The underside ridges leave slight indentations in the compost, which is helpful for sowing in straight lines and remembering where you have sown.
- Water the trays before sowing. This avoids displacing any seeds. Or place the tray in a watertight container to soak from the base.

- For valuable seeds, you can divide a seed tray into sections with green canes or just use half-sized trays.
- Sow only a small pinch, not a palmful. Treat the seed like gold dust. Sowing as thinly as possible is the route to success. Save the leftover seed for next year.
- If your seed is big enough to handle, individually place the seed in neat, well-spaced rows so they can geminate and grow on for a few weeks before needing to be pricked out, without competition from neighbours.

- Cover with a dusting of sieved compost. Peat-free compost tends to have twigs and bits so it's good to sieve these out. Label.
- A bit of basal heat will kick start them and encourage the seeds to germinate quickly. Use a propagator or heated bench, if you have one, at 18–20°C (64–68°F).

Cuttings Care

Tender perennial cuttings (such as those from salvias, pelargoniums and plectranthus) taken in the autumn need to be checked now. They should have been potted on in their own individual pots before Christmas, but if not, do this now, putting them back on a heated bench or propagator to help their dislodged roots settle back in. At this time of year, you just need to check that they are growing well with no signs of botrytis (mould) taking hold.

All cuttings
- In warmer spells plants tend to put on growth and get leggy as light levels are low. Pinch out the tips to encourage bushier more floriferous plants by summer.
- Keep an eye on temperatures and make sure you have some horticultural fleece ready. If prolonged cold is forecast, then we gather all the pots together and make a tent from the fleece over the top of them. This allows us to easily cover them and gives an extra layer of frost protection.

- By February, plants will be starting to grow quite actively and may need a bit of a boost. We feed with a diluted seaweed fertiliser.

Salvia cuttings
After a cold spell, salvias in particular seem to be prone to botrytis and you'll notice mould on the plant and its leaves falling. If this is the case:

- Clear any debris from the compost surface.
- Cut out any evidence of botrytis. Always clean your equipment before and after doing this, including gloves – you need to be careful to avoid transferring the fungal spores to other plants.
- Often there is hardly anything left above compost level. If that's the case, tip the contents out from its pot gently to check for roots. If all looks healthy below the compost, the roots will often send up shoots as the weather warms – don't give up hope!

Pelargonium cuttings
You may find at this time of year that holes start to appear in pelargonium leaves: this is the work of a small green caterpillar which, well disguised, takes a bit of spotting. If you see them, pick them off by hand and give them to the birds. Pelargoniums, like salvias, can be prone to botrytis. If you spot any mould on the leaves, treat them as you would salvias (instructions above).

March

This is the month that sees the garden change the most between the first few days and the last, and that goes for pots as much as anywhere else. In Sussex, it still feels like winter at the beginning of March, but by the end the clocks have gone forward and wherever you look things are growing.

This is one of my favourite moments in the year, with new flowers appearing every day. I'm an early riser and towards the end of March I can easily spend an hour walking round the garden as the sun comes up, checking out the plants and flowers – narcissi, fritillaries and early-flowering tulips – that are new to us, planted in trials in the autumn and now just opening. Every few steps there's something exciting.

At the start of March, we are still mainly relying on small, shallow, terracotta or zinc pots filled with violas, irises, scillas and crocuses, all performing strongly. As in February, these are raised up on metal outdoor tables in prominent places so we really see them. And the shade-lovers – potted hellebores, cyclamen and snowdrops – envelope our back door. As the days pass, more and more pots come up from the polytunnel or are brought out of the greenhouse or cold frames, the flowers pushing up and into bloom.

I love the early spring bulb, glory of the snow, for pots, particularly *Scilla* 'Pink Giant' (syn. *Chionodoxa forbesii* 'Pink Giant'), which has naturalised in the garden borders here now. There are also different varieties of species tulips opening every day. The *Tulipa humilis* hybrids (such as 'Persian Pearl', 'Odalisque' and 'Little Beauty') flower first, followed by *Tulipa*

turkestanica. Then comes *T. praestans* 'Shogun'. Next come
the brilliant pinks of *T. bakeri* (syn. *T. saxatilis* Bakeri Group).
Finally, as March comes to an end, out come the stripy
T. clusiana 'Peppermintstick' and 'Lady Jane'.

These tulips fill our small pots, which emerge from the cold
frames and polytunnel to join the larger zinc and terracotta
containers that stay in situ. In these whopper pots, the earliest
flowering layers of our bulb lasagnes will begin to flower as the
weeks go by. Lots of our pots have a top layer of *Iris reticulata*,
which is still looking good, but from beneath a few invaluable
full-scale and dramatic tulips erupt and take over.

There are some tall tulips pretty much guaranteed to be in
flower with us at some point in March and I love them for that.
For saturated-colour lovers, there's tulip 'Orange Emperor', or
any in the Impression series, as well as 'Orca' and the other
short, but sumptuous Double Early varieties such as 'Chato'
and 'Queen Jewel'. We always try to include these in our pot
designs to lift our spirits in March.

The earliest tulip we grow is 'Ice Stick', closely followed
by 'Purissima', perfect if you like things white and pale.
'Ice Stick' starts the show in the first week of March, with
'Purissima' taking over two or three weeks later, looking good
right through to mid- or late April. This is a valuable duo for
succession. 'Purissima' also makes a great pairing with my
favourite early tulip, 'Exotic Emperor', along with a third
ingredient, *Cerinthe major* 'Purpurascens'. If the cerinthe is
sown early enough (we sow the previous autumn and store
somewhere frost-free until late winter), it arrives at the same
time as the tulips emerge from bud.

This trio is a perfect example of the Bride, Bridesmaid,
Gatecrasher recipe (see p38), which we often follow for our
designs. The tulips go in sometime in October or November,
one layer on top of another. To encourage early flowering, if their
pots are portable, we leave them under cover until they start to
shoot. We find this encourages their flowers to arrive two
to three weeks earlier than if left outside, but it's not essential.
As the bulb foliage starts to grow, we slot in cerinthe by the end
of February. Cerinthe is a stalwart hardy annual which we add
to lots of pots and, as its name implies, it's full of nectar.

Fritillaries are another family that, if we use the right
varieties, give us glamorous and impressive pots for March.

We did a trial of fritillaries recently, all grown in containers, and it was hard not to include every one of the many forms we were judging in our online nursery. As with tulips, there are little and large types. The classic, delicate, miniature *Fritillaria meleagris* (snake's head fritillary) is wonderful in a pot, but it does go over quickly. In contrast, the huge, dramatic *F. imperialis* (crown imperial) or *F. persica* (Persian lily) varieties just keep going, their buds splendid, their flowers triumphant and their seedpods as architectural as any spring plant you'll find.

From our trial, my favourite amongst the greens was *F.* 'Early Sensation' (pictured on p95), one tone fresher and greener than the yellow-green 'Helena' and, as its name suggests, it opens a good week or two earlier. For an orange, it's hard to beat a few bulbs of 'Sunset' in a zinc pot. We have these planted in a plastic inner pot which fits exactly into the zinc tub. The fritillaries can then be hoicked out, plastic pot and all, and stored in a shady, cool spot (against a north wall or in the shade of a shrub or tree) for planting again in autumn. They're expensive to buy initially, but my parents kept fritillaries going in this way in their pots for decades – they truly earn their keep.

Below *Fritillaria imperialis* 'Sunset' with *Tulipa* 'Palmyra'. Next page The Dutch Yard in the last week of March, starting to fill with colour. The most prominent pots here are of *T.* 'Orca' with muscari, *Primula* 'Stella Champagne' and fritillaries, all standing on the wellhead beyond.

Fritillaria raddeana, the species type from the Middle East, flowers even earlier. We sometimes have that opening in February, but it always commands pride of place in its pot by March. I passionately recommend it. We have three bulbs forming the central high point, combined with *Scilla* 'Pink Giant' and the delicate nodding *Narcissus* 'Sailboat', for what's become a classic Perch Hill pot I've named Deborah's Pot Collection, after a friend who particularly loved it in the trial.

We try to have flowers for bees in our pots at all times, and fritillaries really help us out. They are busy with pollinators whenever the sun comes out. You'll see all kinds of bumblebees toing and froing to the tears of nectar collected at the apex of every fritillaria bell. On the invertebrate front, there's one downside to fritillaries: in the *Liliaceae* family, they are a host to the leaf-munching, lily beetle – keep your eye out for these scarlet bugs and remove them before they do too much damage.

Opposite I love this early flowering pot collection with *Fritillaria raddeana*, *Narcissus* 'Sailboat' and *Scilla* 'Pink Giant'. Each one of these bulbs is very perennial.
Below left *Fritillaria* 'Early Sensation' is one of the most dramatic plants for March pots in sun or shade.
Below right *Fritillaria meleagris* is full of pollen and nectar for bees.

Early tulips

Opposite *Tulipa* 'Orange Emperor' flowers in the sheltered Oast Garden from late March, surrounded by *Euphorbia characias* subsp. *wulfenii* 'John Tomlinson'.

I'd love to do a straw poll to find out the most popular plant for growing in pots. Which would be number one? I suspect it would be the tulip. Tulips are just pot perfect: they come in the right size, arrive in a good season, offer a huge range of colours and sometimes they even have perfume. And they're dead easy; if you get them into a pot any time before Christmas (or even, at a push, a bit after) they *will* grow. That's why over the years we have experimented with hundreds of different varieties at Perch Hill, and we particularly look out for ones that flower noticeably earlier than most, so we can have the longest tulip season.

When they flower is mainly down to the group they're in (see p146). The miniature types in the Species group are reliably early, while coming next in their earliness are the Fosteriana and Kaufmanniana tulips. There are some valuable ones in the Fosteriana group (such as any of the Emperor series), while the Kaufmanniana crew tend to have large flowers on short stems and are lacking in grace. That said, 'Ice Stick' is one we like and it truly does flower from early March. Single Early is a great group, but the tulips aren't early enough, opening with us in early April. Whereas, in a sheltered spot, there are a few Double Early stars. As with many of the earlies, some of these are too top-heavy, but luckily there are some exceptions. 'Orca' has vast, many petalled, orange flowers that I used to find too gaudy, but I now adore the show they give so early in spring.

The other thing about double tulips is that the extra petals come from the development of the flower's nectaries, so the doubles are without (or almost without) nectar. They don't draw pollinators in and hence are never fertilised. They keep on flowering, hoping to attract a bee, but it doesn't happen, so on and on they flower. That isn't great for the pollinators, but is for the pot gardener, because they flower for at least 50 per cent longer than a standard single tulip form. We don't forget the pollinators though, and the groves of single tulips and plants like cerinthe, wallflowers and honesty make up for it.

Best of the early tulips

For pots on your doorstep in March, these are the tulips to go for. Can I swear that they will all be fully open in March? I can hear cries of 'no' from those who garden in the north of the UK. And they're right: there's no guarantee that they will flower that early in colder regions. But I still say it's useful to know which beautiful tulips flower ahead of the rest, and these are they.

Standard

These tulips are average in size, standing at around 45cm (18in) tall.

1 *Tulipa* 'Apricot Delight' (Triumph)
The earliest tulip to flower in pots at Perch Hill, with chalky apricot flowers and a tall and elegant form. It looks brilliant simply massed together on its own.

2 *T.* 'Apricot Pride' (Triumph)
A statuesque tulip that's taller than the rest here (about 60cm/2ft). It's a mellow colour with a chalky but not white centre and warm pink wash overlaying the outer petal surface.

3 *T.* 'Chato' (Double Early)
An invaluable tulip for its very early flowering and sumptuous, deep pink, peony-like blooms.

4 *T.* 'Concerto' (Fosteriana)
This was recommended to me by my friend, Dutch garden designer Carien van Boxtel, as an exceptional tulip – and it's lovely in the first spring pot of flowers. It has a look of great serenity, reminiscent, to me, of flowers in a Renaissance painting.

5 *T.* Emperor series (Fosteriana)
Both 'Orange Emperor' (see p96) and 'Purissima' (syn. 'White Emperor') are fantastic for pots and also perfect for picking. 'Orange Emperor' is vibrant and showy, flowering three to four weeks before the main season tulips, while 'Purissima' (pictured) is a fantastic, large, creamy tulip, much like an early 'Spring Green' (see p168). 'Apricot Emperor' is certainly in flower by the start of April, if not before, and is one tone softer than 'Orange Emperor'. It often has a green flash to the outer petals as it opens.

6 *T.* 'Exotic Emperor' (Fosteriana)
A double tulip (also known as 'White Valley' and not in the Emperor series) whose outer petals are more like green sepals than fully blown petals. It looks good from the moment the buds begin to develop until it is about to drop.

7 *T.* Impression series
(Darwin Hybrid)
This lot are really the first
to put on a great show and
come in some glorious pinks,
salmons and, as with the
lovely 'Apricot Impression'
(pictured), apricots. The whole
series features statuesque
tulips that stand proud above
the rest, with flowers that
open early, invaluable for
early season pots and vases.

8 *T.* 'Mystic van Eijk'
(Darwin Hybrid)
A tulip that goes through
many colour changes: when
it first emerges, it's quite
pink, stronger in the heart
of the flower than the outer
petals, which gives it a kind
of radiance. It becomes more
muted as the weeks go by,
ending up a sort of milky
coffee colour, not unlike 'La
Belle Epoque',

but single rather than
double. As a Darwin Hybrid
this is also an early tulip,
which can sometimes flower
with us from early April or
even March, and it is very
perennial, so we always move
it into the garden straight
after flowering.

9 *T.* 'Orca' (Double Early)
'Orca' is an Ascot hat of a
tulip – fabulously vulgar
but undeniably lovely. It
has short stems and huge
brilliant-orange flowers.
It's also scented, which makes
it a complete mood lifter.

10 *T.* 'Palmyra' (Double Early)
This is my friend, gardener
Arthur Parkinson's, favourite
tulip, with huge, fully double,
satin flowers two tones
deeper than red wine. This
is one of the taller earlies
and great for that – it also

flowers longer than any tulip
I can think of, which is what
makes it so good for pots. We
often mix it with 'Orca' to
give the pot a just-as-showy
understorey.

11 *T.* 'Queen Jewel'
(Double Early)
I fell on this new tulip in
a trial field in 2019 as it
seemed even more dazzling
than 'Chato', which is a long-
standing favourite here for
being so glamorous so early
in the season. 'Queen Jewel'
flowers for a good five weeks
and earns its keep five times
over. It has unusual shiny,
bright green leaves.

Miniature

This selection includes those that are smaller than your average tulip, and more delicate. Quite a few of these are scented. They also have great blight resistance, which is so useful as wet springs (in damp conditions, blight proliferates) become more common.

1 *Tulipa bakeri* 'Lilac Wonder' (syn. *T. saxatilis* Bakeri Group 'Lilac Wonder') (Species)
This one has style, like a 1960s Mary Quant dress. I love it in a pot and often have a large, shallow tray filled with it and given pride of place on a table bang in the middle of the cutting garden. It's softly scented. Very similar to *T. saxatilis*, which also flowers in late March.

2 *T. clusiana* 'Lady Jane' (Species)
Very elegant with white interior petals, red-pink outer petals and beautiful glaucous silver leaves. This is an all-out top ranker. Outstanding. Flowers late March.

3 *T. humilis* 'Little Beauty' (Species)
With oval magenta flowers held well above the leaves, this favourite is fantastic when you cram the bulbs, almost touching, into a large pot. Unlike many of the others in the Species group, it flowers for a long time from mid-March.

4 *T. humilis* 'Persian Pearl' (Species)
This has very early flowers in jewel-like colours and a soft, sweet scent. 'Odalisque' is similar.

5 *T. praestans* 'Shogun' (Species)
A brilliant, zingy, clementine-orange colour, this comes up year after year in our perennial pots, with the clumps gradually getting bigger and bigger. We often have it filling two pots with a third pot of 'Orca' next door. Or we use it in tulip lasagnes for succession: this goes in as the top layer to flower late March and go over before the mid-season tulips (such as 'Ronaldo', pictured) emerge.

6 *T. saxatilis* (Species)
Expect very distinct, bright green, glossy leaves and a laxer habit than the other tulips here. This is taller too, with a flower stem of 25cm (10in) compared to the 10cm (4in) stem of, say, 'Little Beauty'. Beautiful in a pot grown with support, and it's scented.

7 *T. turkestanica* (Species)
Flowering early and for the longest amongst this selection, *T. turkestanica* also has seedheads that look architectural for many weeks. This is another softly scented tulip.

Narcissi

Opposite *Narcissus* 'Frosty Snow'
with amelanchier behind, which
flowers from March into April.

I'm crazy about narcissi and feel they're a much underestimated and underused bulb. They're fabulous growing in swathes through grass and, with the right varieties, they make great cut flowers. For pots, there's almost nothing more delicate and lovely for the start of spring. You want tulips, yes, but you want pots of narcissi to mix in with them, or to have in pots alone, backlit as much as possible so you really see their fineness of form.

To me, the difference between narcissi and the other spring queen, the tulip, is like that between the English rose Jean Shrimpton and the American country singer Dolly Parton. They're both glorious and unique but they are truly contrasting personalities. For the perfect March pot scene, I think you want both. There are narcissi, of course, which are more robust and out there, but that's not what I want from my potted daffodils. In all our trials of hundreds of varieties over the last 30 years, there are three characteristics we look for.

Firstly, delicacy needs to be their middle name: delicacy matters both in terms of the flowers and, importantly for pot gardeners, the leaves. The classic daffodil is a triumphant plant with its great yellow trumpet and belt-like leaves, but that look doesn't work in a pot.

Secondly, scent is a lovely thing to have, but not absolutely essential. When it's good, narcissus perfume can be exceptional, and there's none more heavenly than that of my father's favourite miniature daffodil, *Narcissus* 'Canaliculatus', which is in the Tazetta group. You'll see from the divisions on the next pages that many of our top picks have Tazetta and Jonquilla heritage, and that's because these have the strongest fragrance.

To complete our trio of requirements, we look for early flowering. Although, over the years, we've selected the best forms that give a bit of succession over the season, which is why I've made a note of their flowering time in the 'best of' lists on p110.

Narcissus Classification

Daffodils are divided into thirteen horticultural groups depending on their shared characteristics. Often you'll see 'miniature' as a prefix, which just means the flowers are smaller, usually less than 5cm (2in) diameter, but the same division applies.

Division 1: Trumpet
One flower to a stem with a long cup or nose (the technical way of describing this is the corona or, to most people, the trumpet). The trumpet is the same length or longer than the petals. 'Elka' is a miniature member of this group that we like. We don't tend to grow the larger scale ones as their leaves and even flowers can be a bit chunky.

Division 2: Large-cupped
One flower to a stem, with a shorter trumpet than Division 1. We have not gone for these in a big way, as they tend to be on the heavy side, but there are some new varieties in shades of pink grapefruit and apricot that look more elegant. I like 'Pink Charm' and the ivory 'Stainless'.

Division 3: Small-cupped
One flower to a stem, with a trumpet that's no more than a third of the length of the petals. These are sort of flat-faced, which I like – two of my favourites for table centre pots are 'Xit' and 'Segovia', and both are very fragrant.

Division 4: Double
One or more flowers to a stem, with double petals, double trumpets or both. 'Sir Winston Churchill' is a classic of this group, but we don't grow many in pots. They tend to be more for picking.

Division 5: Triandrus

Usually two or more hanging flowers to a stem with reflexed petals. For pots, we grow several in this group including 'Hawera', 'Katie Heath', 'Thalia' and 'Lemon Drops'. They are often graceful and elegant.

Division 6: Cyclamineus

One flower to a stem with very reflexed petals. 'Tête-à-tête' is the famous one amongst these, and we love 'Prinses Amalia'.

Division 7: Jonquilla and Apodanthus

Between one and five flowers to a stem, with a short trumpet that is often wider than it is long, with petals spreading or reflexed. The flowers are usually fragrant. We love 'Sailboat', the small-flowered 'Baby Boomer', 'Kokopelli' and 'Frosty Snow' (pictured on p104).

Division 8: Tazetta

These usually have three to 20 fragrant flowers to a short stem. These are popular as cut

flowers (a top one is 'Grand Soleil d'Or') and we grow lots for pots, including 'Canaliculatus', 'Minnow' and 'Silver Chimes'.

Division 9: Poeticus

The daffs in this division are commonly known as pheasant's eye. Their petals are pure white and the trumpet is very short or even disc-shaped. The flowers are fragrant. This is one of the best groups for naturalising in grass, so we usually grow them there.

Division 10: Bulbocodium

Usually one flower to a stem and a trumpet that looks like a hooped petticoat. I love these very distinctive daffodils and think they look best in smaller pots and containers. They also flower for ages. We grow 'Arctic Bells', 'Golden Bells' and 'White Petticoat'.

Division 11: Split corona

Also known as split-cup, these daffodils have trumpets, and sometimes petals, with split segments. These are too complex and feel a bit mutant to me, but we are soon to trial a few and may find a new favourite.

Division 12: Other

These are the anomalous ones – those that fail to fall into any of the previous categories.

Division 13: Daffodils distinguished solely by botanical name

These are the species, wild varieties.

Best of the narcissi

I have divided the narcissi we grow for pots into two groups according to their palette. The first group are soft and delicate, the second lot are bold and golden. We tend to collect them in these two separate families or concentrate on one colour group with just the odd gatecrasher from the other sprinkled lightly through.

Flowering times
Early: mid-Feb to mid-March
Mid: mid-March to mid-April
Late: mid-April to mid-May

Soft and Delicate

This group features daffodils in soft hues with a petite form to match. It doesn't completely fit with the Soft and Warm palette (see p30) as there are some brighter yellows, but overall these offer softer shades.

1 *Narcissus* 'Canaliculatus' (Tazetta)
This tiny, but hugely and deliciously scented narcissus is the prettiest of the lot. It was a favourite of my father's for small pots on our window ledges when I was a child. It's 100 per cent perennial and will gradually spread and naturalise wherever you plant it, even spreading to fill a pot. Late.

2 *N.* 'Elka' (Trumpet)
Like 'Tête-à-tête', but the most perfect shade of ivory. Ideal for pots and the front of a bed as it's a miniature. Late.

3 *N.* 'Hawera' (Triandrus)
A delicate, almost butterfly-like, highly scented miniature daffodil in a soft, primrose yellow. This is an ideal scale for shallow terracotta pots, which you can bring inside for a temporary house visit. Very late.

4 *N.* 'Katie Heath' (Triandrus)
This has an unusual, peachy coloured perianth that I love, and a pretty scent to match. It can be difficult to find so look out for the similar 'Bell Song'. Mid.

5 *N.* 'Lemon Drops' (Triandrus)
One of the loveliest, multiheaded, delicate daffodils in beautiful ivory and primrose, with elegant, thin foliage, making it excellent for planting in pots and window boxes. We use this in mixed bulb containers combining it with other small to medium bulbs like anemones, muscari and scillas. Makes a beautiful cut flower. Mid.

6 *N.* 'Minnow' (Tazetta)
Brilliant for pots as well as in the garden, 'Minnow' is a dwarf form with flat, pale yellow cups and a wondrous scent. Late.

7 *N.* 'Pink Charm' (Large-cupped)
Fragrant, fashionably peachy, showy, but not overly so. We chose this one from many in our apricot/peach narcissi trials in 2019. A good all-rounder and great for picking. Late.

8 *N.* 'Prinses Amalia' (Cyclamineus)
We trialled this for naturalising in grass, but we had extra bulbs so planted them in pots and even in a bulb lasagne. It triumphed. It's a gentle-coloured daff that looks good and does well wherever we plant it. It's set to become a classic. Late.

9 *N.* 'Sailboat' (Jonquilla)
I love this elegant and petite narcissus with a gentle butter-coloured trumpet and white wings. It's an ideal shade and size to mix with often soft-coloured bulbs such as *Muscari* 'Baby's Breath' and *Puschkinia scilloides* var. *libanotica*. Mid.

10 *N.* 'Segovia' (Small-cupped)
An exquisite, open-faced, highly scented dwarf narcissus with white petals and a small, flat, lemon cup. Grow it in a pot by your front door so you can admire it every day. Late.

11 *N.* 'Silver Chimes' (Tazetta)
With delicate leaves and pretty flowers, this looks good, does well in pots and has a lovely scent. It also looks lovely in grass, bulking up quickly to form clumps, so you could plant it out after flowering. Mid.

12 *N.* 'Sir Winston Churchill' (Double)
All you need is five stems of this by your bed and you wake up in a fragrant cloud. It's bred as a cut flower for perfume and is a multiheaded narcissus with a repeat cropping pattern, which makes it great value. This is one of the only doubles I'd grow in a pot as it is less top-heavy than many of the others. Late.

13 *N.* 'Stainless'
(Large-cupped)
Pure white with a green
eye, this is one of the few
daffodils in the Large-cupped
division that we grow in
pots. It's similar to 'Frosty
Snow' (pictured on p104).
It's lovely cut for a vase.
Lightly scented. Mid.

14 *N.* 'Starlight Sensation'
(Triandrus)
This brand-new narcissus
bowled us over in our most
recent trial, flowering
longer than any other. It
looks perfect in pots (both
with a viola pot topper and
on its own) and has the
strongest and most delicious
citrus blossom scent. It is
exceptionally multiheaded
with some stems topped by
seven or even eight flowers.
It has so much going for it.
Outstanding. Late.

15 *N.* 'Thalia' (Triandrus)
A multiheaded, classic ivory
narcissus. Beautiful in shade
and lovely picked for the
vase. Mid.

16 *N.* 'White Petticoat'
(Bulbocodium)
Planted in a large pot
(we grow them in a copper
one), these look just like
Swan Lake ballerinas on stage.
Early to flower, they are the
prettiest heralders of spring.
Early–mid.

17 *N.* 'Xit' (Small-cupped)
A relatively new discovery
and absolutely beautiful:
dainty, scented, long
flowering and with fine
leaves. It has everything
you'd want from a daffodil
for pots. Late.

18 *N.* 'Ziva' (Tazetta)
The paperwhite 'Ziva' is
a pure white, highly fragrant,
multiheaded daffodil that
makes a classic winter
houseplant. Place one pot on
top of another – like a tiered
wedding cake – for a winter
table centrepiece or plant
into a large shallow bowl
(pictured on p402). Flowers
from November when forced.
Very early.

Bold and Golden

These daffodils are brighter and more striking in their colours, and their forms are a bit more robust than the first selection. They are the rich and golden contingent – powerfully coloured but most have petite and dainty forms.

1 *Narcissus* 'Baby Boomer' (Jonquilla)
A new discovery with a bad name but great characteristics. It looks sweet and delicate and has the finest flowers of any of the egg-yolk-yellow daffs. It's vigorous and super easy to grow. Mid.

2 *N. bulbocodium* 'Golden Bells' (Bulbocodium)
One of the so-called 'hooped petticoat' daffodils, because that's just what they look like: a roomful of ladies dancing in their miniature golden ball gowns. Late.

3 *N.* 'Falconet' (Tazetta)
With individual flowers one size up from 'Grand Soleil d'Or', this is an easy-to-grow narcissus with great scent and good vase life. It was bred in Cornwall for early spring cut flowers. There, the advanced season combined with early-flowering varieties like this one, give Cornwall and the Isles of Scilly a commercial advantage in the cut flower trade. Mid.

4 *N.* 'Grand Soleil d'Or' (Tazetta)
Clusters of scented, multiheaded flowers with bright yellow petals and orange cups on tall stems. Excellent for cutting; a few stems of this will fill a room with scent. This is the earliest to flower here, blooming outside in a sheltered spot from early March. And it can be easily forced, which is why it's so popular in the cut flower industry. 'Martinette' is very similar. Early.

5 *N.* 'Kokopelli' (Jonquilla)
I asked Josie (our head gardener) for her favourite new narcissus and she chose 'Kokopelli'. It is outstanding for its delicate chive-like foliage (so ideal for a pot, lawn or front of border), utterly lovely perfume, multiheads (each one miniature and pretty, but plenty on the top of each stem) and ability to flower for a long time. It's later flowering than the others here, so useful if you want a succession of daffodils flowering from March and well into April. Mid.

6 *N.* 'More and More' (Jonquilla)
I was introduced to this on a tour of narcissus breeders in the Netherlands a few years ago. It's so named because it goes on and on, flowering from March and right through April. It's pretty, petite and scented. Late.

7 *N.* 'Quail' (Jonquilla)
Famed for its length of flowering, this narcissus is hugely fragrant and pretty with it. Each stem has three or four flowers, and it is the ideal scale for a pot. Late.

8 *N.* 'Tête-à-tête' (Cyclamineus)
This miniature, easy-to-grow, live-forever narcissus is excellent value and wins bulb of the year again and again, and with good reason. Mid.

Best of the pot toppers

Pot toppers really help establish the overall feel of a winter and early spring garden, large or small. I love to have a range of things growing in the tops of our pots, many are purely ornamental, others are also edible, giving us beauty and food at times when there's little else around. They also form a lovely ruff around the edge of a pot, providing a softening backdrop to emerging spring bulbs.

There isn't a huge range of things that are happy and hardy enough to look good whatever the weather and its true some of our pot toppers take a bit of a hammering if the winters are severe, but even so, it's worth going the extra mile to include them and to maximise the joy you get from all your pots.

Over the years we've worked out which plants serve the pot-topper role best and which are hardy enough to form the final surface layer over lasagnes of bulbs and be able to withstand any frost, wind, rain and even snow that could be thrown at them. These are the ones that cope through the winter and look good into spring.

1 *Anthriscus sylvestris*
At the gardens of Great Dixter, which are near me in East Sussex, they use green-leaved cow parsley as a foliage companion to bulbs, but I think the black-leaved *Anthriscus* 'Ravenswing' is even better. It survives the winter in a sheltered spot and gives a beautiful, feathery leaf through the cold months, as well as a good backdrop to bulbs in spring.

2 *Cerinthe major* 'Purpurascens'
We grow cerinthe in pots on its own and as a topper for tulip lasagnes. This works for a sheltered spot over winter, but it will suffer in a frost. If you don't have good shelter, plant it out in March, when the worst of the wintery weather is over.

3 *Cynara cardunculus* (Scolymus Group)
We have a few potted globe artichokes (in 2-litre pots) which we tip out and plant with bulbs (in the centre of a bulb lasagne) in autumn. The artichoke foliage, which is pretty much evergreen, gives great presence all winter and then provides a silver foil to the tulips as they flower.

4 Dwarf bulbs
Guaranteed to be 100 per cent hardy are the miniature bulbs, dwarf irises and early crocuses (such as *Iris reticulata* and *Crocus sieberi* 'Firefly'). We cram a top layer of these bulbs in over the double or triple layer of tulips in November.

2

3

4

5 *Erysimum*
Wallflowers are a classic pot topper. With new varieties such as those in the Sugar Rush series flowering on and off all autumn and winter as well as spring, they are invaluable for flowers and perfume when there's little else performing in our pots. Pictured here is 'Sugar Rush Purple Bicolour'.

7 Herbs
Flat-leaved parsley is a biennial grown as an annual – I especially love 'Gigante di Napoli'. Chervil (pictured) is happy outside in rain and snow and gives us a gentle aniseed taste for the kitchen. Regular harvesting keeps the plants looking good and in check.

5

6 *Foeniculum vulgare*
I love fennel as a pot topper, particularly the bronze fennel, *Foeniculum vulgare* 'Giant Bronze'. Its frothy leaves are fresh and perfect as they start to grow in March and April. Fennel does die back in deep winter, but it is early to emerge again come a sunny week in March. Always check the fronds for green fly before adding to salads!

6

7

8 *Heuchera* and *heucherella*
These have become increasingly popular in the last few years and there's an ever-expanding range. I love the pink-crimson *Heuchera* 'Wild Rose' (pictured) and some of the bronze-tinged ones like 'Crème Brûlée' and 'Peach Flambe', as well as × *Heucherella* 'Sweet Tea'.

9 Kale
The crinkly 'Dwarf Green Curled' kale (pictured), dark red 'Curly Scarlet' and the larger 'Redbor' are favourites. All kales are evergreen and truly hardy, but these are the most handsome and hang in there from an autumn planting right through until the middle of spring. At that point, they flower – with typical yellow brassica blooms – which you can remove or leave for the

pollinators (they're stacked with nectar) and as another colour to add to your pot combinations. Repeatedly pinched out, or harvested through the winter, they remain bonsaied.

10 Leafy greens
Rainbow chard is one of the most ornamental edibles you can grow. Pick when the leaves are still small for the best flavour. Spinach 'Rubino' (pictured) has elegant almost-black stems and is the hardiest, making it most suitable for use as a winter pot topper.

11 Salad leaves
I love the spicy Japanese leaf mizuna – the best for pots is the chunkier-leaved 'Red Knight' (pictured), rather than the less substantial green form. Mustards are

also invaluable: 'Red Giant' is pretty hot, 'Wasabina' is also powerful, whereas 'Red Frills' is mild. For salad rocket, try 'Serrata' and 'Dentellata' – both have generous leaves and are strong tasting but not too peppery. These are hardy annuals (unlike wild rocket, which is a perennial).

12 *Viola*
Violas are better than pansies for winter – the smaller flowers are more weather tolerant. We often grow our window box anemones with violas, such as *Viola cornuta* 'Sorbet Phantom' and the hardiest of all, our native heart's ease, *V. tricolor*. These look best if you choose one colour (I love a pot of *V. c.* 'Sorbet Violet' or the fiery viola 'Tiger Eye Red', pictured) or at the most, a harmonious range of two or three colours.

13 *Visnaga daucoides*
(syn. *Ammi visnaga*)
With delicate, finely cut
leaves this forms a pretty
foliage backdrop to soft-
coloured bulbs when they
emerge in spring and gives us
something to look at in the
pot all through winter. It also
seems to be hardier than its
brother, *Ammi majus*, and is
more compact so we can leave
it to grow from spring to
early summer to flower from
May. Its foliage is pictured
here with *Tulipa* 'Orca'.

Next page Curly,
one of our dogs, with
Tulipa 'Concerto' and
T. turkestanica with
amelanchier flowering in
the Dutch Yard beyond.

March

March is our main month for seed sowing. If you sow plenty of varieties and look after them well, you can grow fantastic plants for your pots very cheaply. There are a few plants we sow early in the year – sweet peas are the first seeds we sow in January, together with the slow growers such as snapdragons and cobaea – and a few seeds that we delay sowing until April – zinnias, for instance – as they hate cold nights and aren't safe going out until late May. But overall, March is our busiest sowing time.

Sowing, pricking out, watering and generally being in the polytunnel at this time of year is amongst my greatest pleasures in life. The tunnel feels substantially warmer and more spring like than the outside, and it's full of new life, energy and optimism. I *always* emerge from an hour in the tunnel or greenhouse feeling a lot better – I recommend it.

Having said all that, if you don't have a polytunnel and are without a greenhouse or cold frame, I'd advise buying seedlings online rather than sowing everything into trays and filling up your windowsills. The lower light levels and heat in a house are not ideal for many plants. Perhaps select just one or two to sow, ones that you know are easy, and buy the rest as very young plants. There are more and more great things available online for pots (lots of the plants I mention are available through our online nursery as seedlings or rooted cuttings) and they don't need to be expensive. I'd advise shopping online or

visiting a nursery rather than a trip to the garden centre, where what's on offer can be a bit mainstream.

March is the time for a few other jobs, too. There are dahlia tubers to pot and the cobaea sown in January may well need potting on, and it will also need a silver birch teepee to support it. Caring for cuttings is ongoing (see p87), and if the cuttings look like they are getting pot-bound, they will need potting on too.

There is also a bit of planting to get going with. The frosts are still very much with us, so it's only hardy perennials and hardy

Previous page It's key to pinch
out almost all annuals, particularly
sweet peas.

annuals that can go out this early (and only
with shelter). Cerinthe, calendula, linaria and
sweet peas can all be planted out in March.
Towards the end of the month, hardier salvias
can start to be hardened off by placing in a
cold frame if you have one.

Keep your eyes peeled for more pests as the
weather warms. It's a good time to deal with
early aphids with a jet of water from the hose.

Sowing Methods

We use six sowing methods at Perch Hill,
but the commonest by far for our pots is the
seed tray method.

- **Seed trays** There are lots of plants for pots
  that we sow into these (see p86).
- **Modular trays or Jiffy-7s** We use these
  to sow zinnias (April) and poppies such as
  Papaver rhoeas 'Amazing Grey' (in March/
  April). Famously, poppies are best direct
  sown, but on our heavy clay soil we find
  unusual varieties like 'Amazing Grey' don't
  germinate well, so we use modular trays
  for these.
- **Root trainers** As far as pots are concerned,
  we only sow sweet peas in root trainers in
  January (pictured on p83).
- **Individual pots** We sow our mini
  sunflowers into their own pot, usually
  9cm (3½in) ones, in April (see p173).
- **Direct sowing, straight into the top of**

the pot We sow one or two things straight
into its final pot, mainly seeds that are tiny,
such as linaria or erigeron. This can be done
almost any time in February or March for
linarias, or in February or September for
the erigeron, and no special instructions
are needed: simply take a pinch of seed and
sprinkle it on the compost. Just be as mean
as you can with the seed to avoid the need
for thinning the seedlings at a later stage.

Sowing medium
For all our sowing, we use a peat-free,
sustainably produced potting compost and
place pretty much everything on our heated
propagator mat – the basal heat improves
growth rates. Warmth in general helps speed
up germination, so keep your bags of compost
inside if you can. And water the compost in
the trays with watering cans that have sat
on the hot bench so the water isn't ice cold.

Label
The other thing I never fail to do is label
everything, as it's so easy to forget what's
what. Always start writing at the blunt
end of your label, otherwise you'll be
constantly taking the labels out of the
pots to read them.

Storing seed
If you have any leftover seed, secure the seed
packet and put it in an airtight plastic box,
ideally with a silicone sachet in the corner to

keep the seed dry. Store somewhere cool until next year. We have a special slot in a fridge. You'll then ensure decent germination (for most things) for several years to come.

....

Seeds to Sow in March

For our pots, we do a lot of sowing into seed trays in March. We only need quite limited numbers of a wide range of plants, so seed trays are perfectly suited to the task. We use thin green canes to divide up the seed tray and sow just a few seeds of several varieties into each tray. Seed trays are ideal for some half-hardy annuals, particularly for those with tiny, dust-like seeds that are difficult to sow individually into modules. They also work for things like verbenas, because they have quite large seed which you can individually place and ensure they are well apart. For advice on sowing into a seed tray see p86.

At this time of year, we get going with quite a few things.

Climbers

Contrary to what you might think, climbers are fantastic for pots, offering a dramatic upper storey and making use of vertical space, which is so vital if you have a small garden or balcony. We sow *Ipomoea lobata*, *Rhodochiton atrosanguineus* and *Thunbergia alata* 'African Sunset' now.

Half-hardy annuals

In March, we get going with our annual phlox including *Phlox* 'Crème Brûlée' and '21st Century Blue Star', as well as the grass *Panicum* 'Frosted Explosion' and *Hibiscus acetosella* 'Mahogany Splendor'. It's also the moment for sowing petunias such as our all-time favourites, *Petunia* 'Tidal Wave Red Velour' and 'Tidal Wave Silver'. We sow some of our verbenas (such as *Verbena rigida*) from seed now, as well as our tobacco plants, such as *Nicotiana sylvestris* 'Only The Lonely', which are perfect for pots in shade.

Towards the end of the month, we sow all of our cosmos varieties, including favourites *Cosmos bipinnatus* 'Apricotta', 'Rubenza', 'Sonata White' and 'Sonata Carmine'. Cosmos can't go out until the frosts are over, so we find sowing about four weeks before our last expected frost pretty much gives us spot-on timing for planting out.

Primulas

We sow polyanthus and primroses now for flowers the following year. Ideally sow early enough so the seeds get frosted in their seed tray. Use a fibrous seed compost (not multipurpose one, as the fertiliser levels are too high for these sensitive seeds). Surface sow, don't cover the seeds over. Water lightly and place the seed tray outside in a shady place. We cover with an upturned crate to protect and shade the tray. Make sure the trays don't dry out as excess heat or dryness stops germination. Prick out when the seedlings have reached a decent size.

Spring-flowering violas

Viola seeds are tiny and therefore best sown in a seed tray. Most varieties will flower in eight to ten weeks from sowing.

Dahlias

You can sow some dahlias from seed, including the brilliant dahlia 'Bishop's Children'.

Pricking Out from Seed Trays

Snapdragons sown in February will need pricking out around now, once they have two to three pairs of true leaves. Violas, phlox, panicum and all the other seeds sown in March will usually need pricking out four to six weeks later.

- Prepare an individual 9cm (3½in) pot with peat-free potting compost. Use a dibber or pencil to create a small dimple (not a channel) for the seedling.
- To lift out each seedling, get as much root as you can by pushing a dibber (or you can use a pencil or rigid label) right down to the base of the tray and lift the seedling from there. Avoid touching the stem. Lift the seedling out by the leaves. You may need to tear the roots of one seedling from another a little, but don't worry, as long as they're left with some, the seedlings will be fine.
- Firm it in into its new pot and water. Label.
- Place the pot back on the heated propagator until it's time to harden off.

Planting Dahlia Tubers

For dahlias, make sure you have 3-litre pots. A 2-litre pot is often too small for bigger tubers and you don't want to force them in and damage the root. A big pot also allows the tubers to grow happily until the chance of frost has passed and they can be planted out.

temperatures really start to rise, and even then, take care not to overdo it.

- Once roots appear in the holes at the bottom of the pot, plant out into their final containers, but only if there's no chance of frost.
- When they start to sprout, you can also take cuttings (see p177), but we tend not to do too many for pots, as we only need a limited number of dahlia plants.

Planting Lilies

Lilies can look fabulous in pots, the extra height of the pot making these bulbs look even more statuesque. *Lilium speciosum* var. *rubrum* (and the similar 'Uchida') are excellent for pots and can live in the same one happily for years with very minimal TLC. There are lots of others ideal for pot-growing (see p325).

March is a good month to plant lilies, so that they come out of dormancy and immediately romp away. We plant them en masse in pots on their own, rather than mixing them with other plants. Plant the bulbs so they are almost touching, and buried twice the depth of the bulb, so at least 8cm (3in).

After flowering, we move them somewhere out of sight (they don't look great as they die back). If we need their pots, we deadhead them, leave the foliage in place, then lift the bulbs and replant them in the garden.

- Plant each tuber in peat-free, multipurpose potting compost, just under the compost surface, not buried deeply.
- Water lightly and place on a heated propagator, or somewhere light and frost-free, until they start to shoot (which may not be until the end of April). Different varieties come into growth at different times.
- Only water when the compost starts to dry on the surface. Too much water in the early stages may make the tubers rot. Only increase watering once the plants are growing actively in April or May, and

Planting Out Spent Forced Bulbs

If you have planted bowls of forced hyacinths or narcissi (I love 'Avalanche' and 'Cragford' for this), they will have finished flowering by now – don't chuck them! You can plant them out for flowers next spring. If you don't have a garden, pot them up in a new pot with fresh compost. This does not apply to paperwhite daffodils, which aren't hardy. If you have those, leave the pot somewhere dry and frost-free for next year – reflowering is most likely if you lift them from their pot and replant with fresh compost in autumn.

- Choose a sunny spot.
- Dig a hole that's big enough to take the bulb with the base of the leaves buried just 2–3cm (1in) deeper than they were in the pot for extra stability. Line the hole with grit.
- Turn out the bulbs into the hole. Then cover over with more grit mixed into the soil. Leave the foliage intact, rather than cutting it back.
- If they continue to photosynthesise well for another month or so before the leaves die back, they'll flower well next spring.

Planting Out Sweet Peas

If you sowed your sweet pea seeds in January or February (see p83), the seedlings should be romping away now. Once you've got bushy seedlings that are 5–7cm (2–3in) tall, with roots coming out of the bottom of the root trainer, you need to plant them out.

From all our testing and growing sweet peas (in pots and in the ground) over 30 years, I'm convinced that the middle of March is the best time to do this, and that's particularly so with pots. Sweet peas are cold-weather plants and they're also not perfectly suited to pots. They're hungry and thirsty and need a really rich, deep root run, but we find, planted in tall pots from the middle of March, they can get their roots down deep while it's still cold and wet, well before the demands of flowering in late May and June.

If your pots are all full of tulips at this time, pot the sweet peas on into a deep 1-litre pot to buy yourself another few weeks, but you must get them into their final planting pot by the end of April. I'd recommend having special sweet pea pots to avoid this clash if you possibly can. Before they go out, we have their pot teepees ready and waiting (see p202).

- We line our terracotta pots with old compost bags to keep the moisture locked in as much as possible.
- I recommend using your largest, deepest pots and plant one sweet pea seedling to each upright. That will give your structure good coverage, while two could become top-heavy.
- The plants will need to be spaced at 15cm (6in) around the base of a teepee, and 5–7cm (2–3in) away from the support.
- Sweet peas are some of the hungriest and thirstiest plants we grow, so fill the pot with peat-free compost mixed with farmyard manure to a ratio of 3:1. The small amount of manure acts like a sponge and slowly releases food and water.
- Dig a good, deep hole for each plant, water the hole and plant the seedlings.
- Tie them into the base of the teepee using twine or twist ties.
- If you have a problem with slugs, top the pots with grit or apply Vaseline or copper tape around the pot. We encircle the base of the pot with a strip of horticultural grit 30cm (12in) wide and 3–4cm (1½in) deep.

April

April is a triumphant month for pots. It's when most of the bulb lasagnes we planted in autumn are looking their best and, along with August and September when the half-hardy annuals, dahlias and tender perennial climbers reach their peak, April is when pots are in the spotlight. By late summer and autumn, the garden is packed with colour and flowers, but in April that's not yet the case, so it's pots that really take centre stage.

When you walk into the Dutch Yard and Oast Garden you're hit by the sight of whopper pots bursting with tulips, narcissi and wallflowers, with hyacinths and hellebores still flowering away to add to the fiesta. At the other end of the scale, we have small pots as table centre pots, pretty with grape hyacinths, soft-textured pansies and violas and the first of the *Primula auricula*. I can hardly bear to tear myself away.

As well as thinking carefully about colour combinations, we keep in mind a few key factors when it comes to pot design. I'm a great believer in raising up pots to make them more visible. As they start to look good, we lift pots onto the plinths of our brick walls and the flat surface of our wellhead (we have a well that is surrounded by a low circular wall), as well as placing them on the many tables throughout the garden. Window boxes are a way of elevating pots too. I have a small London garden where my pots are my window boxes on generous, deep sills. They're key to the pleasure of life inside as well as out, and for many city dwellers, they are the garden.

If pots are raised, you see what they're made of, so the material of the pot becomes important. All of our pots, whether small or large, are either terracotta or metal. Amongst the metals, our pots are usually zinc, but some are cast iron and our repurposed water troughs are made from galvanised steel. We also have some huge French metalwork urns, which we line with moss – these provide great impact placed either side of an entrance. We stick with those materials because they mellow well with age and are visually quiet. I want the plants to do the talking, so I'd advise against bright, glazed pots. I have tried a few and all but the smallest have now been banished.

I also find playing with scale is a winner – little and large. Big pots take a fraction of the looking after compared with small ones (bigger volumes of compost need less feeding and watering), though I love both. Tables are ideal for highlighting delicate collections of plants in smaller pots, as are plant theatres. We love to layer muscari, polyanthus, primroses, pansies and fritillaries on plant theatres.

We also fill the stone sink in what we call our Chelsea shed with three auriculas that we find easy to grow and are reliably perennial: *Primula auricula* 'Purple Pip', the coppery 'Lunar Eclipse' and the deep red 'Black Jack'.

Previous page A repurposed Hungarian enamel cooking cauldron with *Tulipa* 'Dreamer' growing amongst fresh rose foliage at the start of April. Even though this is a Double Early, you can see it's still being visited by bees.
Below Looking out of the barn over a table of containers massed together. Plants include *Tulipa acuminata* (syn. *T.* 'Cornuta'), *Armeria pseudarmeria* 'Ballerina Red', tulips 'Slawa', 'Honky Tonk' and 'Vovos', and violas.
Opposite Tiered pots filled with *Muscari* 'Pink Sunrise' at the centre of a table. The seedheads are almost as good as the flowers.

Like most primulas, these thrive in cool shade, so they love it in the shed, flowering away happily for a couple of months. We fill the sink every three or four days, leave the pots sitting in water for half an hour and then drain. As a general rule, this is more effective for small pots than watering from the top. Flood them from the base for a short period, drain and repeat a few days later, or even every day in summer.

Muscari are excellent in mini-pots in a series along a windowsill or down the centre of an outdoor table. Most start flowering in March, but it's April when they come into their own. For me, tulips are the brouhaha for spring, great for medium and large pots, but muscari are equally valuable for something delicate and fine. The bright blue, silver-dusted grape hyacinth 'Big Smile' is guaranteed for early March, while the pure white 'Siberian Tiger' and pale 'Pink Sunrise' flower in March and into April, with the blue and white-tipped 'Helena' and the pale blue 'Esther' perfect for late April into May. Their seedheads all last for ages and are handsome too.

At the other end of the scale, we go large. We top the table at the centre of the Perennial Cutting Garden with just one

Previous page **The Oast Garden from above at its pot peak in April. The tulips in the whopper pots down the central path are filled with our Venetian Tulip Collection (also pictured on p145).**
Below **Our grape hyacinth collection:** *Muscari* **'Pink Sunrise',** *M. armeniacum* **'Valerie Finnis' and** *M. aucheri* **'Blue Magic' growing in an old sink.**

huge pot, filling the space. And I adore two giant wirework urns that we pack with a mix of tulips for spring and a combination of tall and trailing drought-tolerant salvias for summer. These have twice the impact of a clutch of medium-sized containers.

April pots are also good for supporting garden wildlife. As always, we're keen on plants reliably dense with pollen and nectar to feed our pollinators. Crab apple trees in blossom are brilliant for bees and early butterflies like orange-tip, peacock and brimstone. We're starting to introduce more of these trees into our permanent pots at Perch Hill and we're doing a trial of them, including *Malus × robusta* 'Red Sentinel', *M.* 'Evereste' and *M.* 'Comtesse de Paris'. We'll be looking at their performance growing in pots, the beauty and pollinator appeal of their blossom, their autumn leaf colour and how dense a crop of fruit they provide for garden birds.

Last but not least for April pots, we want scent. Wallflowers (*Erysimum*) are the name of the game for perfume in spring. I've grown wallflowers at Perch Hill for as long as I've been there – I love their old fashioned look and fragrance. There's been great breeding in the last couple of decades, and we have the Sugar Rush series flowering lightly from winter right through spring, joined by the Spring Breeze series in March. This is a good month earlier than the traditional varieties like *Erysimum cheiri* 'Fire King' and *E.* 'Blood Red', and they're compact and floriferous for pretty much the whole of spring.

With tulips as your upper storey, including a good crowd of scented ones, and wallflowers as the carpet through which they grow, April pots can smell as good as they look. That's our aim.

Main season tulips

I've covered early-flowering tulips in March (see p96), but April is true tulip heyday. Here I've divided them not in terms of scale (as in March), but into the four colour palettes we use in our pots at Perch Hill (see p26–33).

The colour density and saturation of tulips means that getting colour combinations right is so important, more so than with many other plants. You can't fudge it: it's either right or wrong, magnificent or… just plain hideous. By dividing tulips into four distinct colour families, you can have a group of pots that work together and have plenty of contrast and variety, without needing to mix in any of the other palettes. Splitting them in this way gives you joyful combinations and prevents pot collections from becoming too hectic.

I'd advise not only keeping the colour palettes apart from one pot to the next, but also in the whole visual field. So decide on which you fancy for a particular area, say, around one side of your house, and then select colours from the same palette for all the pots in that spot. You can do a bit of borrowing from other palettes, just don't get carried away. If you look at all the photographs throughout the book, you'll see the pots contain either tulips exclusively from one palette, or with a small daub of one colour borrowed from another.

There are some overlaps between the palettes and a few colours that, depending on the light quality and age of the flower, can slide between one palette and another (see p34 for more advice). Sometimes I dither when I'm looking at the flowers as to whether a blackcurrant purple should go in the Dark and Rich or Boiled-sweet Brilliant category. If it glows on the day, then it's to the brilliants I allocate it; if it's densely saturated in colour, then it's to the darks. Oranges can also be difficult to place sometimes, particularly as some change in tone as they develop. But if they're coppery brown, a sort of gingernut, then it's into the Dark and Rich group they go.

The Dark and Rich crew are quite earthy, a characteristic they share with the Soft and Warm family, which allows these two palettes to mix well. I find the crimson and bronze from Dark and Rich is very useful, just a smattering, to prevent the Soft and Warm being a bit cloying.

I play around with photographs of the plants I want to use, cut out from catalogues or printed out, and then I assign them where they seem to sit most easily and quietly in a colour group. And then from there, I filter down further into three or four tulips for a pot in a single planting scheme.

When you're choosing a palette for an area, the colour of the surrounding plants is key. You don't want a great, white-flowering shrub like a choisya as a backdrop to your dark and dramatic tulips. Just as a splendid acid-green euphorbia will not enhance the beauty of a pot of tulips in soft, warm shades – the euphorbia is noisy, they are quiet, and it will jar.

There's just one other hazard to be aware of when bulbs are coming up to flower, as well as during the months since planting, and that's bulb-eaters (namely grey squirrels, rats and even pheasants, though pheasants only become interested

Below A classic tulip recipe (see p38) in the Dark and Rich palette (see p26). 'Palmyra' (Bride), 'Continental' (Bridesmaid) and 'Amber Glow' (Gatecrasher) in terracotta pots.

in bulbs when they can actually see them). These can be a major issue. I used to say squirrels were more of a problem in towns and cities, particularly in leafy, tree-filled areas or near parks, but to be honest, with the numbers of grey squirrels in Britain, it's a problem almost everywhere. See p400 for advice on how to protect your pots from pillage.

Perennial Tulips for Pots

Annoyingly, the longevity of tulips is not straightforward when it comes to pots. We know some tulips reappear reliably year after year when planted in the garden, but with every tulip (bar perhaps those in the Species group, see p146) we've trialled in pots, the first year is undoubtedly the best, with the flower show just as you might expect and, after that, it really goes downhill.

In a pot, the bulbs get hot and the heat of summer spurs them on to reproduce. The bulbs then make babies, bulbils produced around the base plate of the parent bulb. You'll see this if you turn out the bulbs from a pot in autumn: there will be many mini-bulbs and the main bulb will often look rather shrivelled and done for. The baby bulbs have taken the strength from the mother and compromised her survival. In time (two to three years), the bulbils will grow strong enough to reach flowering size, but until then your pot, left to its own devices, will feature quite a bit of leaf the following spring and rather meagre flowers.

In the Netherlands, where bulbs are cheaper than elsewhere, it's common for potted bulbs to be discarded. But at Perch Hill we worry that this is rather unsustainable. Chucking out huge numbers of tulips from pots does not seem right. Instead, we plant new ones in our pots each year, and move the ones that have performed that season to elsewhere in the garden. This method works especially well with the ones we know to be reliably perennial. We lift these bulbs out of their pots as they're going over but the flowers are still visible (this helps to identify them when they're planted out), and we plant them straight away, somewhere in the cutting garden for future picking or in amongst our shrubs, perennials and roses. Bury at least 10cm (4in) deep, leaving the leaves on, and support

them by pushing the soil up and around the base of the stem and leaves. It's worth adding a potash-rich fertiliser (such as comfrey pellets) around their planting site as you go. Label and then deadhead them. The plants continue to photosynthesise and should flower the following year or, if not, certainly the year after that. If you don't have a garden, see p175 for tips on storing your bulbs.

One other thing you could do with perennial varieties (for example 'Mistress Mystic' or one of the Viridiflora tulips, like 'Spring Green' or 'Orange Marmalade') is to dig a clump up from the garden as they start to emerge in spring, pot them up to enjoy them in pride of place, and then replant them in the garden as they're going over. That's a bit of a palaver, but it is perhaps the most sustainable way of doing things.

Sadly though, left in pots year after year, they just don't perform. Getting one incredible show from your tulips is easy, extending it is hard.

Opposite Another Dark and Rich tulip combination in the Rose Garden, including tulips 'Slawa' and 'Brownie' with 'Queen of Night' just coming up to flower. The apricot edge of 'Slawa' lightens and brightens this group.

Below I've been putting this tulip collection (we call it the Venetian) together for 20 years and I still love it. 'Couleur Cardinal' (red), 'Prinses Irene' (orange) and 'Havran' (purple-black) are planted with an understorey of wallflowers in huge terracotta pots in the Oast Garden.

Tulip Classification

In the 'best of' list I've named the group the tulip belongs to. I don't think this classification matters hugely, but it can be an indication of general characteristics, for example how perennial a bulb is. The Darwin Hybrid, Viridiflora and the Species tulips (featured in March) are reliably perennial, but there are some other less obvious long-performers too. Particularly for pots, you'll find I mention tulips from six or seven groups more than the others, but for the sake of clarity here are 15 official groups.

Single Early

These are quite short yet elegant tulips in saturated colours, often with equally fine foliage that features a silvery wash over the green. They are early to flower, usually opening in Sussex in early April. Examples include the classic 'Prinses Irene', a key component in our longstanding, bestselling Venetian Tulip Collection (pictured on p145).

Double Early

The proportions feel a bit wrong to me in this group: they have rather large heads on short stems. Their nectaries have been bred to be secondary petaloids, so they are sterile. This is bad for the pollinators but means they can flower for often twice as long as the singles. There are some noted exceptions to the proportion mismatch, such as the deep pink 'Chato' and tangerine 'Orca', which are both early, showy and look like a very early peony.

Triumph

In the 19th century, breeders were looking for a tulip that was suitable for both forcing and for the garden, and the result was the Triumph group. They stem from crossings between early tulips and the large-flowered, late-flowering tulips. They are called Triumph because of the big flowers, strong stems and huge colour variation. The blackcurrant 'Havran' is a longstanding favourite here, while boiled-sweet-purple 'Negrita' is a classic that, wherever you put it, usually comes back well every year.

Darwin Hybrid

The whopping great Darwin Hybrids look like a tulip a child might draw. They are reliably perennial, but with some you'll find them reverting to the sort of flat shades of red and yellow you might associate with municipal planting. I grow and love the Impression series and 'Ivory Floradale'.

Single Late

These are as they sound. Usually tall single varieties with large flowers. They flower later in April into May. A reliable group; we particularly value the deep purple 'Caviar' and, one of the most famous tulips, 'Queen of Night'. 'Blushing Lady' is also a favourite, standing at nearly a metre tall!

We trialled a few new multiflowering tulips (these have multiple small flowers atop every stem and are basically a group in their own right) and the Single Lates 'Blue Heaven' and 'Flaming Club' emerged as definite keepers. In fact, 'Blue Heaven' is now one of my favourite tulips for its unique colour.

Lily-flowered

These are very slim, elegant varieties, and often referred to as the catwalk models of the tulip family. Not only visually beautiful, they also include the must-have, scented 'Ballerina' and also my namesake, 'Sarah Raven', which is not as tall as the rest.

Fringed

The name gives it away: the petals of these tulips appear to have been cut with pinking shears. I haven't always been a fan of this lot, but have fallen hugely for 'Louvre Orange'. It's perennial, elegant and the perfect partner in a pot with 'Brown Sugar'. I also like 'Green Mile' and 'Bastia'.

Viridiflora

These tulips are known for the green flash on their petals. They are incredibly reliable at reappearing and many come up and flower brilliantly every year for us, including 'Spring Green', 'Artist' and 'Groenland'.

Rembrandt

With striped and stippled petals, these tulips have similar markings to those caused by a virus in the 17th century. These modern forms arc virus-free.

Parrot

Like Parrots that have landed in the garden, these tulips are frilly and flamboyant and often feature several colours over a main base colour. We find some to be reliably perennial and often use the scarlet 'Rococo' on its own for head-turning pots.

Double Late

One of my favourite groups, Double Late features lots of brilliant varieties. They are sterile (as with the Double Earlies), but the proportion of stem height and flower size are balanced. 'Black Hero' is a favourite, with 'La Belle Epoque' newer to the party. Double Lates are some of the best tulips for pots because they flower and look good for a long time.

Kaufmanniana

These tulips are the earliest of the earlies. They can feature rather large heads in relation to their stem length, but there are a few notable exceptions that look good, including 'Ice Stick' and 'Concerto', which flower long and hard and are super perennial.

Fosteriana

Known for their reds and yellows, Fosteriana tulips are often the earliest to flower. I love the ivory 'Purissima', which is perennial and very early, as well as the elegant 'Exotic Emperor' (also known as 'White Valley'), which is one of my favourite tulips and in flower here from mid-March often until the end of April.

Greigii

These tulips tend to be top-heavy, much like Kaufmanniana tulips. We don't really grow them.

Species

These are ones collected from the wild or the hybrids that have been crossbred from them. They will self-sow and naturalise, thriving even in grass. We grow lots of these for small, early pots (see p102).

Next page Pots of tulips in the Soft and Cool palette (see p30) in the Farmhouse Garden. They contain 'Exotic Emperor', 'Silver Cloud' and 'Françoise', just coming through, with a splash of brightness from 'Silver Parrot'.

Best of the main season tulips

I am listing the tulips I would miss if they weren't out there growing in pots from April into May. We have a big garden and an absurd number of pots, so there is a wide range to choose from. I've tried to select a broad colour spectrum so you can make your own recipes referring to the advice in the design section (see p15).

Dark and Rich

This lot are from palette 1 (see p26). It includes all the saturated colours with a certain depth of pigment to them, and they tend to have a good texture to their petals too.

1 *Tulipa* 'Abu Hassan' (Triumph)
A lovely old tulip that's been around for at least as long as I've been gardening. It can be difficult to find, with the nearest alternative being 'Amber Glow', which is similarly a mix of crimson and gold, but not quite as rich. Very perennial.

2 *T.* 'Bastia' (Fringed)
A crazy tulip that I don't love in a border, or to be honest on its own, but it turns a tulip pot (or vase) combination into something stellar.

3 *T.* 'Bellville' (Triumph)
This provides a new and unique colour amongst tulips: plush gold to turmeric with a softening smoky crimson stipple on the outer petal surface. Very perennial.

4 *T.* 'Black Hero' (Double Late)
The deep colour of this tulip reminds me of the horse Black Beauty. It is the darkest of all tulips and so glossy. Flowers for ages.

5 *T.* 'Black Parrot' (Parrot)
A tulip with a beautiful shape and a subtle and sophisticated mix of crimson, black and green in every flower. Great at all stages, right the way through to when the petals drop.

6 *T.* 'Brown Sugar' (Triumph)
This is in my tulip top ten. It has tall stems and large, orange-to-gingernut flowers that come early, plus a sweet and slightly spicy scent.

7 *T.* 'Brownie' (Double Early)
I love this tulip, which has huge heads like a handful of coppery silk or the richest gingernut. It provides the perfect understorey to many rich colour combinations in pots and is a very long-flowering and long-lasting, perennial tulip.

8 *T.* 'Cairo' (Triumph)
Like an amber lantern lit from within, this can look orange in some lights, but the petal hue is richer and more like cinnamon.

9 *T.* 'Dream Touch' (Double Late)
This reminds me of a splendid plum or blackcurrant meringue pie. It has the richest crimson-purple base with a narrow white rim to each petal. Any whiter and it wouldn't fit with this palette, but the pencil line provides a beautiful contrast.

10 *T.* 'Havran' (Triumph)
I remember falling for this in the wholesale cut flower market at Covent Garden about 30 years ago. It is the first dark tulip to emerge (together with 'Queen of Night') and is lovely for its pointed, slim, elegant petals – not a bowl, but a goblet of a flower. I keep being told this is soon to become unavailable – I'd mourn it. Having trialled many dark tulips over the years, I know this has the best shape.

11 *T.* 'Merlot' (Lily-flowered)
A distinctive tulip with huge flowers on tall stems in rich blackcurrant with a touch of carmine. Lovely satin texture.

12 *T.* 'Ridgedale' (Double Late)
Every spring I travel to the Netherlands to see tulip breeders and visit Keukenhof gardens, a living museum of bulbs, all growing cheek by jowl. This subtle peony-like tulip with quite a small flower might be too demure for some, but I adore it for its overlay of chestnut brown on crimson. There's nothing quite like it. Late flowering right into May.

13 *T.* 'Sarah Raven'
(Lily-flowered)
My parents had a tulip like this in their garden when I was a child. It had that typical, elegant, pointy-petalled, lily-flowered shape and was a true crimson-black. I remember it so well and have been on the look out for it ever since. I've trialled various tulips such as 'Purple Dream' and 'Burgundy', both the right kind of shape, but purple in colour, even though that is not how they are pictured in catalogues. They were not what I was looking for. Then, during a visit to a tulip trial field about ten years ago, feeling slightly grumpy, without the right gear in the pouring rain, I spotted, several rows off, what is now called 'Sarah Raven'. I fell on it and was able to bring a few bulbs home. We've nurtured this unique variety ever since.

14 *T.* 'Slawa' (Triumph)
A newish tulip, with an apricot edge to a crimson heart. Like 'Dream Touch', it looks like a pudding – and sophisticated with it.

Boiled-sweet Brilliant

Next comes palette 2 (see p28). These colours have a luminosity, a radiance like a stained-glass window with the sun shining through. The key here is the clarity of colour, there's no cloudiness to it – this is due to having no, or almost no, white in the hue, and that makes a real difference.

1 *Tulipa acuminata* (syn. *T.* 'Cornuta') (Species) My parents grew this very old tulip in their garden, where it naturalised. I love it for its slight madness: it is bright yellow and scarlet, though anything but gaudy with its spidery petals and elegant silhouette. It's one we raise onto a table so you see it, as often as possible, backlit by the sun. It's late flowering and perennial.

2 *T.* 'Amazing Parrot' (Parrot) Huge, crinkly and glamorous in coral and orange like a Vivienne Westwood dress with many layers. Late flowering.

3 *T.* 'Attila Graffiti' (Triumph) This is a luminous raspberry-pink colour and it stands out a mile off.

4 *T.* 'Ballerina' (Lily-flowered) Probably my favourite tulip in a clear, boiled-sweet orange with a great luminosity to it. Tall, elegant, showy and with a delicious scent. I also like 'Request', which is more terracotta in colour, so fits better in the Dark and Rich palette.

5 *T.* 'Campbell' (Double Late) A new introduction and a glamorous one at that. It's a double form in a similar orange to 'Ballerina' and with the same delicious freesia scent, but peony-flowered. Outstanding in our most recent trials.

6 *T.* 'Doll's Minuet' (Lily-flowered) This is a dancing tulip in an intense, saturated pink. Its strongly divided petals form an almost star shape when viewed from above. It's short in stature and very long-flowering, with a good lot of Viridiflora genes mixed in. That's what gives the elegant green stripe to the centre of the petal and makes the flowers robust and long lasting.

7 *T.* 'Estella Rijnveld' (Parrot)
A true raspberry ripple of a flower. Red is its main colour (hence its inclusion in this palette), with a feathering of white. I love to bring this inside – mixed with another bicolour, such as the multiflowering 'Flaming Club' (as pictured), it makes a splendid table centrepiece.

8 *T.* 'Flaming Parrot' (Parrot)
People divide strongly on the merits of this tulip. With a vanilla ice cream-coloured base and red stripes, it can be too OTT for some. I planted just nine bulbs in a 30cm (12in) terracotta pot and stood it in the middle of a table in my London garden many years ago. It looked good from late April and all through May. I've loved this tulip ever since.

9 *T.* 'Green Mile' (Fringed × Viridiflora)
You won't see many yellow tulips in my collections. Gold and turmeric, yes. But not many sharp yellows. This colour can be marvellous with purple and it's okay with white, but there's a limited number of colours it mixes well with, in my view. I love this tulip, though, for its pure citrus zestiness. Tall, elegant and late to flower.

10 *T.* 'Helmar' (Triumph)
Buttercup yellow with red markings, this is reminiscent of a tulip as painted in a Dutch still life. Back in the 17th century, it was a virus that gave the tulips unusual markings, but this one is strong, healthy and pretty perennial. It's excellent at providing contrast amongst the Dark and Rich crimsons.

11 *T.* 'Louvre Orange' (Fringed)
You'll see from all the tulips selected for this book that I'm not crazy about many fringed forms (this is one of just three here). I think they can look good cut for the vase, but not so good in the garden. However, this one can really work in a pot. The frilly petal edge, as with the Parrot group, adds to its glamour and glory.

12 *T.* 'Mariette' (Lily-flowered)
A clear, radiant pink with a beautiful shape on top of tall stems. 'China Pink' is one tone paler and lovely too, but doesn't have the same depth and saturation of colour.

13 *T*. 'Nightrider' (Viridiflora)
Not always easy to find, but
worth looking out for, this
is such a glamorous tulip.
The citrus green is a perfect
contrast to the boiled-sweet
purple. It's late, long-
flowering and fabulous for a
mixed pot and a vase.

14 *T*. 'Orange Marmalade'
(Viridiflora)
A new tulip that has shot
to the top of my list. I've
always loved the Viridiflora
group and the short-
stemmed 'Artist' is one of
my favourites, but it is more
terracotta than orange.
'Orange Marmalade' is tall-
stemmed, large-flowered and
a deep orange mixed with
lime. It's glorious and I'm
pretty sure will turn out to
be very perennial.

15 *T*. 'Orange Princess'
(Double Late)
The double version of 'Prinses
Irene' and later flowering.
This has short stems and
large flowers but is still
elegant. We often use this
as a lower storey plant in a
pot collection.

16 *T*. 'Prinses Irene'
(Single Early)
This is one of the first tulips
I grew. It has been around
for decades, has stood the
test of time and is still
widely available. It's a lovely
tangerine orange, with so
many other colours washed
over the outer petals that it
feels like a calm and truly
classy flower. I love gaudy
sometimes (see 'Orca' on
p100) but this is orange with
style. Perennial.

17 *T*. 'Rococo' (Parrot)
A scarlet Parrot with many
other colours overlaid,
including gold, green and
smoke. This is one of the
earliest of the Parrots and is
good for forcing, so a welcome
ingredient in a Valentine's
Day bunch. Ideal for a pot as
it is showy, but unlike many
Parrots, not too long-stemmed,
top-heavy or busy with colours.
It's great planted en masse
on its own. We plant it in
dolly tubs on the balcony and
it's strong enough to hold its
own there, mainly seen from
a distance.

18 *T*. 'Royal Acres'
(Double Early)
The epitome of boiled-sweet
purple, radiant and clear
with fully double flowers
on medium-length stems.
We use this in lots of our
pot collections.

Soft and Warm

Palette 3 (p30) is what I think of as the cashmere jersey colours, based on lots of white with differing amounts of colour density. They share a kind of chalkiness, so that even if they're bright, like the orange tulip 'Menton', there is an opaqueness to them.

1 *Tulipa* 'Apricot Beauty' (Single Early)
A tulip that's been around for ages. It's utterly lovely, pretty but not too sugary sweet. We find this very perennial, so always plant this straight out into the garden after its pot performance.

2 *T.* 'Apricot Copex' (Triumph)
Created by the same breeder as 'La Belle Epoque', this is unique: a single tulip with an apricot petal base and a smoky, crimson overlay. I think of this as the younger sister of 'La Belle Epoque'.

3 *T.* 'Apricot Foxx' (Triumph)
Together with 'La Belle Epoque', this is the queen of this palette because it's so beautiful and so distinct. It opens a chalky terracotta, or a fox orange, and then gradually fades to apricot. We use it a lot in our tulip pot mixes and I love it.

4 *T.* 'Blue Heaven' (Single Late)
I've long loved the tulip 'Bruine Wimpel' for its warm copper colour with a silver wash on the outer petal, but it has disappeared entirely (apparently it's prone to the fungus fusarium). That's why I jumped on this one when I saw it in the trial field of one of the best tulip breeders in the Netherlands. It's an exceptionally beautiful colour, moving from copper to an almost mauve as the flowers develop. I love the clutch of balloon-shaped flowers that top each stem. It's one of the deepest colours in this palette and is a good bridge to the Dark and Rich shades.

5 *T.* 'Blushing Lady' (Single Late)
A statue of a tulip, standing almost twice as tall as every other tulip we grow with huge, elegant, lily-shaped flowers. Each one looks like an elegant vase in the softest primrose with blush pink feathering on the outer surface. A truly impressive beauty.

6 *T.* 'Copper Image' (Double Late)
Opens a soft coral colour, fading to milky coffee after a week or two, and it has a lovely sweet scent.

7 T. 'La Belle Epoque'
(Double Late)
A remarkable tulip that took
the florist world by storm
about ten years ago. Its
milky, coffee-coloured petals
feature lots of other tones in
green, smoke and crimson,
particularly as it emerges
from bud. Hugely pretty.

8 T. *linifolia* Batalinii Group
'Bronze Charm' (Species)
A beautiful mix of colours
between the soft apricot
flowers (which are larger
than many of the petite
species tulips) and the
silvery green leaves. Left in
their pots, and stored after
flowering somewhere cool,
these reliably come up year
after year.

9 T. 'Menton' (Single Late)
One of the most statuesque
tulips standing sometimes
70cm (2ft) tall, which with
the added height of a pot is
quite something. Its coral
colouring makes this a
fabulous Bride or
Gatecrasher (see p38) for a
pot combination. And we
often use it for exactly that,
and to add a splash of contrast
to the ivories and whites.
This is my favourite colour
amongst what are often
described as the French tulips
– several varieties that are
similarly tall and elegant, all
named after French towns
and districts, such as the
tangerine 'Dordogne' and
bright coral 'Avignon'.

10 T. 'Pink Star' (Double Late)
A spring peony lookalike.
When I have this cut in a
vase, visitors often ask how
we have peonies so early.
This is the loveliest mix
of colours with beautiful
ruffled and rippled petals.
Short stems mean you need
to pair it with other compact
varieties, such as 'Harbour
Lights' and 'Groenland'.

11 T. 'Sanne' (Triumph)
This was one of the
outstanding tulips in
our most recent trial:
exceptionally long-flowering,
strong and healthy (and in
a wet year, which is bad for
tulip fire). The colours soften
as the flowers age, but I love
this in all its stages.

12 *T.* 'Silk Road'
(Double Early)
This reminds me of a
crumpled ivory silk
handkerchief, slightly messy
and chaotic in its petal
form, but rather good with
it. We mix it with other
peony-type tulips such as
the similar 'Crème Upstar',
'Copper Image' (pictured on
p140) and something like
the sultry, copper-crimson
'Ridgedale' to give the group
a bit of depth and contrast.
Both 'Silk Road' and 'Crème
Upstar' are scented.

163

Soft and Cool

Finally, palette 4 (p32) features plenty of white in the base colour, mixed with a splash of a cool colour. These are the cleanest shades. Chic, crisp and feminine, I think of these as the Champs-Élysée shades.

1 *Tulipa* 'Boa Vista' (Double Late)
A bizarre-looking tulip reminiscent of a globe artichoke with green petals that look more like leaf scales. I wasn't sure about it when I first saw it, but love it in container mixes as it gives a kind of solidity and architectural presence for the lower storey. The flowers are scented. 'Harbour Lights' is a similar, so-called artichoke form, but with white flowers and variegated leaves.

2 *T.* 'China Town' (Viridiflora)
Light on its feet, this soft pink tulip would fit in with the Soft and Warm palette too, but it has variegated leaves, which I feel make it more compatible with this family. As a Viridiflora, it's long-flowering and very perennial, so we transplant it to the garden after its initial pot performance.

3 *T.* 'Dreamer' (Double Early)
One of the earliest soft pink doubles to flower, up to a month earlier than 'Angélique', which is becoming tricky to find. It can even hit March in a mild year. This is a more pure pink compared to 'Pink Star'.

4 *T.* 'Finola' (Double Late)
The strongest pink tulip in this palette, but with plenty of white in the base colour, so it fits here rather than in Boiled-sweet Brilliant. One of the last doubles to flower, and it's tall for a double, too. 'Foxtrot', a more recent introduction, is very similar.

5 *T.* 'Florosa' (Viridiflora)
Tall, stately and elegant, with flowers in ivy-green with a soft pink wash – it looks like a Lily-flowered tulip crossed with a Viridiflora, with the lovely characteristics of each group. It's ideal as an upper storey tulip in a pot, mixed with other whites.

6 *T.* 'Françoise' (Triumph)
If you're choosing just one ivory tulip, this should be it. Its huge, shapely, almost oval flowers are reminiscent of an ostrich egg. It's tall and invaluable for shade, shining light into a north-facing corner. That's how we often use it, on the north face and in the shade of our barn.

7 *T.* 'Green Power' (Triumph)
You may wonder why on earth you'd want a green tulip, but we find this useful and rather lovely for two reasons. Firstly, it creates a good foliage-like foil for some of the brighter pinks or whites in our pots. Secondly, it's very late to flower, so gives us tulips right to the end of May. For these reasons, it combines well with 'Green Wave' and is lovely with the other very late Parrot tulip in this palette, the mauve 'James Last'. We also grow the similar 'Green King'.

8 *T.* 'Green Star' (Viridiflora)
Another one with twisting, turning petals, which must mean it has some Lily-flowered genes. It almost dances, and has great architectural presence. It is ivory and green, and I love it paired with 'Exotic Emperor', which comes

early and crosses over with 'Green Star', which then takes up the baton to keep going well into May.

9 *T.* 'Green Wave' (Parrot)
In my top ten of all tulips, 'Green Wave' is one we've grown for years. Its huge heads in green, white and pink are as good when they first open towards the end of April as they are when their petals drop towards the end of May. Super perennial too.

10 *T.* 'Groenland' (Viridiflora)
A beautiful pure pink tulip with the classic Viridiflora green stripe. I love using this in pot combinations and vases as it almost plays the role of foliage, with enough green to calm any combination. Hugely useful and, like all Viridifloras, very perennial, long-flowering and long-lived.

11 *T.* 'James Last' (Parrot)
I am not the greatest fan of mauve tulips, but this, and the similar 'Blue Parrot', are notable exceptions. They have great glamour and style with wonderful shapes and a mix of purples and mauves. It is one of the last tulips to flower.

12 *T.* 'Mistress Mystic' (Triumph)
A one-off colour: pink washed with grey. I'm never quite sure of the difference between this and 'Mistress Grey' and think, perhaps, they are indeed the same thing. When we use this in pots to give a more subtle, smoky pink to a combination, we always transplant it into the garden as it's one of the most perennial tulips we grow. Late flowering, going on well into May.

13 *T.* 'Rems Favourite'
(Triumph)
A little reminiscent of the
tulips you see in 17th century
Dutch paintings, the time of
the tulipomania craze. It has
lovely blackcurrant ripple
swirls through meringue
white petals. A very healthy
grower, ideal for mixing in
with bright whites to give
a dash of light contrast,
without being blocky.

14 *T.* 'Silver Cloud' (Triumph)
The prettiest and most
ethereal tulip we grow, in
a colour that seems to be
fashionable at the moment:
a soft mauve, though each
petal also has a hint of green
over it. I particularly love
this when it's just emerging
from bud.

15 *T.* 'Spring Green' (Viridiflora)
The classiest of tulips and a
garden classic. In ivory with
green flashes, it goes with
almost everything. Super
perennial, it has been coming
up in the same place at Perch
Hill for 20 years and it's
tolerant of shade. One of our
classic pot combinations is this
with 'Green Wave'.

16 *T.* 'Tropical Lady' (Triumph)
One of the few variegated
foliage tulips we grow. I
usually feel stripes can make
the foliage look a bit sick, but
I like the soft pink mix of the
flowers alongside the leaves.
Tall, elegant and unusual, it
is great for both pots and
vases, where it is the perfect
contrast to whites, as well as
stately on its own.

17 *T.* 'White Star'
(Lily-flowered)
I came across this at Keukenhof
gardens in the Netherlands a few
years ago, around the time it was
first released, and I loved it. With
fully open flowers it is properly
star shaped, each petal with a
great twist and turn making it
look dynamic and elegant in all
its phases. If you can't find this,
go for the similar if less starry
'White Triumphator', or the
earlier flowering and shorter
stemmed 'Très Chic'. There is a
new, truly star-shaped one called
'Healthcare', which we love.

18 *T.* 'White Touch' (Double Late)
We grow quite a few white
Double Early tulips, with this,
our favourite Double Late. It
flowers for ages, at least to the
middle of May. Like many in this
group, you can confuse it for an
early peony, all the more so as
the flowers are big.

April

April, in pot world, feels like a continuation of the first three months of the year, with everything waiting for the frosts to be over. That is usually early next month here in Sussex. We can't risk putting anything tender out until then, so the polytunnel and cold frames are bursting at the seams.

We're still doing a bit of sowing (sunflowers and zinnias) and it's the month for pinching out, with any seedlings shooting for the skies pinched when they have two or three true leaves. This helps to keep roots and side shoots growing strongly. When you're pinching out your cosmos and other seedlings at this time of year, include your dahlias too. They should be properly starting to grow. You can use the pinched tips as cuttings to grow your collection (see p177).

Cuttings taken last autumn usually need some TLC around now. We always have cuttings of *Salvia greggii*, *S. mircophylla* and *S. × jamensis* varieties growing strongly – they are all great for pots. We tend to give them a delicate overall haircut at this time of year, and within a week or two they'll be covered with a new flush of green buds and leaves.

Cosmos sown at the end of March germinates and grows so quickly, so the seedlings will need pricking out (see p128), ideally when they have three pairs of true leaves. It's easy to pinch them out as you move them into their own individual pots – they'll be there for a month or so before they're safe to go out in the garden. I try to spend a couple of hours, every Saturday in April if possible, with the radio on, doing some therapeutic pricking out. And when everything is pinched, pricked out and potted on, we shuffle everything around, taking the more mature hardy annuals – and, by the end of the month, half-hardy annuals – outside during the day to harden them off, before beginning to plant them in their final pots.

If you've bought seedlings, your online orders will start to arrive now. With all these nascent plants, whether bought or homegrown, make sure you keep them frost-free if they're tender, in good all-round light (or as near to that as you can provide) and watered, but not drowned. Many shop-bought seedlings will also need pinching out and, if you've got the smallest seedling size (rather than jumbos), they'll need to be potted on into 9cm (3½in) pots. If they are in Jiffy-7 pellets, always remove the net before you pot them on.

Finally, April can be quite dry weather wise, so make sure containers out in the garden are watered. Tulips will soon hang their heads if the compost is too dry. If you want to hold back flowering, move containers to a shady and cool spot. Our pots on the north side of the barn flower slightly later and fare better if the weather becomes suddenly warm, as it often does at this time of year.

Below Sowing zinnias into peat-free
Jiffy-7s – these need to be soaked
for a few minutes to rehydrate.

Sowing

Sowing continues, with anything we have left over from March (see p127), plus a few additional plants such as zinnias, sunflowers and primulas that specifically need sowing a bit later as they struggle with cold nights.

I love zinnias for pots, particularly those in the harmoniously toned Queen Lime series. They famously hate root disturbance, so we sow these into modules towards the end of April to avoid the need for pricking out. They struggle when the nights are cold, so can't be planted out into their final pot until the end of May. In a month's time, zinnias can be crammed in, 12 or so seedlings, into a 40cm (16in) pot.

Sowing into modular trays

When sowing in modules, whether pre-made Jiffy-7s or modular trays, you don't have to prick out. You might possibly need to pot on, but quite often you can plant module-grown seedlings straight into their final pot. This works well in terms of saving time, money and plastic. We increasingly use FSC-certified rubber trays to minimise our use of those flimsy plastic cell trays that only seem to last a year; you can recycle them, but it's a hassle to find places that do that.

Modular trays and Jiffy-7s are quite shallow, so we only use them for raising a specific group of plants for our pots, namely those that struggle with root disturbance. We used to use them for cosmos, but have mainly reverted to trays for those as they are so fast growing that they struggle with the shallow compost. At this time of year, we sow zinnias and sometimes annual poppies such as 'Amazing Grey'.

- Fill the tray with peat-free compost, breaking up any lumps. Water the trays before, not after sowing. If using Jiffy-7s, they'll need rehydrating in a watertight barrow or crate for 5 minutes before you sow.
- Plant two seeds per cell (or for Jiffys, into the dimple at the top of each pellet).

- Label and place in a cool, light, frost-free place with basal heat if you have it.
- Check every day whether they need water. Keep their compost well-watered, but never dripping wet.
- Allow them to germinate or shoot. If both seeds germinate, remove the weakest-looking one after the first has been showing for about a week. Just pull it out and chuck. This avoids the need to prick out.
- Once roots appear at the base of the tray, and the tops have three pairs of leaves, pinch them out, removing the apical bud between your thumb and forefinger.
- When planting out or potting on, if you're using Jiffy-7s, don't forget to remove the pellet's net to allow the plant roots to run free. They settle in much quicker without anything holding them back, and that's even if you destroy a few micro-roots as you take the net off.

Sowing into individual pots

I love to grow cobaea and sunflowers from seed for our big pots, and I start them off in individual 9cm (3½in) pots. They both have very large seeds that are difficult to get into Jiffy-7 pellets and the seeds also rot easily in a compact space. Cobaea was sown in January (see p84), sunflowers we do now. For pots, we use the more compact ones such as *Helianthus annus* 'Ms Mars' and 'Micro Sun'.

- Fill 9cm (3½in) pots with a peat-free compost. Water the compost.

- Push the seed in to a depth of 2.5cm (1in). Push it in vertically (blunt end down with the sunflower, rather than flat). The compost usually folds over the seed and buries it, but you can cover with compost if this hasn't happened.
- Label. There's no need to water again straight away. Put on a heated propagator until they germinate.
- Once germinated, water every few days when the compost starts to dry on the surface.
- For sunflowers, harden them off briefly and then plant out into your garden pots once you see roots appearing in the holes at the bottom of the pot, usually in about a month's time.

Sowing primulas

Primula malacoides finishes flowering early and runs to seed in April. This seed is hard to find commercially so it's best to save your own. Do so by plonking a plant, still in its pot, bang in the middle of a large seed tray or crate filled with peat-free compost. The primula will shed plenty of seed straight onto the compost, which will germinate by summer.

Come summer, lift the seedlings from where they are and pot them on into their own 9cm (3½in) pots. Keep them somewhere cool, but with good light (such as a cold frame) and water once a week or so. Bring them undercover before the first frost. They will be ready to flower in the new year.

Below Top dressing pots of the perennial agapanthus, just as it starts to shoot in April.

Pinching Out

For all seeds you plant, once the seedlings have three pairs of leaves, pinch out the leader (the growing tip). Just squeeze it off between your finger and thumb. This promotes vigorous root and side shoot formation, with the energy of the plant going into growing down and out, rather than up – it makes for a more floriferous and long-living plant.

Planting Out Hardy Annuals

Hardy annual seedlings can go out into pots now. We try to get sweet peas planted in March, but all the others are sitting, ready and waiting, including our scabious plants and briza grasses, as well as our hardy annual cut flower mixes for pots.

If you don't have much outdoor space, creating a cutting garden in pots is ideal, and I recommend growing cut-and-come-again plants such as annual linarias, or our classic trio,

Euphorbia oblongata, *Calendula* 'Indian Prince' and *Cerinthe major* 'Purpurascens' (pictured on p209). Rather than deadhead, you live-head – not only will your house be full of flowers, your pots will look good for twice as long.

We plant hardy annuals in big pots, as these need less looking after than a series of smaller pots. When planting them, you can space them more densely than you would in the garden – in the garden they might be about 45cm (18in) apart, but in a pot it's more like 25cm (10in). Picked regularly for flowers inside, you can cram more plants in.

Dismantling Pots

Out in the garden, our larger pots are mainly still brimming with tulips, but towards the end of the month, early tulips, plus hyacinths or narcissi, will be going over and the pots can begin to be dismantled.

If we're lifting and replanting in the garden, all the bulbs need deadheading before they're planted out. If you don't have a garden, lift the bulbs with the leaves left on and lie them out somewhere light but, importantly, cool. Once the foliage has dried, remove the last bits of shrivelled leaf and any bulbils that may have formed around the bulb base. Discard these and pack the bulbs away in paper bags, labelled. Store them somewhere cool, dry and dark until autumn.

Move any perennial pot toppers (see p118),

such as primulas or heucheras, from their pots into the garden too. Dappled shade is ideal for both. If you don't have a garden, pot these into their own individual pots to transplant back over bulb lasagnes in the autumn.

Perennial Pot Care

At the start of April we tend to our perennial pots. Plants such as agapanthus, honeysuckle and buddleja are all low maintenance, but they do need a mini-annual makeover.

Top dressing plants
Top dressing encourages perennials to be extra flowery over summer.

- Scrape off the top 5cm (2in) of compost and replace with fresh compost mixed with some slow-release, pelleted fertiliser. Top with a shallow layer of grit to smarten them up for the new season.

Dividing pot-bound plants
If any perennial plant has been in its pot for years, it may be pot-bound and would welcome being repotted. Agapanthus do like to be quite packed in, but after three years or so, they usually need dividing and repotting.

- To test if a plant is pot-bound, push in a bamboo cane close to the edge of the pot. If it sinks in relatively easily, there's room for

root growth. If the pot is packed full of roots, you won't be able to get the cane in and you'll know that the plant needs repotting.

- At this stage of the year, the spear-like leaf tops of agapanthus plants are just emerging. Tip the clump out of the pot, split it in half (you may even need a saw to do this) and repot both halves. For each half, use the same pot size as the original.
- Water and top dress the pot with a handful or two of grit to keep it looking smart and to prevent weeds seeding into the pot surface.

Propagating Dahlias

You can easily turn one dahlia tuber into several plants, whether they're new this season or stored from the previous year. You can do this in one of two ways and with both methods the propagated plants will have formed tubers of their own by the end of the season and should be treated like any other dahlias in your garden.

Dividing dahlias
Large, mature tubers can be divided in spring.

- Slice the tuber into sections making sure that the narrow part at the top of each tuber has an eye. This eye is sometimes difficult to spot, and not all tubers will have eyes – but if the section doesn't have an eye, propagating won't work. Make sure each section has one good stalk emerging.

- Insert the new sections of tuber into gritty compost with the eye above the surface.
- Water lightly, then don't water again until the compost has dried out.

Taking dahlia cuttings
Dahlias usually start to shoot towards the end of March. Once the shoots have reached 5–6cm (2in), you can take some of the shoots as cuttings, aiming to leave four or five on the mother tuber to ensure you still get a good show in summer.

- Slice off short, stout shoots with a sharp knife, aiming to slice a little off the tuber with the cutting if you can.
- Pinch out the tips – the growth hormone is then diverted from pushing the plant upwards into strong root growth.
- Push the cuttings into a gritty mix of compost, spaced 2.5cm (1in) apart, positioning them around the edge of a pot.
- They will root more quickly with a bit of basal heat, so put them in a propagator if you have one. We find black plastic pots work well as they absorb the heat.

These will be established enough to plant out in a couple of months and will grow so rapidly that they're almost indistinguishable from the mother plant by the end of their first season. These rooted cuttings will flower a little later than the mother plants and will continue on a little longer too, extending your dahlia season.

May

Most of our large containers are still chock-full of tulips, so
the first half of May is partly a continuation of April. Late tulips
such as the Parrots 'Green Wave', 'Blumex Favourite' and 'James
Last', along with some of the Double Late ones – 'Angélique',
'Ridgedale' and 'Dream Touch' – are at their best and, even
with their petals dropping, I love them. I now start to pick
bunches for the house from the pots as well as the borders,
as I want to make the most of them. Whether it's from the
huge Danish pots in the Farmhouse Garden or from the more
modest pots around our doorstep, I pick just one flower
in three and find the pots carry on looking good while giving
us a vase for inside too.

May seems to be the moment for slightly crazy tulips. I'm
mad about the spidery-flowered, ethereal *Tulipa acuminata* (syn.
T. 'Cornuta'), the brazen tulip 'Flaming Parrot' and the bicolour,
red-on-yellow 'Helmar'. These are too gaudy for some, but not
me! They're tulips straight out of a 17th century Dutch still-life
painting and should, in my view, occupy pride of place. Every year
we grow them in a series of pots raised up on the wellhead, so
we see them silhouetted by light whenever we leave the house.
That's how they work best, these flamboyant forms, not in
borders, but as prima donnas in pots, dominating their stage.

By the middle of the month, all but the green tulips such
as 'Green King' and 'Evergreen' (these have quite leathery
flowers and are very long lived), are starting to tire, but luckily
the pansies and violas thrive in the spring heat. We find these
are often at their best now, either in pots of their own or as

Previous page *Tulipa* 'Queen of
Night' creating the silhouette
above *T.* 'Blumex Favourite', and
Viola 'Martin', surrounded by the
long-flowering *Salvia rosmarinus*
'Benenden Blue'.

pot toppers amongst tulips. One of our head gardener Josie's
favourite pots in recent years was the combination of the Parrot
tulip 'Blumex Favourite' underplanted with *Viola* 'Martin'.
The pot sat on the sunny south-facing doorstep of her office and
the viola flowered well for the whole of spring and, with the
late tulip flowering in May, it put on a decent show before being
drowned – violas will gradually get choked by the tulip foliage
in all but the outside edge of the pot, but it's still worth doing.

I know violas and pansies are small, but they're a Perch Hill
favourite, used here in pots, in vases and as edible flowers to
dress up salads and puddings. We'd be bereft without them.
Joining violas are some other invaluable small tabletop fillers
to help keep the pot performance going as we dismantle the
tulip pots and plant them up with dahlias and tender plants.
It's worth knowing and growing a few good May gap fillers so
you have something lovely to look at and enjoy while waiting
for newly planted pots to hit their stride.

I'm a big fan of *Euphorbia hypericifolia* 'Diamond Frost' for
just this reason. We like to plan ahead so that we have snowball
domes of 'Diamond Frost' in pots for our tables by May, either
by bringing our existing plants under cover from autumn until
spring or by taking cuttings in autumn, which by May will
have put on great growth. There's been quite a bit of breeding
of the euphorbia clan recently, and 'Breathless Blush' is another
favourite for its crimson-splotched leaves. These two euphorbias
are not hardy, but are perennial and super low-maintenance.
Kept through the winter protected from frost in a greenhouse,
cold frame or shed with a window, they can come out into the
garden once the risk of frost has passed to flower in May (top
them with fleece if a surprise cold snap is forecast).

We now do the same with an increasing band of plants that
are tender perennials. It seems to work with the New Zealand
native *Plectranthus ciliatus*, the whole South African daisy brigade
– the arctotis, gazanias and osteospermums – as well as some
nemesias. We bring them under cover over winter, pot them on
into fresh compost in March and then, when the frosts are over,
bring them back out. The roots continue to grow slowly through
the winter, gradually building up substantial root balls as they
would as perennials in their native habitats. And, importantly, it
ensures much earlier flowering. They give impact straight away
in May, and become invaluable pot performers.

It doesn't work with everything and sometimes the more mature plants seem to be less flowery, but with foliage plants in particular, it's proven to be more than worth it.

Nurserymen friends in the Netherlands have taught me you can do this very effectively with the elegant, trailing foliage plant dichondra. They repot them into fresh compost, hang their pots inside over winter, then put them out again as soon as the frosts are over. With this easy system, they have hanging baskets of *Dichondra argentea* 'Silver Falls' looking fantastic straight away in May, like a miniature Niagara Falls; delicate, but hugely impressive, tumbling down almost 2m (6½ft).

Pelargoniums are much the same. We find that certain varieties, if given just a light haircut in January and potted on at the same time (or any time until the end of March), can look wonderful in May. Treated like this, the handsome-leafed *Pelargonium* 'Chocolate Peppermint', as well as 'Tommy' and 'Orsett', are May troopers, as is the brilliant-pink 'Ashby' and the non-stop flowering 'Aurora'. The boost of the new compost pushes them on and all five are covered in bold and brilliant flowers just when they're needed.

Below *Euphorbia hypericifolia* 'Diamond Frost' in a line of terracotta pots placed down the middle of the table outside the barn. They are drought tolerant and low maintenance and thrive there until the frosts start.

Next page Pots on the wellhead at this time of year include *Tulipa acuminata* (syn. *T.* 'Cornuta'), *T.* 'Gavota' and *Heuchera* 'Wild Rose', all great in silhouette.

In Sussex, we can bring these out from the greenhouse by this stage of the year, but those further north will need to watch the forecast and bring them in again if cold nights are in the offing.

One must never forget the ever-invaluable Mexican daisy, *Erigeron karvinskianus*, which also earns its keep, perhaps more in May than at any other time. Already in flower, it is happy as Larry from one year to the next, not even in need of repotting. Think about where you see it in a garden – in all the nooks and crannies in steps, paths and walls – and you'll realise what a tough old bird it is, ideal for low-maintenance pots. And supremely pretty with it. There's almost nothing better than a row of terracotta pots filled with erigeron running down the centre of an outdoor dining table.

Finally, not for glamour but scent, is the alyssum, *Lobularia maritima* 'Snow Princess' or the soft mauve 'Lavender Stream'. Easy to grow from seed and widely available as young plants, these are hardy annuals, lovely in terracotta pots positioned on a window ledge or table. Late spring and early summer is their peak (albeit short) flowering time. They fill their corner of the garden with intense honey scent, which takes me straight back to being five and having honey sandwiches for tea. That's a cheery thing!

Below *Lobularia maritima* 'Snow Princess' in a terracotta pot.
Opposite *Pelargonium* 'Ashby' is one of our stalwarts in May as it flowers reliably early. Behind it is the fern-like *Asparagus setaceus*, which also looks good at this time of year.
Next page *Erigeron karvinskianus* in a line of pots on the table on the south side of the barn – it's a fantastic table centrepiece pot plant for summer and autumn.

Violas

Opposite Our outdoor eating table in the Dutch Yard with its centre topped with pots of all shapes and sizes filled with *Viola cornuta* 'Antique Shades', with the architectural silver foliage of *Allium karataviense* for contrast.

If it's muscari that provide the size counterbalance to tulips in April, it's violas and pansies that we turn to in May. Violas and pansies may be small, but particularly for pots, they are perfect. Their length of flowering, ease of growth, range of colour – not just across the genus, but in just one flower – combined with perfume and one of the richest textures you'll find anywhere in the plant world, make them pretty stellar in my view. For a pot garden, you've got to grow them.

Some of the violas planted in autumn have been flowering since the start of spring and there might even be ones like 'Sorbet Phantom' or the classic heart's ease (*Viola tricolor*), or the even longer-flowering, newly bred 'Sorbet Lemon Jump Up', that have bloomed lightly right through the winter. But it's in May, with so much going over, that these plants become truly invaluable.

I think the whole viola clan provide the very best velvety richness – just think of those famous classics, like the almost-black 'Roscastle Black' and 'Molly Sanderson', or the gingernut 'Irish Molly'. I've grown these now for over 30 years, but more recently, I've fallen for the soft peachy colours of violas like *V. × wittrockiana* 'Mystique Peach Shades'. The muted, dusky shades are the epitome of the cashmere jersey colours I love.

With delicate-flowered things like these, give them big pots with tons of plants massed together, or lots of small pots in series. I love them used like this, rather than mixed with other plants. That's when they're in danger of looking too twee. I think this is fundamental to their success in pot design, though we feel they work with tulips because the bulb foliage is so architectural.

Using the Bride, Bridesmaid and Gatecrasher system (see p38), we mix three violas together in a large table centre pot, two purples and one copper or bronze. And just two slightly contrasting colours, but the same flower size and shape, is a good recipe too. I love the combination of the yellow-tinged 'Green Goddess' with the copper-brown 'Irish Molly'. They make a great pair, as does 'Tiger Eye Red' with 'Antique Shades'. Those two look great in a pot together or in individual pots alternating down a table. One year we combined them with pots of *Allium karataviense* for its foliage, and that was a real success: the crisp pleated nature of the allium leaves and their smoky-silver colour was the perfect foil for the sugary violas (pictured on p188).

Violas are fashionable at the moment and some are being bred to have taller stems so they can be used in floristry. With their stem ends seared in boiling water for a few seconds, they do make good cut flowers and, of course, all violas and pansies are edible. With the larger-flowered forms, pull the petals off the base of the flower and scatter, and with the small-flowered violas, use the whole flower, scattering over salads and puddings. By live-heading, we don't need to deadhead, so picking them has a double benefit.

Varieties come and go a bit. But, with most being seed-raised, there are new ones being bred all the time. If one does go, there's usually something similar coming along to take its place. The classics like 'Tiger Eye Red' and 'Green Goddess' seem to stay put. Every year we trial more and more, and it's rare that I don't fall in love with at least one or two new ones.

Below I love our butler's tray plant stand jammed with violas in terracotta pots. The ones here include lots from the slightly crazy Frizzle Sizzle series and Ruffles series, including 'Ruffles Soft Lavender', 'Ruffles Wine', 'Frizzle Sizzle Lemonberry' and 'Ruffles Dark Heart'.
Opposite *Viola × wittrockiana* 'Nature Antique Shades'.

Best of the violas

I've started this list with my favourite small-flowered violas. These tend to be more tolerant of summer heat and winter cold than the pansy types, though it's still best to move them into partial shade at the height of summer. The bigger-flowered violas we know as pansies fall under the name V. × wittrockiana – there's a selection of these at the end.

1 *Viola* 'Antique Shades'
This is one of the *Viola cornuta* varieties, which are all perennial but usually grown as annuals or biennials as they tend to struggle in the heat. A mix of colours from one packet of seeds isn't usually a good thing with violas, but with 'Antique Shades' you get a beautiful combination of copper and purple. It's one step more glamorous than the British native, heart's ease.

2 *V.* 'Brush Strokes'
This is the perfect thing for a series of terracotta pots on a window ledge or table. It's as if each exquisite flower has been painted with delicate stripes, so you want to see them closely. We pick them, rather than deadhead, to prolong flowering and they're wonderful in mini-vases.

Sow in spring for flowers all through summer.

3 *V.* 'Green Goddess'
I've always loved a green flower and this fits the bill, with its greenish tinge over gold and copper. It makes a great companion to 'Irish Molly'.

4 *V.* 'Irish Molly'
Copper and bronze flowers rank very highly with me. I've grown and loved this viola for at least 20 years.

5 *V.* 'Martin'
The most reliably perennial viola we grow, with small flowers in a vibrant purple held on long, wiry stems above low-growing foliage. It has a lovely soft scent. It's great as an understorey to tulips (pictured on p178).

6 *V.* 'Sorbet Phantom'
With flowers in rich, deep purple and a central white halo, this has a compact habit, so it's good for combining with spring-flowering bulbs, and it's scented. This is the hardiest viola and, if the weather is mild enough, the easiest to encourage to flower all through the winter of any we've trialled. We grow it in window boxes and pots inside the greenhouse for a reliable and continuous winter show.

7 *V.* 'Tiger Eye Red'
This is as it sounds: like the semi-precious stone, rich and rather exotic. I loved the tiger eye stone as a girl and am naturally drawn to these coppery coloured, ink-patterned flowers. They are brilliant for pressing and sticking on to card for Christmas gift tags.

Viola × wittrockiana

These pansies have larger, more showy flowers than the classic viola.

8 *V. × w.* 'Coolwave Raspberry'
Not really raspberry coloured at all, this newly bred hybrid is a shade of amethyst and flowers long and hard. It also survives the rain surprisingly well without getting stains and blotches over its velvet petals.

9 *V. × w.* Frizzle Sizzle series and *V.* Ruffles series
The Frizzle Sizzle series violas look as though the outer petal edges have been gathered on a thread. They divide people strongly: you'll either find them impossibly froufrou or love their craziness. I'm mad about them, and I also love the similar Ruffles series, and grow more and more each spring. Some of my favourites are 'Frizzle Sizzle Burgundy' (hard to beat, it's like a handful of silk velvet, pictured) and 'Ruffles Wine', which is a similar colour, but not quite as deep. 'Ruffles Soft Lavender' is pretty mixed with one of the soft apricot shades – use it as the Gatecrasher in a mixed pot. And finally, there's something vaguely Shakespearean about 'Ruffles Dark Heart', with its rich purple petal and a wide gold edge – fabulous in May

in the centre of a table. All violas, but particularly the Ruffles and Frizzle Sizzle ones, press fabulously and look great mounted onto black card.

10 *V. × w.* Matrix series 'Matrix Rose Fire' (pictured) is an example of plant breeders getting it spot on. I adore this variety for its wonderful mix of colours in one plant. 'Matrix Sangria' is an amazingly rich wine colour, brilliant for impact on cakes. It's a great favourite: we grow it in pots and in the greenhouse and use it to top almost every salad we serve in winter and spring.

11 *V. × w.* 'Mystique Peach Shades'
Like a cashmere jersey in hue and texture, this one is hard not to swoon over. With large, soft flowers, it is vulnerable to bad weather and only comes into its own in April, or even May, but it's worth the wait.

12 *V. × w.* 'Nature Antique Shades'
This is my current favourite. It fits perfectly in the Soft and Warm colour palette, but comes with its own contrasting crimson at the centre of the flower. There's also a beautiful tonal variation between one flower and the next. Very long-flowering and prolific.

May

May is the great changeover, with spring bulbs coming out of the pots and our summer and autumn schemes being planted. Whether it's huge terracotta pots staying in place in the garden or the more portable tabletop zinc pots, it's time to pull them apart and put them back together again.

The polytunnel and cold frames are crammed with tender annuals and perennials waiting to fill our pots. As soon as we're sure the frosts are over, our wheelbarrows are almost permanently full. All our pot-compatible plants – the more compact dahlias, scented-leaf pelargoniums and the drought-resistant tender lot, such as nemesias, petunias, snapdragon, salvias and osteospermums – are at the ready, and out they all come into the garden.

We have a few stalwart perennial pots that just keep going (more on those in July), but with the majority of our containers, it's time for a refurb. We tend not to open the garden in May for just this reason. It makes the place feel a bit transitional, but I love this time of year – it's full of optimism and creativity as we work out designs, confirm pre-planned ones, mix form and colour as we plant and make the place sing for at least the next five months.

Dismantling Bulb Pots

It's sad to see the pots of spring bulbs go, but with their petals now dropped, it's time to move on.

Dismantling tulip pots

So, first, what to do with the tulips? Sadly, if you leave them in their pots, they will not flower as well in their second year, producing lots of leaves but very weak flowers. After much experimenting with different systems, we now recommend lifting the tulips from the pots and planting them straight into the garden. They then die back in their new garden position and the idea is that they continue to photosynthesise and store enough starch in the bulb over the next few weeks to flower the following year and for many years after that. In truth, they may not put on a fantastic show in their first year in the garden, but after that they do seem to do well. See p143 for more on planting out pot tulips.

How well they take depends on how perennial the varieties are. Tulips in the Fosteriana, Viridiflora, Darwin Hybrid, Species and Lily-flowered groups, as well as certain individual ones (such as 'Mistress Mystic', 'Green Wave', 'Apricot Beauty' and 'Negrita'), are reliably perennial.

To make tulip growing sustainable, it's worth giving every tulip a try with replanting. If you don't have a garden, see p175 for tips on storing bulbs. And if you're really short of time or space, treat tulips as annuals: remove them from their pots, chop them up and add to the compost heap. You need to chop up the stems and leaves with shears and then the bulbs with a sharp spade – slicing them into sections means they compost quicker.

Previous page One of our whopper pots in the Oast Garden. We fill the base with plastic pots overlaid with fleece to reduce the amount of compost needed.

Dismantling other bulb pots

With species tulips, all narcissi, muscari and fritillaries, different rules apply. They come back happily and look just as good year after year. If we can spare their pots, we leave them where they are. If their pots are needed, we transfer them to a plastic pot.

Either way, they need to be deadheaded and given a liquid seaweed feed. Then we put these pots out of sight (beside our polytunnel), leaving the bulbs to build up strength. The leaves will gradually die down and we leave the bulbs to bake without watering through the summer. They only need watering while the leaves are still green.

The pots will then need a feed in July or August, before the bulbs start putting down roots again at the start of autumn.

If you had an annual pot topper above the bulbs, wait for it to go over and then remove and add compost. If you had a perennial pot topper, remove and plant into its own pot or out into the garden.

Replanting Pots Between Seasons

We have quite a nifty system here to avoid a total colour lull in May. We use robust plastic inner pots for as many of our dolly tubs and long toms as we can. The tulip lasagnes are planted in those (see p399), as are the plants we plan to follow on with. This means that when the tulips start to look ropey, the whole inner pot can be whipped out and the next combination slotted straight in. This system is only suited to shallow-rooted plants and regular feeders – we can't use it with our largest pots for climbers or hungry feeders such as dahlias, which we plant straight into the pot to give their roots more room.

The one downside of this succession system is the inner pot's black plastic rim. This can look ugly, at least until things have grown enough to cover it. So rather than propping it on the rim of the outer pot, we now allow it to sink down, by just an inch, supported from the base with empty, upturned plastic pots or empty compost bags. This system is practical and works aesthetically and, with half the volume of potting compost required, it is cheaper too.

Preparing Pots for Planting

We have different methods depending on the size of the pot.

Whopper pots

These instructions are for pots approximately 60cm x 60cm (24in x 24in) and for planting straight into the container (without the use of a plastic inner pot). In spring, we empty these whopper pots entirely and start again with new crocks, fillers for the bottom of the pot and compost (pictured on p196). In autumn, we only refresh the top layer of compost.

Below Pot liners make succession planting so easy. You can just remove the spring combinations and slot in another pot for summer and autumn. It doesn't work for everything (for example, dahlias need a deeper root run) but it's a great cheat.

- Fill the bottom of the whopper pot with crocks to 15cm (6in). We sadly tend to have quite a few broken terracotta pots, so we use these, but empty compost bags do a similar job.
- Cover this layer with old fleece or newspaper or torn-up cardboard boxes. This is to stop the compost falling into the spaces between the crocks and being wasted.
- Add a mix of compost and manure, 2 parts to 1. We make this ourselves with our own well-rotted organic farmyard manure. Fill to a depth of about 30cm (12in).
- We finish the top layer with 10cm (4in) of multipurpose peat-free compost. This stops weed seed germination, which sometimes happens with manure. Fill to the final level, which should be 3–4cm (1–1½in) below the pot rim.
- We then plant into this, just as you would into soil in the garden. I've found that digging into the compost to plant is better than placing each plant and then filling the compost in around it (it's hard to get the compost into all the nooks and crannies around the plant's roots and you're often left with big air pockets). So simply dig and plant as you would in a border.
- If you can move the pots, rock them a little to settle the compost, but if too big, this is not essential.

Medium pots

These pots that are about 30–40cm x 30–40cm (12–16in), and I include the long toms in this batch. As with whopper pots, we usually only change the compost entirely for these once a year in May. We use the spent compost as a mulch in the garden.

If you're not using an inner plastic pot, follow the same steps for whopper pots, but adjust the depth of the layers to the size of the pot. Bear in mind that Mediterranean-type plants (such as rosemary, lavender and fig), as well as pelargoniums, like a free-draining medium. In this case, add horticultural grit or sand to the compost/manure medium. Four parts compost, 2 parts manure and 1 part grit is a good mix.

As with whopper pots, fill the pot to almost the top with compost and then dig in the plants, don't position and then fill around with compost. After planting, rock the pots to settle the compost.

Small pots

These pots are less than 20cm x 20cm (8in x 8in). With these smaller pots we change the compost entirely twice a year in spring and autumn.

Follow the instructions for whopper pots, but put just one crock over the hole in the bottom of the pot to prevent it getting blocked up with roots and compost. There may only be room for the compost (always peat-free) and one plant. That's it – don't overdo it! Fill about one third of the pot, add the plant and then tease compost around the edge of the plant's root ball before filling with more compost. Tap the pot down on a flat surface a few times and fill again to ensure no air pockets.

These smaller pots need more watering, which means more feeding as the nutrients are flushed out. We often have saucers below our small pots to reduce the amount washed away.

Planting Into Pots

In terms of quantity of plants per pot, I recommend being quite generous. If you have several plants in a pot, as a general rule, you can pack them in tight, at twice the density you'd space them in the garden, then you get a better show and there's no room for weeds. If you're planting seedlings or rooted cuttings, still plant densely, but be mindful that these young plants will more than double in size by the end of their season.

For a whopper pot, add three Pillars (such as the climber *Thunbergia alata*), three Spillers (such as *Lotus berthelotii* or *Pelargonium* 'Chocolate Peppermint'), and either one or three dahlias as the Thriller or Bride, depending on the variety's size.

For medium pots, choose one Thriller/Bride and a couple each of a Pillar and Spiller.

As you plant, make sure each plant is in the right position, with the climbers at the base of the vertical supports and trailers ready to cascade over the edge of the pot.

For small pots, it's best to stick with one plant per pot. There's nothing more striking than erigeron, *Euphorbia hypericifolia* 'Diamond Frost' or a compact pelargonium such as 'Lavender Lass' or even 'Attar of Roses', just one to a pot, and potentially several pots of the same plant in a series. I love creating a group of five pots, filled with perhaps three pelargoniums (each to a pot) and two erigeron plants, all running along a window ledge or outdoor table.

For more on plant quantities, see p82.

Planting rooted cuttings and half-hardy annual seedlings

- Fill a barrow or a watertight trug with water. Stand all your pots of cuttings and seedlings in the water before planting. This ensures their roots go in good and moist, which encourages them to settle in quickly.
- With a trowel, dig a decent hole in the

compost, aiming at twice the depth and width of the seedling's root ball.

- Water the hole so that the base roots will be in damp compost.
- Knock the seedling out of its pot with a firm strike to the pot base, tease out the roots a little if they're knotted, then plant.

Planting climbers

You'll need a large climbing frame for their final pot and this is best made before you plant (see p202). Climbers such as cobaea and thunbergia will be in large pots when they come out of the polytunnel and will already have a climbing frame over which the seedling plants have grown.

When planting these, tip them out of the pot taking care not to disrupt this frame. Don't try to separate them, just lean the pot frame onto the large final teepee and tie it in. With no root or top disturbance you'll get uninterrupted growth. Already up to a good height, with everything left intact, they romp away.

Planting dahlias

Dahlias thrive in a rich, moist soil, so it's worth upping the organic matter in their pots, aiming for a mix that's half well-rotted manure and half peat-free compost. As you plant the dahlias, look out for any shoots that are starting to get leggy and pinch them out. This promotes axillary bud formation and makes them bushy, giving you more compact plants and more flowers.

Major slug and snail patrol is important when dahlias first go out. Dahlias are some of their favourite foods, so if you know you have a slug or snail issue, plan ahead and add copper tape or a good smear of Vaseline to the pot rim. Also be on frost alert – if a late frost is forecast, cover the plants with fleece.

For all pot sizes and plants

- Once your planting is done, water in well. We use a very diluted seaweed mix to do this (about one third of the recommended concentration).
- Add labels to the pot edge so you have a note of the plants you've loved, or not. That's key for us when trialling things, and is always helpful when you're planning next year's combinations.
- Water as necessary through the season. Start feeding with seaweed feed after a month and don't forget to deadhead when required.

Below Making a silver birch teepee
for our tender perennial climbers.

Pot Supports and Teepees

Our large-scale pots often have a woven teepee
or frame for climbers and/or they may contain
dahlias, which also need support. For climbers,
we usually add silver birch or hazel teepees.

Once dahlias have reached 60cm (2ft), and
this can happen by late May, they need to be
staked. You can make your own supports or
use decorative frames (simple iron hoops will
give enough support). We make our own birch
domes or rings (see p229).

Making a pot teepee

Teepees can be made from bamboo canes,
or hazel or silver birch. The supporting canes
or branches, referred to as uprights, need to
be at least 1.5m (5ft) tall. You can supplement
these with smaller sticks pushed in between
each upright, around the base. With bamboo
canes, you need to add a network of twine
between the uprights to create an efficient
climbing frame, which doesn't look as good,
but does the job. For hazel and birch, you can
use bundles of thinner side branches to wrap
around the uprights. The twiggy nature of
the thinner branches makes the best climbing
frame, giving the plants plenty to grip onto
as they climb.

- Whatever you choose to use, push a circle
  of 4–8 uprights into the pot (depending on
  pot size), sinking them a good 20–30cm
  (8–12in) deep. It's key to secure the sticks
  well into the compost so they don't ping out
  as the climbers grow. You'll probably need
  to work from a stepladder.
- Gather the uprights together at the top and
  tie with a robust flexi tie or piece of twine.
- If using birch or hazel, you need to wrap
  the smaller branches around the structure.
  Start at one upright in the circle, gather
  all the thinner side branches about 30cm
  (12in) from the rim of the pot and hold
  them together in your right hand. Twist
  horizontally. Carry on twisting until
  you get to the next upright and twist the

second bundle, binding and weaving it in with the next and so on until you get to the beginning again, reversing back on yourself to tie off any loose ends.

- Next, move 45cm (18in) up towards the top of the teepee and do another layer in the same way.
- We also make teepees with one long spiral from the bottom to the top of the teepee, so the whole thing looks like a helter-skelter. To do this, keep twisting up and around, gathering as you go, until you reach the top.

Planting Out

Potted hellebores

If you've been growing hellebores in pots, plant them in the garden now. Tidy them up by removing any tatty leaves and seedpods, then plant in a shady spot, adding plenty of organic matter to the planting hole. Mulch the plants with well-rotted manure or leaf mould as they start to die back for their dormant season. They'll thrive with this friable, humus-rich addition to their soil, and the extra nutrition will help protect them from black spot, to which *Helleborus niger* in particular is prone to.

Potted primulas

The primroses and polyanthus that have been flowering since February or March are now going over. The more robust ones, such as 'Stella Champagne', can be lifted out of their pots. The large clumps can then be gently teased apart to create several smaller sections to be replanted into the garden or into new pots for next winter.

With the more delicate forms, such as the green-flowered 'Francesca', and particularly auriculas, repot into fresh, well-drained, gritty compost once they've finished flowering. We like to make a mix of loam-based John Innes No. 2, leaf mould and grit to a ratio of 4:2:1.

Top any pots with grit after planting. For auriculas, keep them shaded, just moist over summer and always protected from heavy rain. Move them into a cold greenhouse or cold frame over autumn and winter and reduce watering to a bare minimum. You don't need to protect them from frost. In early spring, start to feed with a weak liquid seaweed, move to part shade and resume watering.

With all potted primulas, it's also key to protect against vine weevil. Plants permanently living in pots are particularly prone to attack. Keep an eye out for notched holes on the leaf edge: a sign of adult vine weevil. We use biological control on these (see p225), as well as on heucheras, which are also susceptible plants.

June

When I walk out into the garden in June, it's flowery and fragrant, full of poppies, roses and sweet peas. But I have to say, our whopper pots are still building up steam for their next extravaganza. By the middle of the month, some of the more compact dahlias such as 'Dreamy Nights' and 'Dalaya Devi' have a few flowers starting to open, and 'Josie' and 'Totally Tangerine' usually join in by the end of the month. But most of our dahlias and the bulk of the half-hardy annuals and tender perennials won't start flowering until the middle of July. However, we have discovered, over the years, how to plug this flower gap.

It's our small, tabletop zinc pots and smaller, more portable terracotta containers that we rely on for flowers and colour in June. These are shifted and collected to stand in groups around doorways or up on walls or on outside tables, essentially wherever they give the most impact. And they're filled with what we've learnt are the most reliable flowerers.

We have two groups that have proved invaluable. The first lot are a few specific tender perennials that naturally come into flower early. I've already mentioned several pelargoniums as early summer stalwarts in May (see p181), and I'd add nemesias to these. Fragrant, compact and, with modern breeding, now long-performing, these give us a mass of fabulous colours in June and July. We try to have as many nemesias as possible, as singles or in mixed colour collections with reliably early-flowering calibrachoas – the smaller-flowered, more compact cousins of the petunia.

The second crucial group are hardy annuals and biennials, planted out into their pots as soon as the worst of the winter cold has passed. I have a particular soft spot for the delicate looking annual toadflax, *Linaria maroccana* 'Little Sweeties Mix'. Its flowers have a top and bottom lip, like a snapdragon but a quarter of the size, with one mini-flower stacked on top of another in a dainty spire. You can sow and grow these in single colours, but I love the simple sugary mix of pink, mauve, yellow and white. It reminds me of a packet of Love Hearts sweets and they are softly scented. We often have linarias in a pot on our sunny, south-facing terrace, surrounded by cascades of *Erigeron karvinskianus*. I pick the linaria to put into mini-milk bottles to run down the centre of our kitchen table. With stem ends seared for a couple of seconds in boiling water, they last about a week.

We sow both linaria and erigeron in mid-February into seed trays. Linarias make quite spindly plants, which we prick out for planting into their final pot in early April. You can also sow a meagre pinch of either straight into the containers you want to grow them in. Be as stingy as you can with the seed

Previous page Moving a pot of *Erigeron karvinskianus* to our outdoor eating table – it makes a low-maintenance table centre pot for summer.
Below Delicate flowers like these double campions *Silene pendula* 'Sibella Carmine', 'Sibella Lilac' and 'Sibella White' look best en masse in a whopper pot to avoid any sense of fussiness. They're scented too.

to prevent overcrowding once they're up and growing. Keep the pots under cover until April to speed up flowering. With linarias, you'll need to push a few silver birch twigs into the pot, through which the fine stems can then grow supported. This is key to keeping them upright. And then it's just pick, pick, pick (or deadhead) for continual flowers for much of summer.

Schizanthus, the butterfly flower, is perfect now too and should be grown in a similar way. It's a borderline hardy annual, slower to flower than linaria. We sow this twice, first the previous summer, to make sure we have it flowering under cover in spring, and then again in early spring to flower from June. Like linaria, it needs support, ideally not with chunky canes and string, but a few small silver birch or hazel branches picked from the garden and just poked in. This plant was popular with the Victorians, grown for colour in their greenhouses, filling their pelargonium plant theatres with flowers from April. For pots in the garden, we find it's at its best in May or June, and we love it for its cheery, almost orchid-like flowers. One of the common names of schizanthus is, in fact, poor man's orchid.

We're also fans of the double-flower campions in the Sibella series, which were bred for hanging baskets. We don't use these annuals in baskets, but in table centre pots, mixing all three Sibella colours in one container: the red *Silene pendula* 'Carmine' with the soft pink 'Lilac' and a dash of 'White'.

We sow these in March in seed trays and they are quick to germinate. Like schizanthus, campions don't flower for hugely long (perhaps eight to ten weeks), but they come at just the right time, and we use them in a large, low pot in one of our most prominent spots, bang in the middle of the Perennial Cutting Garden. It's into this garden that our visitors first arrive and this particular pot is one of the first things they see in June. We replace the campions later with a mix of late-performing plants such petunias, salvias and pelargoniums (pictured on p272), but for early summer, we couldn't be without this trio. Like the wild white campion *Silene latifolia*, the varieties we use have a faint, slightly clove-like scent and, even though they have been bred to produce double flowers, they're still packed with nectar and continually busy with bees, as well as species of the much ignored but crucial pollinator, the hoverfly.

Like a puff of pink smoke, we also grow the mini *Psammophiliella muralis* 'Gypsy Deep Rose' (syn. *Gypsophila muralis* 'Gypsy Deep Rose') and the taller, beautifully elegant *G. elegans* 'Kermesina'. Bred for pots and therefore compact and delicate, these hardy annuals look brilliant planted alone in small terracotta pots. We love using a series of these to run down the centre of an outdoor table or on a wall. The flowers are pretty individually as well as en masse and, elevated above ground level, you really see them. These are best sown into modular trays in late February/early March and planted into their final pot to flower in June and through the summer.

Heliophila coronopifolia (syn. *H. longifolia*) is our final elegant and dainty June must-have hardy annual. It's known as false blue flax, and looks just like annual flax with the same sky-blue flowers, but they're even finer and more delicate. I adore this sitting on our doorstep in dappled shade, its flowers standing out against the lichen greys and silvers of our stone trough. It is over quite quickly but is so worth the minute of sowing required, which we do around Valentine's Day, a tiny pinch straight into the pot where it will grow.

Cutting Patch Pots

Euphorbia oblongata, *Cerinthe major* 'Purpurascens' and *Calendula officinalis* 'Indian Prince' are my number one group for cut flowers from a pot. I'm often asked, if I had nothing but pots in an urban yard or terrace, what would I grow? This group would be a strong contender. Not only do these plants look handsome in pots, they also provide countless vases of flowers, meaning you can have a cutting patch without the need for a garden.

All three are cut-and-come-again, the last two prolifically. We plant and harvest them together, but the cerinthe and calendula go over more quickly – when this happens, we lift the euphorbia and replant it into the garden. Remember, if you do harvest or move euphorbia, do so with gloves on and even then take care not to put your hands to your face: its sap can cause an allergic reaction.

No garden, whether it has pots or borders, should be without cerinthe. It has elegant, hanging, silver-hooded stems and purple flowers, and it cuts brilliantly for the vase (sear the stem ends in just-boiled water) and I love the look of it.

It's also stacked with sugar-rich nectar for bees and butterflies, hence its common name, honeywort. A wildflower of the Mediterranean, it can be in flower by May after a March sowing, but reaches its peak now, in early June.

The final player is the English marigold 'Indian Prince'. With its crimson reverse to each petal and rich orange front, it's like a blood orange in flower form – and what could be nicer? Sown with the cerinthe in March, this will be at peak flowering for June. I love its richness of colour in a pot or picked for a vase. We use it as an edible flower too, scattering it over rice and couscous salads like strands of saffron. It's a stellar plant.

Cerinthe looks great in a pot on its own and even better with the structure and flowers of the others in this trio. The euphorbia acts as a natural corset, supporting it as it grows, while the marigold studs the pot with orange Catherine wheels, contrasting perfectly with the cerinthe.

Last, but absolutely not least, are sweet peas, an obvious winner for June. At Perch Hill, we mainly grow these in the garden over extensive arches and frames, but there's something luxurious about having them right there on the doorstep growing in pots so we can walk into the house through a perfumed arcade.

Early planting and growing is key with sweet peas for pots; the ideal time for getting them into their final pot is March (see p130). As far as varieties go, we've tried all sorts for pots. There are semi-dwarf forms that have been bred over the years to be specifically suited to pots, but in our experience they don't do as well as they should. Instead, I'd recommend *Lathyrus odoratus* 'Matucana'. It is the most strongly scented sweet pea you can grow, lovely to pick but with its shorter-than-average stems, rather suited to a pot. There's also 'Blue Velvet' and 'Anniversary': with almost twice the length of flowering season, these two are good in pots, lasting well not just through July, but into August, and that's unusual. Most recently we've had success with the purple and white-flecked 'Nimbus' and 'Earl Grey'.

So, there are flowers to pick and flowers full of fragrance from our June pot supremos. It's not a peak pot moment, but there's still plenty out there to enjoy.

Nemesias

Opposite *Nemesia* 'Lady Lisa' shot straight into my top ten container plants after a recent trial. I love it growing in our leaf-embossed zinc planters.

Nemesia 'Lady Lisa' is my most recent and favourite plant for pots. Newly bred, this beauty is a great mix of two of the richest colours: its top lip is indigo, the bottom Liberty-bag purple. And it's correct to talk in terms of lips, as nemesias are cousins of the snapdragon and have similar, though smaller, flowers. With flowers densely packed on a stem, and in such saturated colours, they remind me of alternating ribbons on a maypole.

I only discovered this family after a wildflower trip to South Africa a few years ago. In the wild, they're crazily glamorous and one can hardly believe, as you come upon them, that such a flower hasn't been planted. That's what many of the wildflowers in South Africa feel like: exquisite and extraordinary and beyond what feels possible in nature. But of course they *are* wild and southern Africa is the original home of so many of our garden plants. It's an exhilarating place to go botanising.

Whether hybridised or in the wild, most nemesias are deliciously scented, with a perfume slightly reminiscent of vanilla and sugared almonds. And many of them have petals that look like they've been cut from silk velvet. Nemesias are short-lived perennials, often grown as annuals and propagated by seed or cuttings in spring or summer. But we find the plants easy to overwinter under cover, which ensures we get larger and more floriferous nemesias from one year to the next, and they flower earlier too. If you have a cold frame or greenhouse, this is worth doing.

The species varieties tend to flower here from May to early July, and then go off when the heat starts to rise, but this has been extended to at least September or October with most of the new hybrids we've trialled. They may have a rest at the height of summer, but if deadheaded and fed, they soon bounce back. We give them all a liquid feed every two to three weeks – especially after deadheading – and on and on they go.

In the same family as nemesias, diascias are great June flower-givers. We particularly love *Diascia personata*, which can be perennial in a sheltered spot in the garden, but in a pot will need to be brought under cover in autumn. As insurance, take some cuttings in the early autumn to make sure you have plants for the following year. With its coral-pink flower spires, this stands at about five times the height of 'Lady Lisa', so is a different thing altogether: rangy, even a little gangly, but clearly from the same tribe. Because of its height and more open, airy habit, we tend to plant this in the ground around other pots, rather than in a pot itself, to create a coral halo in the background. We also love *Diascia barberae*, more suited to the patio and reliably hardy – look out for *D. b.* 'Blackthorn Apricot', which has an RHS AGM.

With new varieties appearing all the time, this whole clan of plants (nemesias in particular) are worth keeping on one's radar. We intend to trial new ones every two to three years.

Below What we call our Summer Fruit Salad Container Collection growing in a window box at my home in London. It follows the usual recipe of Bride (the brilliant orange *Nemesia* 'Sunsatia Plus Papaya'), Bridesmaid (matching *Calibrachoa* Superbells Unique 'Tropical Sunrise') and Gatecrasher (the purple *N.* 'Framboise').
Opposite One of the softer coloured blue nemesias, 'Mirabelle', which has a lovely scent.

Best of the nemesias

Following lots of recent breeding, navigating the range of nemesias can feel like a maze. I've organised them here by series. They all seem to behave in much the same way and flower for much the same time.

1 *Nemesia* Fairy Kisses series
These have bushy, upright growth, with bicoloured flowers that are scented and fruity, hence they're all named after fruits that fit their flower colour. They don't set seed, so have a long-flowering period – cutting back and feeding in midsummer should reboot them to flower again. 'Boysenberry' (pictured) is one of our favourites, with a fabulous fragrance. Rich pink upper petals meet a paler shade below. It flowers all through summer and well into autumn.

2 *N. fruticans*
Neat, compact, upright and bushy, 'Framboise' has very large, upward-facing, raspberry-coloured flowers with a dark eye. It's a great partner to nemesias 'Myrtille' (pictured) and 'Mirabelle'

(pictured on p217), which also have very large flowers and are compact and bushy. 'Myrtille' has inky-blue, sumptuously dark flowers with red-tinted eyes on robust stems – very dramatic. And 'Mirabelle' is strongly scented and has very versatile lavender-mauve flowers, which work well in a bright, rich or pale palette. 'Wisley Vanilla' is a good variety that has been around for some time and has possibly the strongest and most distinct scent of all nemesias. We still grow this for its earliness – it starts to flower in May, but it's usually over by July, so these days it has been rather outdone by longer-flowering, newer hybrids.

3 *N.* Karoo series
The nemesias in this series don't set seed, so they keep blooming for longer without the need for a midsummer cut-back. They are early, long lasting and tough plants. 'Karoo Dark Blue' (pictured here with *Diascia* 'Little Tango') is one of our favourites: a single-colour flower and good for that reason, because it's easy to mix with other things in a pot without making the collection too busy. A perfect, rich, background filler flower, with scent.

4 N. Lady series
Newly bred in the UK, these
were real winners here at
Perch Hill, though they
are only lightly scented.
They have remarkably
large flowers with the most
unique deep colouring. 'Lady
Anne' (pictured) is a shade of
unwashed denim, which gives
it an eye-turning richness;
only salvias and gentians come
near the density of this blue.
'Lady Lisa' (pictured on p214)
is a more classic dark and rich
bicolour. It came top in our
most recent trial for being
fragrant, flowery and long-
performing – and it shot into
my top ten container plant
must-haves. 'Lady Ruby' is a
real ruby amethyst, as its name
implies. Densely flowery and
earlier than the other two,
flowering from April or May
and then going over earlier
than the other two.

5 *N.* Maritana series
The flowers are sterile in this series, so they keep going all through the season. 'Blue Lagoon' (pictured) is genuinely lagoon coloured, with pretty, almost violet-shaped flowers.

6 *N.* Nesia series
Another band of new varieties. The plants in this series grow to about 30cm (1ft) tall and wide and have large flowers on good strong stems. 'Nesia Burgundy' is densely flowery for the whole of summer – the flowers open nearly scarlet and then deepen to ruby and burgundy as they age. 'Nesia Tropical' is one of my favourite colour combinations, with orange and burgundy flowers that become richer and deeper as they age. 'Nesia Tutti Frutti' (pictured) is exceptional for its density and length of flowering – unparalleled in our trials. We almost felt this was too dense in its flowers, but rather remarkable with it. Pictured with it is *Penstemon* 'Garnet' and Miss Willmott's ghost, *Eryngium giganteum* 'Silver Ghost', beside it in the border.

7 *N.* Sundae series
Beautiful, sweet-perfumed plants that continuously flower from spring to autumn. Loved by bees and pollinators and, once established, hardy through very mild winters. 'Blueberry Ice' (pictured) is unusual amongst the ones we've trialled in that is has unwashed-denim-blue upper petals with white below. It's good for breaking up rich blues or pure whites and it's more compact than the others.

8 *N.* Sunsatia series
This lot are early to flower and come in bright colours. 'Papaya' (pictured) is our head gardener Josie's all-time favourite nemesia, partly due to its colour, but also because it forms a big enough plant to make its presence felt at around 30cm (1ft) both tall and wide. This is a key player in our bestselling Summer Fruit Salad Container Collection, which is pictured on p216, as well as on the wall pillar in the photo on p210.

Next page **A scented-leaf pelargonium collection of 'Attar of Roses', 'Sweet Mimosa' and 'Prince of Orange', with potted figs creating great silhouettes behind.**

June

June is a busy month in the pot garden. Watering has now started in earnest and, since we have so many pots, we've evolved a system to keep them well-hydrated. There's a whole section on that here. This is also the month that we concentrate on deadheading, giving all the flowering pots a good going over at least once a week. It makes a huge difference, not only to how they look, but to how long they flower. We're relying on the annuals and biennials for colour at this time of year, so deadheading them is particularly key. Sweet peas in pots need picking or deadheading twice a week.

With most of our containerised plants, the fertiliser in their compost will sustain them for four to six weeks from planting, so we don't start feeding until July, but sweet peas, even with the extra manure we add to their pot mix, benefit from a fortnightly potash-rich feed. We make our own comfrey liquid fertiliser for this job, but an organic tomato feed will also work well. We start feeding hungry dahlias now too – they benefit from an extra food boost of seaweed fertiliser.

Sowing for this year's pots is over now, but next year comes onto the radar. Sowing biennials, such as wallflowers, Iceland poppies and even foxgloves for pots in shade, is best done in June. We are also at the tail end of planting out, with cold-sensitive plants such as zinnias left until last, but we aim to have even these planted out early in June.

Finally, if the primulas or heucheras are collapsing, and we know we've given them plenty of water, we check around the roots for vine weevil larvae. Grown in pots, these plants are particularly susceptible. The larvae look like fat maggot grubs – if you spot one, there are usually more. We uproot the plant and have a bit of a rummage; we then feed the grubs to our hens or leave them out for garden birds. We've also had good results with the biological control Nemasys Vine Weevil Killer.

Watering

In dull or cool weather, stick your finger in the compost to see if it's damp and water according to what you find.

When it's hot and sunny, small pots dry out incredibly quickly. To keep them hydrated, sit them in saucers to catch the water as you water from the top and allow them to soak the extra up. If it's really dry, plunge them into a bucket or barrow of water for five minutes or so, until the bubbles stop rising from the compost.

With medium or large pots, we have a double (or in very dry weather, triple) watering technique that from June to August usually has to be done three times a week. We have set watering days on Monday, Wednesday and Friday, so we know where we are and don't forget. In a heatwave, this can increase to every day.

Previous page Lifting a large pot to
see if it needs water – the lighter it is,
the drier it is.
Below Comfrey ready to be cut down
so we can turn it into potash-rich
plant feed.

If you've missed a watering and the compost has really dried out, water can quickly run out through the holes at the bottom and it's easy to think this means the container has had enough, but that's usually not the case. Dehydrated, the compost can't hold on to moisture. In this case, you need to give the pot a really, really good drenching. Josie – our head gardener – also recommends pressing the compost against the edges of the pot if it has shrunk away. Add fresh compost if there is a big enough gap.

If it's particularly scorching, always water pots in the evening, not the morning.

This avoids excess evaporation under the day's sunshine. And use a hose pipe not a watering can if you can. It makes the task so much easier and quicker considering the volume of water required. We have water butts and rainwater harvesting tanks around the garden to fall back on if there is a water shortage and with it a hosepipe ban.

We have lots of pots, so our method is to collect them into groups. Every pot in each group is watered thoroughly. We spend a good minute on whopper pots to give them a real drenching. If it's rained in the last day or two,

this first stage may not be necessary. We then go around the group of pots again, but not for quite as long, watering for more like 30 seconds. By then, the whole plant root ball is well hydrated, with water right down to the micro-roots. With our whopper pots, in a drought, we do a third round of watering.

For advice on irrigation, see p266.

....

Making Pot Feed

Liquid seaweed fertiliser is an excellent organic option which we have used here for years, but increasingly we try to make our own. As a team, we are all keen at Perch Hill to make the garden sustainable and self-sufficient and that includes making our own container plant food.

Luckily, in the garden we have plenty of potash-rich comfrey and nitrogen-packed nettles. These two plants provide us with the raw material to make fertilisers.

Potash is necessary for good root, flower and fruit formation. Nitrogen is the major component of chlorophyll and is necessary for photosynthesis and leaf growth. Various feeds use varying quantities of these, but when making your own fertilisers you can apply them separately or mix them together for a more broad-spectrum feed.

Feeding our pots only starts in earnest in July (see p266) but now is a good moment to get the brews ready.

- Cut the plant (comfrey or nettles) back to the ground. At this time of year, they will grow back quickly for a later harvest. Gather up all the stems and leaves in a trug or wheelbarrow.
- Chop everything up (you can include the flowers) and pile into a bucket or water butt. Ideally, your container will have a tap in the base (such as a water butt), so you can extract the liquid, and a lid is useful as the mixture starts to smell as it breaks down, but any watertight container is fine – even wine or beer boxes with a tap at the base work well. Cut the cardboard top off and make a small hole in the bag, which you can then stuff with leaves. Whatever you're using, fill up the container with water, add a lid (or secure a bag with a peg) and leave somewhere outside.
- After 3–4 weeks extract the liquid and store in bottles somewhere cool and dark. Alternatively, just take liquid from the mixture as and when you need it, always topping the mix up with more water and plant material.
- To use the fertiliser, dilute with water to a ratio of about 1:10, then apply to the pot plants.

Below Deadheading *Verbena rigida*, which we do from now right through summer and into autumn.

Deadheading

Picking or deadheading annuals and tender perennials such as verbenas and pelargoniums is already important by June to ensure they go on flowering for as long as possible. Cut back the ageing flower to a leaf or an already formed axillary bud. Do this every week to ten days from now until October. We always try to have snips in our pockets and deadhead whenever we have a spare minute and pass a plant which needs a bit of tidying. It makes such a difference.

Sowing Biennials

Sowing biennials such as wallflowers, foxgloves (for pots in shade) and Iceland poppies in seed trays is much the same as any seed sowing (see p86). There are, however, a few things to look out for, particularly when sowing biennials with tiny seeds.

- As a rule you should think of your seeds as gold dust and individually place all but the very tiniest (it'll save you time later when pricking out). With dust-like biennial seeds, such as foxgloves, you just can't do that. For these, we use deep, large trays or polystyrene crates for sowing, which we recycle from the local greengrocer and fishmonger.
- To sow, don't pour straight from the corner of the packet – put a small number of seeds into the palm of your hand. Scatter the seeds as far apart as you can over this wider-than-usual surface area. This is best done fast, in a quick swoosh of the arm, and from a height. Do the first swoosh at one end of the tray, the next over the middle and the final over the other end, trying not to scatter over the same area.
- We usually sow wallflowers first. They are spring-flowering and benefit from an early sowing. We aim for May or early June. By the end of June, they may be ready to prick out.

Making Supports

It's time to give May-planted dahlias and half-hardy annuals a bit of attention as they're growing quickly now. In pots we tend to create a cage-like dome, rather than just using a single stake. It looks architectural and supports the plants well. For thunbergia, cobaea and other tender-perennial climbers, you can make a pot teepee, just as we do for sweet peas (see p202).

Making a pot dome

To make a dome, start by checking the final height of the tallest plant in the pot, and aim to create a structure that is about one third to one half of this height. For heavy-headed plants such as dahlias, aim for the taller end. If you have smaller plants with lighter stems, such as salvias, just one third of the height is fine.

- Arrange 4–8 uprights (depending on the pot size) vertically inside the edge of the pot, pushing them to at least a depth of 20cm (8in), but ideally 30cm (1ft) so they don't ping out as you start to weave. Silver birch is perfect, as is willow, though you need to bark the stem end you're burying, so it doesn't root.
- Choose a pair of opposite uprights, bend them into arches, then twist to secure them to each other. Continue to pair up the uprights, bending them one below and one above the previous pair, until you have bent all the verticals into a dome.

- Finally twist horizontals of willow or hazel 15cm (6in) above compost level to encircle the whole frame, twisting in and out with several lengths until the frame is firmly bound together.

Making a pot ring

Some light-stemmed plants (such as salvias) only need a ring of support around the edge rather than a domed cage.

- Arrange 4–6 uprights (depending on the size of the pot) standing vertically inside the edge of the pot (as with the dome).
- Bend the first upright over at a right angle to itself to touch the upright next to it. As you reach the next one along, do the same, bending it at a right angle and so on.
- At about a third of the ultimate height of the pot's contents, weave the uprights together horizontally. Carry on bending the uprights over and integrating them until you're back at the start, finishing off by twisting the twigs backwards to secure.
- If the top of the pot ring is more than 45cm (18in), I suggest adding another layer between the top of the frame and the pot rim. This looks nice and helps to support and strengthen the structure. Twist the twiggier horizontals of willow, birch or hazel to encircle the whole frame, twisting in and out with several lengths until it's all bound firmly together.

July

At this midsummer moment, our world of pots is a source of joy, with flowers opening wherever you look. In the Dutch Yard, we have to pick our way through a jungle of container plants. The wellhead is packed with pots, as are the metal tables around the yard's edge and the tiered plant theatre at our back door. There are containers galore covering the bricks at ground level, enriching the view, and the contents of our huge terracotta pots now tower well over our heads. From the moment you come into this space, you feel enveloped. It's true the climbers might not reach the tops of their frames yet, but they're well on their way.

As fans of the dahlia, we always have container-compatible varieties on trial, and it's exciting to see new ones starting to show their true colours about now (more on those in August). Petunias may have been flowering for a month or so, but by this time of year they, and their smaller cousins the calibrachoas, have grown enough to swag the edges of many of our pots. There are few plants that can compete with the flower size and texture of a petunia, and they're so easy to grow from seed or cuttings. They're one of my top ten container plants. These join pelargoniums, also here in large numbers, as our highlight in July.

This is also the month when most half-hardy annuals come into flower and there is, of course, a good range that's excellent for pots. Planted into their final garden pots about six weeks ago as the frosts ended in May, many of these are now in full bloom.

Cosmos is one of the very prettiest and longest-performing half-hardy annuals you can grow. There have long been compact forms suited to pots in white ('Sonata White'), pink

('Sensation Pinkie' and 'Pink Popsocks') and deep red ('Sonata Carmine'), but the last five years have seen great breeding of this ever-popular family, mainly in Japan. I love the soft apricot 'Apricotta', with its pronounced pink halo providing a beautiful contrast at the centre of each flower. At about 90cm (3ft), it's a good height for a pot if given a bit of support. 'Apricot Lemonade' is a beauty too, a gentle yellow with the same pink halo as 'Apricotta', but with the pink bleeding out as a wash right to the petal edge. It's a bit shorter at 70cm (28in).

For bright shades, there's 'Xsenia', which is the same height, but pink with a bronze tinge, particularly when it first opens. And for a dark number, we love 'Rubenza', which opens the deepest deep red-carmine, gradually brightening as the flowers age. It's a similar size and will also need staking to stay upright. The beauty of cosmos is that rather than deadheading, you can pick and fill your vases. The pots look all the better for the picking and the house is full of flowers.

I also love snapdragons for this time of year. We grow *Antirrhinum majus* 'Appleblossom' and 'Giant White' together as a pastel-coloured pair, along with the open-faced, softly scented

Previous page *Agapanthus* 'Midnight Star' in a series of pots with *Salvia viridis* 'Blue' paired with tagetes in another. *Trachelospermum jasminoides* fills the whole place with perfume in July and well into August.
Below *Cosmos bipinnatus* 'Sonata White' (Bride), *Phlox* '21st Century White' (Bridesmaid) and *Osteospermum* 'Akila White Purple Eye' – its purple eye provides a light-touch Gatecrasher (see p38).
Opposite *Cosmos bipinnatus* 'Velouette', *Petunia* 'Tidal Wave Red Velour' and *Salvia microphylla* 'Cerro Potosí'.

plants of the Chantilly series in pale shades such as the fragrant 'Chantilly Light Salmon'. Magnificent too are the tall-spired snapdragons in the Sonnet series, which come in a true boiled-sweet mix of blackcurrant, orange, cherry and raspberry. This is one of my favourite mixes for a pot in the strong-coloured Oast Garden, paired with an equally saturated orange, terracotta or mahogany thunbergia trailing out over the pot's edge. For all our snapdragons, as with cosmos, we pick rather than deadhead – that helps them look their best well into autumn and gives us months of single stems and mixed bunches for vases.

Last but not least amongst the half-hardy annuals are the verbenas. These look great in pots in July. I've long loved the bright pink, low maintenance, drought tolerant and reliable *Verbena* 'Sissinghurst' (syn. *Glandularia* 'Sissinghurst'), a perennial verbena if stored frost-free. It has rightly been awarded an RHS AGM for its general health and floweriness from May until the first frost. It's simple yet glamorous planted in the four handsome bronze urns at the arched entrance at Sissinghurst Castle or, more modestly, in a zinc pot as a table centre here at Perch Hill.

Besides annuals and tender perennials, we always have a few hardy perennials in our pots growing steadily, year after year, without needing much care or attention. July is a good moment for many of these. One of my all-round favourites is the hardy perennial *Verbena rigida*, great interplanted with the tender perennial *Dahlia* 'Bishop's Children' in a large container. Both are quick and easy to grow from seed in March and flower together long and hard, the verbena just the right height to create a pretty purple skirt below the dark-leaved dahlia, which is an intense mix of reds, purples, yellow-ochre and orange. Both are super pollinator plants, busy with butterflies and bees. The verbena also has seed that the finches seem to adore. Our pots are regular feeding grounds for goldfinches once we get into autumn, occasionally joined by the now rare greenfinch.

Quite new on the horticultural scene are a whole tribe of familiar shrubs and climbers that are usually too big for an average pot, but now come in more compact forms. We've experimented with quite a few of these plants over the years, but not all have been a success, and that includes many roses said to be good for pots. In our experience, most roses are too susceptible to fungal diseases to be worth all the watering and feeding that they need in containers. A good general rule: roses are best in the ground.

The honeysuckles, on the other hand, *Lonicera periclymenum* 'Chic et Choc' and 'Rhubarb and Custard', are both beauties and grow happily here in large terracotta pots. We tend to keep them in the same pot for three or four years and then transplant them into an even larger pot with entirely new compost, or sometimes into the ground to romp away and clad a wall. It seems you can keep these honeysuckles sort of bonsaied for a bit, but not forever.

We've also been experimenting with herbaceous, non-climbing clematis for pots and are very keen on a couple of outstanding ones: 'Blue River' and the purple, hanging-bell form, 'Alionushka'. Both excelled in our last trial. Bred from the non-climbing *Clematis × durandii*, 'Blue River' is similar in colour to the ever-popular 'Prince Charles', with large starry flowers in a blueish mauve. It's perfect for a pot if it's given a frame and it flowers all summer. It's not too vigorous, but yet with its lovely twisting and turning stems, has a great shape.

One of my favourite plants ever is *Hydrangea paniculata* 'Limelight', which looks good in our north-facing alley at the back of our house from May until Christmas. You could use this

Left A good example of balanced form (see p43), with *Hydrangea paniculata* 'Little Lime' (Thriller), with *Coleus argentatus* 'Silver Shield' (Filler) and bacopa (Spiller). Right *Buddleja davidii* 'Buzz Lavender' with *Heliotropium arborescens* 'Midnight Sky' and *Pelargonium* 'Attar of Roses'.

in a massive water trough, or if you need something a little easier for containers, its compact brother 'Little Lime' is less than half the size. Its flower buds are a beautiful soft green, like the guelder rose *Viburnum opulus* 'Sterile', though a bit flatter in shape than the guelder's pompoms. The flowers of 'Little Lime' last four times as long as the viburnum, morphing from green to ivory then white, then developing a pink hue as autumn begins, only browning with the first hard frost. They give splendid value in pots.

The new varieties of buddleja are equally good, with many different colours of the Dreaming and the Buzz series trialled here over the last five years. These are really compact compared to the buddleja you see growing along railway sidings, and they have an elegant habit, creating an arching dome with trailing branches that cover a pot's edge. We have a pot mix that has been one of our bestsellers for years, combining *Buddleja davidii* 'Buzz Lavender' with *Heliotropium arborescens* 'Midnight Sky', and my favourite, the scented-leaved *Pelargonium* 'Attar of Roses'. Each of those plants give fabulous fragrance (you'll need to squeeze the leaves of the pelargonium as you walk past), and all three perform long and hard.

If I was allowed to choose just one perennial for pots there's no doubt it would be *Agapanthus* 'Midnight Star' (syn. 'Navy Blue'). We started growing this 20 years ago and it's held a prime position at Perch Hill ever since, the sole resident of a series of pots lining the path in the Oast Garden. It is a cracker for its colour – the loveliest blue, intense and rare in its saturation. Its flowers are strong yet delicate-looking and very long-lasting. When the petals have dropped, the seedheads are pretty too, like green faceted beads on starry stems. Also, unlike many agapanthus hybrids, it has narrow, elegant leaves, which look good from when they first emerge in April right until they die back in November – that's key for pots. We've also found 'Midnight Star' to be reliably hardy without too much hassle. It doesn't like it cold and wet, but if you place it somewhere out of the rain, it is fine down to −5°C (23°F). We started with four plants, each in their own 30cm (12in) pot and have divided them every three or four years, and there are now more than 20. We move all our potted plants into our open-sided barn as the frosts start in late November and out again in early April and have never lost this agapanthus in all the years it's been here. Tall, elegant, in a strong blue, yet airy, it's one of the best plants for summer pots.

Pelargoniums

Opposite Pelargoniums take pride of place in the greenhouse all summer, with all the rich and bright colours mixed together. We keep the softer shades apart – these sit on a shelf around the edge.

When you walk into the greenhouse in July, you'll be greeted by a tiered stage of pelargoniums. They live in plain terracotta pots, which I find balances the richness and colour these plants give so brilliantly. We gather the saturated-coloured varieties in the middle and leave the softer colours – the whites and soft pinks, as well as the ones we grow more for their foliage – on a single shelf that runs all the way around the edge of the greenhouse. The saturated colours really pack a punch and deserve to sit in pride of place, while the softer pinks, greys and greens lead the eye outside and merge more easily with the fields and woods beyond. I don't think these two palettes complement or enhance each other – they jar when mixed – but I love to have both in different places.

Some pelargonium hybrids will have been flowering since May, but others are just coming into full bloom, often carrying on until Christmas. July is the crossover moment, with both the earlies and lates in flower, so this is the time of year we have the widest range. Lots have wonderful fragrance and the scented-leaved ones in particular are super vigorous. Maybe the essential oils give them extra antioxidants and keeps pests and diseases at bay. Lots are even flowery enough to give you cut flowers.

Pelargoniums, hailing from southern Africa, are one of the few plants that will thrive even in the intense heat we can get in the greenhouse on a sunny day. Most of them don't seem to bat an eye. I love them, too, in wavy-edged pots and placed at the centre of every table in the marquee when we have our open garden days. Cut flowers struggle in that environment, wilting fast in the heat, but not good old pelargoniums. Of course, through the summer they don't need a greenhouse – they are happy in almost any sunny corner. We include them in many of our mixed containers or pot them up just on their own and have them right through the garden.

I divide pelargoniums into three groups, with the second group also subdivided. The first lot are the ones that flower well in spring – these are useful when we have our pot-colour lull in May. The second group flower from now in July right until winter. When a frost is forecast, we put them in a wheelbarrow and bring them under cover in the greenhouse. We have an old Scandinavian wood burner in there to help keep the space frost-free. It's a wonderful place to be, the pelargoniums providing a remarkable amount of colour until well into the new year, when we cut them back. This is the largest grouping, so I subdivide this lot by colour and tone, and you'll see that in the 'best of' list on the following pages.

The third group features the ones we grow for leaf more than flower. Many of them (such as 'Chocolate Peppermint' and the fern-leaved 'Filicifolium') give a handsome backdrop to more flowery things in containers. But we also use their leaves for teas and cordials (their flowers are edible too) and we pick sprigs in summer and autumn as scented foliage for vases. Many of the foliage varieties stay bright and fresh until Christmas, so they're perfect picked for a Christmas wreath – they last three to four weeks in a wreath if poked into a reusable water vial. The pelargoniums will be cut down by the weather, or us, at some point through the winter, so they offer a guiltless harvest.

Pelargoniums are easy to grow and most are a cinch to propagate. You can root cuttings easily almost any time between March and October, but we tend to take most of ours in late summer (see p311). August coincides with what would be spring in their native home, and they seem to be quickest to root just then. We take cuttings to create extra plants, but also as insurance against any losses over winter.

There's one other practical thing we've learnt with the tougher pelargoniums: we can leave them in the ground here in the south of England and they'll emerge again the following April or May. Sadly that doesn't apply to pelargoniums in pots, where the frost can not only get to the plant, but to the roots too. They must come in through the winter and be stored frost-free, but they can happily stay in the same pot, so they are still low maintenance. If you're short of indoor space, you could try planting them out in a sheltered spot in September so they have time to get their roots established before the winter cold. They may well survive if the winter isn't too severe.

It's hard to think of better things to fill your pots with at this time of year, and there's a huge range. Take your pick!

Best of the pelargoniums

I have divided my favourite pelargoniums into three groups. Group 1 collects together the ones that reliably flower early for May. Group 2 is the largest posse – these are invaluable from July until winter – and I've further subdivided these by colour palettes. Finally, Group 3 covers the ones we grow mainly for their foliage.

Group 1 – Early

1 *Pelargonium* 'Aldwyck' (Regal)
This becomes so covered in flowers that at times it can become almost solid magenta and wine red. It's early to flower (from April or May) and has super soft petals and a saturated colour. 'Regalia Chocolate' is similar but a little later to flower. Reliable and easy to grow.

2 *P.* 'Ardens' (Species Hybrid)
A wonderful cross of *P. fulgidum* and *P. lobatum*, this has grey-green soft foliage and pillar-box red petals calmed by deep crimson markings. It's supremely elegant and classy. Very early to flower from March, it becomes dormant in early summer and loses its leaves, producing new ones in early winter. It can be a bit temperamental in our cool, grey climate, but it also likes a bit of shade so is ideal on a north- or east-facing window ledge. It's easy to over water this one, so don't stand it in a pot tray and keep watering to a minimum during the dormant season.

3 *P.* 'Ashby' (Decorative)
Bright pink petals with a wine-red heart. This one is a prolific flower producer, quick-growing and easy to look after. We love it for its pretty showiness and the fact that it is already covered in flower by the middle of May and it often continues right through the summer, though fades out in autumn. It is also pictured on p185.

4 *P.* 'Aurora' (Zonal)
A classic 'bedding' pelargonium (you'll recognise it from parks and pub hanging baskets), this has typical lily-pad leaves that have strong bronze markings forming a halo within the leaf edge. I know people can be snobby about Zonal forms, but if you like full-on colour, this is one for you. Its large pompom heads are the brightest fuchsia and it almost never stops flowering. Don't think it gaudy, think it glorious! I love it. It's also pictured as a houseplant on p385.

5 *P.* 'Clorinda' (Unique)
An unusually tall pelargonium, which I've seen in brilliant pink flower in February, trained up a wall in a greenhouse. If left unpruned, or at least supported by a triple layer of bamboo canes, it can get up to a couple of metres tall. And, protected from frost, it can go on growing from one year to the next.

6 P. 'Marion Saunders' (Decorative)
Bright pink petals with a strong crimson blotch on early flowers (often from April) that go on and on. We deadhead this one quite religiously as it really seems to make a difference. 'Pink Aurore' (pictured on p18) is similar and equally wonderful, with flowers one shade brighter.

7 P. 'Orsett' (Scented-leaf)
Flowering from April to September, this has pink upper petals broken up by dark red markings. This is one of the most reliable pelargoniums we grow, surviving from one year to the next. With a bushy, strong habit, it's also easy to prune into neat globes or even standards.

8 P. 'Tommy' (Ivy-leaf)
A hugely long-flowering ivy-leaved form that has the darkest, richest pompom flowers of any we've trialled. This needs regular deadheading to keep it flowering. We also have one in a pot on a kitchen shelf and it trails about 75cm (20in). It has a break from flowering over winter, but it's still lovely, fresh and green year-round. Easy to grow and very healthy.

Group 2 – Main Season

Rich and bright
I've collected together the pelargoniums that fall into palettes 1 and 2 (see p26 and p28), covering dark and sumptuous shades, as well as more saturated brights.

1 *Pelargonium* 'April Hamilton' (Ivy-leaf)
A deep, rich red, long-flowering, shiny-leaved variety that tumbles. I love this in alternating pots with its bright pink brother, 'Surcouf' (pictured on p243 and p256). Super reliable and easy to grow.

2 P. 'Barbe Bleu' (Ivy-leaf)
A similar ivy-leaf to 'Tommy', but one tone brighter and later flowering. It's just as lovely and plush in texture.

3 *P.* 'Dark Venus' (Regal) This was given to us as a cutting from our Sussex neighbour Parham House and Gardens, which has an impressive pelargonium collection in its Victorian glasshouse. It flowers long and hard with large, cup-shaped, single flowers in wine red. Supremely saturated in colour and velvety too.

4 *P.* 'Dragon's Breath' (Stellar) Introduced to me by my friend, the gardener Arthur Parkinson, this is a compact form that becomes an ideal houseplant once the frosts start. Bright scarlet petals form flowers like firework explosions.

5 *P.* 'Lara Starshine'
(Scented-leaf)
With a lemon-scented leaf and brilliant pink flowers, this is supremely pretty and ideal for filling a window box or two – you'll only need about three rooted cuttings per box.

6 *P.* 'Lord Bute' (Regal)
Offering one of the richest, darkest crimsons of the very showy Regal types, this flowers longer than most in this group. It gets better the bigger it grows, so we store it in its pot from one year to the next, out of the frost. Very easy to propagate from cuttings.

7 *P.* 'Mystery' (Unique)
The perfect mix of bright and rich, with a scarlet-crimson petal base and an almost black heart to the flower, all standing out against bright green, crinkly leaves.

8 *P.* 'Pink Capricorn'
(Scented-leaf)
The most floriferous of the scented-leaf lot with large, pink flowers above bright green leaves. The leaves are scented but not as distinctive as the other scented-leaf forms we grow. You might also find this under its synonym, 'Pink Capitatum'.

9 *P.* 'Shrubland Rose'
(Scented-leaf)
An unbelievably long and prolific flowerer on truly minimal TLC. We put this in our farthest flung pots – we know they tend to get a little overlooked compared to those in the heart of the garden, but 'Shrubland Rose' does fine. We plant this with the equally tough-as-old-boots (and just as showy) *Cuphea subuligera* and *Argyranthemum* 'Grandaisy Deep Red'.

The trio make one of my favourite pot combinations.

10 *P. sidoides* (Species)
This species form seems to be hardier than most and has survived outside in the ground here for ten years. I love its deep red, almost black, delicate-looking flowers in contrast to its ruched skirt of silver leaves. It's petite and elegant in a line of pots.

11 *P.* 'Tornado Red'
(Ivy-leaved)
This variety's lacquer-red flowers work well when it's planted in a chic line in a window box or a series of small pots on a table or up some steps. 'Ville de Paris Red' and 'Decora Red' are more petite versions with flowers that are one tone brighter.

Soft and pale

These are the pelargoniums that sit in palettes 3 and 4 (see p30 and p32) featuring the paler, softer shades.

1 *Pelargonium* 'Deerwood Lavender Lass' (Scented-leaf) I'm fond of this delicate plant as it reminds me of the wild forms of pelargonium I saw on a wildflower botanising trip to South Africa. On its own in a pot or mixed with something similarly simple and elegant, such as a delicate lobelia or erigeron, this is an ethereal beauty.

2 *P.* 'Designer White' A classic, long-flowering pure white variety that thrives in a pot. We have it in lines or groups in our white garden collections around, and on the table in the middle of, the lawn.

3 *P.* 'Horizon Appleblossom' (Zonal) This is one of the pelargoniums you can grow easily from seed, so it gives great value. This is the single form, the double is called 'Appleblossom Rosebud'. Not the most exciting flower or colour, but it has a hugely long-flowering season.

4 *P.* 'Prince of Orange'
(Scented-leaf)
This has delicious citrus-
scented leaves and simple pink
flowers all through summer.
It is easy to propagate and
look after and is one of our
stalwarts for the pot garden
and greenhouse. We use the
leaves for flavouring sugar,
cordials and ice cream and
the flowers for decorating any
plate. (Also pictured on p222.)

5 *P.* 'Sweet Mimosa'
(Scented-leaf)
Many of the scented-leaf
pelargoniums have soft pink
or white flowers (much like
this one), but the flowers
are not really why you grow
them. 'Sweet Mimosa' is
different – it has pretty, large
flowers through much of
summer and autumn. (Also
pictured on p222.)

6 *P.* 'Viletta White'
(Ivy-leaved)
The prettiest of the ivy-
leaved trailing pelargoniums
that we've trialled in recent
years. It reminds me of the
cascading flower curtains
you see from chalet window
boxes in the Alps. This
just flowers and flowers.
'Supreme White' is also good
and very similar.

Group 3 – For Foliage

1 *Pelargonium* 'Attar of Roses'
(Scented-leaf)
For the fragrance-obsessed
gardener, this stellar
pelargonium is an essential
classic. It has pretty pink
flowers, though not showy
or prolific, and bright green,
strongly rose-scented leaves.
It is a quick and easy grower,
almost cut-and-come-again,
so we pick it quite a bit, even
from pots. We use its flowers
in arrangements and the
leaves for making tisanes and
cordials – I think it's more
delicious than elderflower.
(Also pictured on p222.)

2 *P.* 'Chocolate Peppermint'
(Scented-leaf)
If you cross *P. tomentosum*
with *P. quercifolium* you
get the hybrid 'Chocolate
Peppermint', which has
many of the attributes of
both its parents. Its leaves
are beautifully felted and
have distinct and handsome
markings and good scent.
We use this as a plush,
downy, tactile foliage layer
under more floriferous
pelargoniums such as the ivy-
leaved and trailing 'Tommy'.

3 *P.* 'Filicifolium'
(Scented-leaf)
The so-called fern-leaved
geranium is unique, with
very finely cut leaves that
make it look very much like
a fern. We use it as perky,
aromatic foliage for pots.

4 *P. graveolens* (Scented-leaf)
A pelargonium one
sees in pots all over the
Mediterranean where it's
grown more for its intensely
fragrant, rose-scented leaves
than its quite inconspicuous
flowers. It was used by mid-
20th-century cook Elizabeth
David for flavouring puddings
and sugar for cakes.

5 *P.* 'Orange Fizz'
(Scented-leaf)
Distinctly orangey in smell
and taste, this is lovely for
making cordials and tisanes.
There are also various lemon-
favoured ones like *P. crispum*
'Cy's Sunburst', which has
small, crenulated leaves.

6 *P. quercifolium* (Species)
Called the oak-leaved
pelargonium because of
its leaf shape, this species
is a trouper, looking good
pretty much year-round.
It has a strong cedar scent
and a mahogany splotch at
the centre of every leaf. It's
excellent for picking and lasts
nearly a month in water.

7 *P. tomentosum* (Species)
Strongly scented with a minty
perfume, this has the softest
texture of any plant I know.
It is also one of those rare
pelargoniums that thrives in
dry shade. It makes a great
houseplant once the frosts
threaten. It's shy to flower
and, even then, the flowers
are small and delicate. But it
is so worth growing.

Petunias

When it comes to petunias, the richer and more intense the colour, the better in my view. That's why the silk-velvet-petalled *Petunia* 'Tidal Wave Red Velour' is my favourite. Everything about it is strong: its colour, its texture and the way it grows. It germinates quickly and easily from seed (or you can propagate from cuttings taken in autumn) and then it grows fast once pricked out, romping away as soon as it's planted into its final pot. Within a couple of weeks, you'll have crushed-velvet swags growing out and over the edge of your pots. And it keeps going with minimal TLC. We'll tidy it up and deadhead it once every couple of weeks, and it's included in our three-times-a-week watering regime, but that's it. This makes it the perfect Spiller (see p43) in a large pot mix. In fact, it's such a romping grower, if you provide it with a climbing frame and tie a few of its shoots to go up, not trail down, it will reach well over a metre and become a fantastic Pillar plant. We started to use this as a cut flower last summer: with stem ends seared for a few seconds in just-boiled water, it lasted nearly two weeks in a vase.

If pale colours are more your thing, there's another petunia in the brilliant Tidal Wave series called 'Tidal Wave Silver' – we grow this in our cool area around the lawn. It opens white with delicate purple veining, which then washes over the trumpet flowers to turn them soft mauve. This is as densely covered in flower as its red relation, but one step down in terms of vigorous growth.

It seems that the paler petunias (which are more closely related to the species *P. axillaris*) often have scent. 'Tidal Wave Silver' doesn't, but the double 'Tumbelina Priscilla' has a good perfume that, rather like the winter-flowering shrubs *Sarcococca confusa* or wintersweet (*Chimonanthus praecox*), catches you almost unawares as you walk past. We have trialled, but rejected, 'Lavender Sky' (it looks like it's spent the night in the rain) and 'Lightning Sky' (too overworked and fussy). And there are a few we've trialled which are just too bright.

Even in our much-loved Tidal Wave series, I find the purple variety too synthetic, beaming out like neon from a hundred feet away.

As well as petunias, we mustn't forget the calibrachoas, whose flowers are usually about a third the size of petunias and have even more of them. Another difference is their leaves are not sticky (like petunias) and their flowers have a much milder scent. Calibrachoas are commonly known as million bells or superbells and they really are the epitome of plush curtain tassels, or that great word *passementerie* – fussy but lovely ornamental trims. Their overall habit is more compact and petite than petunias, but they're still strong growers with a hugely long-flowering season. We love them here for small table centre pots. They can be grown in part shade, but the number of flowers you get is related to the amount of sun exposure. They don't need deadheading, but we do pick them over and, occasionally, cut back stems to encourage branching and fresh growth. They are quite tolerant of the forgetful gardener, but when their leaves start to wilt, they need a good watering.

Then there's the petchoa – a newish hybrid between the petunia and calibrachoa. For me, they are the new stars. Brilliant performers and quite weather tolerant, they are very flowery (like calibrachoas) with larger flowers (like petunias). We grow and love several of these. I'm really fond of the rusty 'BeautiCal Cinnamon' and pale custard-coloured 'BeautiCal French Vanilla'. These seem classy and sophisticated, with an overall sepia, vintage look and feel. They also cut brilliantly.

In terms of planting, it's best to keep the brights and the pales in separate pots and areas. Though, really, we'd rarely put two petunias, petchoas or calibrachoas in one pot together anyway. Even in two different but complementary colours, they'd merge and look too samey.

It's worth knowing that even the single petunias are not a great source of food for pollinators, although the hummingbird hawkmoths feed on the singles as they can reach into the throats.

Best of the petunias and calibrachoas

As one of the world's most popular bedding plants, there's continuous breeding of petunias with new subgroups appearing all the time. Here are our favourites, which have stood the test of time at Perch Hill, including the petchoas and surfinias.

Rich and Bright

This lot fall into palettes 1 and 2 (see p26 and p28), with saturated bright shades and intense, rich ones too.

Petunias

1 *Petunia* 'Black Velvet'
I am often tempted by black flowers, particularly when they're velvety, but you have to be careful that they don't create an undefined black mass. You want them to stand out, so have something sharp and bright as a backdrop. 'Black Velvet' is marvellous if combined with lots of bright or acid-green plants.

2 *P.* Tidal Wave series
'Tidal Wave Purple' (pictured) is almost luminously bright and if you want something super showy, this will do the job. It's hugely flowery but not really for me in terms of colour. 'Tidal Wave Red Velour' (pictured on p23) is first class in all ways. You'll see it in endless container collections here and on its own. It climbs as well as trails. A stellar plant.

3 × *Petchoa* BeautiCal series
'BeautiCal Bordeaux' (pictured on p256) is a classy deep red, one shade brighter than 'Tidal Wave Red Velour', but not as prolific. 'BeautiCal Cinnamon' (pictured) is a sophisticated colour which moves from cinnamon to crimson, sometimes with a wash of gold. You'll either love it or hate it. It's quite a difficult shade to combine with other plants, but it holds its own in a pot. I've grown it to great effect in large terracotta long toms running down the side of the path in the Perennial Cutting Garden.

Calibrachoas

4 *Calibrachoa* Can-can series
'Orange Punch' (pictured) genuinely looks like a fruity punch in a clear glass bowl, perhaps an orange juice mixed with Campari. A good and long performer. 'Black Cherry' is a lovely single and almost black. Billowing out from a large, low table centre pot, this looks like a swag of velvet. And 'Double Can-Can Wine Red' (pictured on p44) is one of my favourites for its mahogany richness and length of flowering. We include this in quite a few of our summer and autumn pot collections.

5 *C.* Million Bells series
There are quite a few orange calibrachoas and we've grown 'Million Bells Crackling Fire' for more than a decade now – it has stood the test of time. 'Million

Bells Red' is a deep ruby shade with single flowers ('Cabaret Red', in the Cabaret series, is a good substitute). 'Million Bells Terracotta' (pictured) is one we've grown for ages and it looks fantastic with nemesias.

6 *C.* Superbells series
These ones are all doubles, which means they don't have forage for pollinators because their nectaries have been bred to be secondary petaloids, so they are infertile. It does mean each flower lasts longer than the singles, making them low-maintenance, with minimal deadheading needed. 'Double Ruby' (pictured) is a truly rich red and is also quick growing, strong and healthy. 'Doublette Love Swept' is a bright yet nicely fading peach-pink.

Soft and Pale

These live in palettes 3 and 4
(see p30 and p32) with plenty
of white and soft colours.

Petunias

1 *Petunia* × *atkinsiana*
Surfinia Group
We love to grow these trailing
petunias. We're not looking for
them to hang down the edge
of a pot, but more to spread
out their shoots from a shallow
tabletop pot and send soft-
textured saucer-sized flowers
in all directions. 'Blue Vein'
is lovely for this. It has deep
purple hearts and veins that
elegantly break up the white
petal base. 'White' (pictured)
has a green eye and soft green
veining over the petals.

2 *P. axillaris*
A species petunia that is easy
to grow from seed. It has a
wonderful perfume and the
petunia's classic, very sticky
buds and leaves.

3 *P.* 'Sophistica Lime Green'
I'd like this to be a touch more
acid-green, but it has its place
in white pot mixes where it
brings freshness and contrast.

4 *P.* 'Supertunia Latte'
In the Supertunia series, this
has a wonderful creamy-white

base with chocolate markings. A long and late flowerer.

5 *P.* Tidal Wave series
'Tidal Wave Silver' is a massive favourite here for being an excellent, reliable flowerer. (Also pictured on p20.)

6 *P.* Tumbelina series
This series features small-flowered varieties with blooms halfway between petunias and calibrachoas. The mauve 'Priscilla' (pictured) has a stock-like scent.

7 × *Petchoa* BeautiCal series
'BeautiCal French Vanilla' (pictured) is in the same series as 'BeautiCal Cinnamon' and is similarly sophisticated in a subtle colour, which I love. This reminds me of crème brûlée: soft, creamy yellow with a burnt sugar top (in fact, a heart in this case).

Calibrachoas

8 *C.* Can-can series 'Appleblossom' (pictured) is a pretty, single, white flower form with pink throat and markings. A good performer offering a long season. 'Double Apricot' is a rather wonderful mix of muted apricot moving to peach, but its double flowers (like crumpled tissue paper)

also have deep red hearts and markings. Very pretty. For the best sort of smoky, vintage mauve you can't beat 'Double Dark Lavender'. The colours fade as the flowers age to give a good mix of tones. And 'Double White Improved' is completely covered in snowball blooms, almost like a bacopa in its floweriness all summer and autumn.

July

July is the month when we can ease off from practical jobs in the pot garden and just enjoy all the things we planted in May. Having said that, it does differ from year to year. July 2022 saw some of the hottest days ever recorded in the UK, so a lot of effort went into alleviating the effect of the heat on the pot garden, while July 2023 was notably wet so there was less watering to do.

Gathering pots together is a good thing. They then create their own microclimate. Clumped together, the larger plants shade the ones below and, packed in, the group can hold on to a higher level of humidity after watering. Grouping pots also makes watering quicker and easier.

Another thing to be aware of is your pot materials. Zinc and metal containers sitting in full sun will get extremely hot. If they're portable, move those to sit in the shade, at least for the hottest part of the day. Troughs will be too heavy if full of compost and plants, so before planting up in May, they need to be lined with waste polystyrene, which insulates against both heat and cold and will help to keep conditions regulated.

Watering and deadheading are in full swing in July and being diligent with both will keep plants looking good. It's now that we add feeding to our pot regime.

We are still doing the odd bit of sowing in July, finishing off any of the later-flowering biennials such as foxgloves and Iceland poppies, and pricking out others such as wallflowers that were sown last month. Our spring-flowering pots of violas are grinding to a halt, so we sow a few quick growers such as the trusty toadflax (*Linaria*) and non-climbing nasturtiums to plug those gaps. Some sweet peas (such as 'Matucana') will start to look ropey this month, so it's good to have a few quick-growing annuals coming along to replace them. Climbing nasturtiums are ideal if you want to leave the sweet pea frames intact and train another climber on the same teepee.

Many of our larger pots are topped with tender perennial climbers – thunbergia, ipomoea and rhodochiton. They'll be racing skywards now, so we keep tying in their new growth to their hazel or silver birch teepees. If they've reached the top of the frame, we pinch them out to contain them and to encourage flowering.

Some plants (erigeron and some of the nemesias, for example) will take a rest around now. Cut these back by about a third and feed to give them a boost. This will encourage a second flush with the nemesias and speed up reflowering with the erigeron.

And last but not least, we continue to look after the birds by regularly cleaning and filling bird baths.

Watering

Watering is the job that takes the most time in the summer as it needs to be done regularly. I've covered it in more detail in June (see p225), but keep a close eye on your pots in July, which

Previous page Watering containers
of mint.

can be the hottest month. In extreme heat, smaller pots will need watering not three times a week, but every day.

Ideally, look at your plants in the morning when the leaves should have rehydrated a little over night. If the leaves still look wilted, then more watering or pot soaking is needed. At cooler times, wilting may be a sign of overwatering, so always check the compost by poking your finger as far down as you can and see whether the compost is in fact wet or bone dry.

To help plants in portable terracotta pots, submerge the pots in a trug of water to really soak the terracotta. This will help cool the root ball as the water evaporates. We also use watering spikes in medium pots. Made of terracotta, these are hollow tubes you can sink into the compost and fill with water. Add these in as you plant up your pots. The water gradually leaches out into the compost during the day. We trialled them during the drought in 2022 and they seemed to work well.

We also find that a few plants (such as salvias and fuchsias) shed their leaves in extreme heat, but when temperatures cool again, they send out more leaves and flowers. So don't despair if some of your plants look a bit stressed.

watering for five years and has become a bit of an expert in irrigation. If set up well, an irrigation system can use less water than watering with a hose or can, so with the likelihood of more summer droughts, I think they're worth seriously considering.

To install one, your pots must be in set places, which might not suit everyone. The amount of watering varies through the year. In spring and autumn, my friend recommends switching it on for two minutes once a day. From July right through the summer, she ups that to three minutes twice a day. Of course, how much water you give your pots depends on what you're growing and how wet or dry the season is, but something like dahlias like a good dousing, so this sounds about right to me.

The system she recommends is by Gardena and is readily available at most garden centres. It is reliable (we use this brand in the greenhouse at Perch Hill) but you need to keep an eye on it all. Disasters include the little nozzle heads flying off, leading to great water geysers spraying up into the air. The batteries in the timer also eventually run out, so replace them before you go away for any length of time.

Irrigation

Last summer I had a lesson from an old friend who gardens only in pots over three city terraces in Athens. She has not done any hand

Feeding Pots

Good compost will have enough nutrients in it to keep plants growing well for four to six weeks from planting. That time's up now, so

Next page The Oast Garden at its summery peak with salvias, petunias and agapanthus filling our pots with flowers from now until late autumn.

feeding pots becomes important. We garden organically here, so we use seaweed feed or our own homemade mix of comfrey and nettle fertiliser that we make in June (see p227). Strictly speaking, seaweed is a biostimulant as it doesn't provide much in the way of nitrogen, phosphate and potassium (the main minerals that plants need). We have also found that a big bucket of mature cow manure topped with water works well. Pour off the top liquid into a watering can, then water the pots. Refill the manure bucket with water until next time.

Whatever you use, feed your pots once a week, on the same day so you don't forget!

- First, water your pots as normal (as described on p225 and p265). Then make up the feed in a watering can, diluting according to the instructions. At this time of year, don't increase the strength as the plants can't take it up, so it's a waste. In September, with some plants, it's worth doubling the strength to keep everything looking lush for a few extra weeks. We do this with pots of pelargoniums that we'll be moving into the greenhouse.
- Add the rose attachment to the watering can nozzle to widen the watering beam for maximum coverage. Water the plants from the top so the water lands on the leaves as well as the compost, as the plants can take up the feed through both leaves and roots. Take care with this approach on a bright, sunny day as the leaves can scorch.

Pests and Diseases

We try to have a set day each week when every pot in the garden is preened: the dead flowers and any yellowing leaves are removed and we do a swift check for pests and diseases. We particularly keep our eyes peeled for aphids and powdery mildew, as well as lily and rosemary beetle.

All the dead flowerheads go straight on the compost heap, but we'll dispose of any leaves if there's a chance they're blighted with fungus.

In a hot, dry season, mildew can become a particular problem and we start taking preventative measures by spraying with a homemade solution.

- 1 teaspoon bicarbonate of soda
- 500ml (17fl oz) water
- ½ teaspoon vegetable oil
- A few drops of pure liquid soap to help the solution stick to the leaves

Add all of the ingredients to a spray bottle. Give it a good shake and then apply – try to spray the underside as well as the tops of the leaves. Apply once a week, starting now and continuing until the end of September when the temperatures cool and it's more likely to rain. With that, the chance of mildew declines.

August

We open the garden to visitors as often in August as we do in April. These are our two garden high points, with pots playing a key role at both times of year. In April, it's tulips that deliver. In August, it's mainly down to dahlias.

The pots in the Oast Garden are full to the brim with dahlias, accompanied by petunias, salvias, tagetes and snapdragons, all flowering away. And you really have to pick a path through the Dutch Yard now: pots are encroaching on all the usual routes through it – from gate to back door, back door to the Oast Garden, and through the yard down to the Rose Garden – in a joyous and abundant way. I love this space at this time of year, and we have dinner here whenever we can; solar lights and a fire pit add to the loveliness. I'd sleep out there, in pot heaven, given half a chance.

Pots on the wellhead, including all the rich and brilliant beauties such as gazanias, gerberas (in zingy orange) and pelargoniums, are all pumping colour. And we have salvias from the Lake series in pots on their own and also mixed with petunias in harmonious or contrasting colours for a velvet-curtain look. These all manage drought well, so are still thriving in August.

Zinnias – sown in April and planted at the end of May – are opening now, more and more by the day. The compact Aztec series give you a very low-maintenance pot with each flower lasting over a month. And I'm mad about the Queeny Lime series in all its tones. These have stood the test of extreme temperatures during some very hot summers.

Previous page The Dutch Yard at dusk jam-packed with all my favourite pot combinations. There's a sweet pea (sown late) in the foreground, with dahlias, *Ipomoea lobata*, gazanias, verbenas and gerberas. I love eating in this sheltered yard while it's still warm enough to do so.
Top Our huge central pot in the Perennial Cutting Garden containing the spectacular combination of *Salvia* 'Lake Onega', *Pelargonium* 'Tommy' and *Rhodochiton atrosanguineus*.
Bottom left Looking through the barn. We have collections of pots all year on the north side as well as the further south side.
·Bottom right The end of our rosemary bench is punctuated with a great pot of towering *Diascia personata* and the fragrant *Petunia* 'Priscilla' spilling out beneath.

Around the lawn, our repurposed animal water troughs are billowing with petunias, cosmos and pelargoniums, all in a soft palette to keep this area calm in feel. That's what we aim to achieve here with tulips in spring, and we continue this theme right through the year.

Moving round to the south face of the barn and into the Rose Garden, salvias are really hitting their stride in August. And it's here that we also have delicate and unusual plants in pots outside of the gardeners' office. We walk past these buildings and pots many times a day – the plants here need a little extra TLC, so it's good to position them in a high-traffic area. We grow glory lilies, such as *Gloriosa superba* 'Tomas de Bruyne', which is exquisite, but must be moved into a sheltered spot if wind is on the cards. And we also have a potted pomegranate here, which is easy to grow, but to get fruit to develop, needs to be kept out of chill winds and brought inside for a bit of protection.

Out in the Perennial Cutting Garden, on the far side of the drive, colour reaches a high point in August, with all our mass plantings of half-hardy annuals at their peak in the beds and borders. The pots in this part of the garden have got to be quite something to hold their own against the level of floweriness in the borders, so we tend to go for robust, long-flowering and showy plants that don't take too much looking after. This garden is the outlier at Perch Hill, with only one tap. It's not an area we walk through tens of times a day, so it's easy to overlook deadheading and watering.

Pelargonium 'Shrubland Rose' is a perpetual winner here, tried and tested to be both drought tolerant and happy with only occasional deadheading. We also have a huge pot of the super low-maintenance *Argyranthemum* 'Grandaisy Red' on the central table (pictured on p6). And I love a gargantuan pot of *Sparrmannia africana* (pictured on p281), with its vast lily-pad leaves. As people leave the garden, we have this on the left and *Lilium speciosum* var. *rubrum* (pictured on p286) on the right. They're hard to beat for pot impact in August.

Drought-tolerant plants

Whenever I'm asked about which container plants are best able to cope with periods of heat and drought, I think of things I've seen growing in the wild, thriving on walls and in nooks and crannies where there is little or no organic matter and rain is the only source of water. Churchyard walls and steps are a good pointer – you'll see things like erigeron, ivy-leaved toadflax (*Cymbalaria muralis*) and aubrieta growing happily. And in the city, railway sidings and building sites offer good ideas. Buddleja always thrives in these places, and there are now many varieties bred to produce a longer-flowering season and a more compact habit, so they're ideal for pots.

For half-hardies, I think back to a botanising trip I made to South Africa. It was September (spring there) and I saw fields of self-sown orange and yellow daisies reaching far into the horizon – arctotis, osteospermums, bidens, argyranthemums and gazanias all growing wild (some are native, others from similarly warm regions), coping with minimal or little rain. I know they can put up with harsh conditions.

And finally, whenever I'm on holiday in the Mediterranean in July and August, I make a mental note of what seems to be coping in the baking heat. That's where I realised gaura was a good bet and, of course, pelargoniums (many of the species have their roots in southern Africa). And then there's the lily, *Gladiolus murielae* (syn. *Acidanthera murielae*). That appears to thrive with minimal watering too.

Best of the drought-tolerant plants throughout the year

With our increasingly hot summers, it's good to be aware of the plants that can definitely take intense sunshine and dry conditions. Here are the ones we've tried and succeeded with for every season.

1 *Agapanthus*
Having seen agapanthus naturalised amongst the sand dunes in the Isles of Scilly, I know how tough this whole genus is. The plants can cope in salty air too. Pictured here is 'Midnight Star'.

2 *Agastache*
There is a huge and increasing number of these drought-resistant plants – they're set to become as popular as salvias. There has been great breeding in recent years, with a beautiful palette of colours emerging. I particularly love the pinks and terracottas, like *Agastache × hybrida* 'Arizona Sandstone' pictured with the pot-compatible *Lavandula angustifolia* 'SuperBlue'.

3 *Argyranthemum*
Known as marguerites, these Canary Island daisies flower from May until November on minimal TLC. There are some I think of as rather dull white ones, but some are beautiful, long-performing deep reds and pinks. Pictured here is 'Grandaisy Red'.

4 *Buddleja*
The new Buzz series varieties (such as 'Buzz Wine', pictured) are bred to be more compact, with an arching, slightly trailing habit. Like their wild counterparts, they're tolerant of harsh conditions. They will need deadheading though.

5 *Diascia*
Hailing from South Africa, diascias are drought tolerant and supremely pretty. They are the cousins of nemesias, but we find they fare a little better in prolonged heat. Go for *Diascia personata* (pictured) for lovely pink flowers.

6 *Echeveria*
With their padded leaves and glaucous colour, these succulents are built for heat. I think they look best in a collection of terracotta pots, with the contrasting forms of different species and varieties adding interest. Pictured here is *Echeveria elegans*.

7 *Erigeron karvinskianus*
Look at where this naturalises – in all the driest nooks – and you'll realise how little water it needs.

8 *Gaura lindheimeri* (syn. *Oenothera lindheimeri*)
This is a very tolerant plant. 'The Bride' is easy to grow from seed, and we also like the deep pink 'Whiskers Deep Rose' (pictured). They flower long and hard, but as short-lived perennials, they need replacing every few years.

9 *Gazania*
These southern African daisies (such as 'Daybreak Bright Orange', pictured) lead the way for colour in drought and sun; however prolonged or strong, they don't bat an eye. Osteospermums (see p368) are similarly robust.

10 *Gladiolus murielae*
Known to many as acidanthera, this is the scented, white cousin of the wild gladiolus. Hailing from parts of Africa including Ethiopia and Mozambique, it will take drought and heat.

11 *Lantana*
Another tender perennial from across Africa and South America. It can become invasive in its home countries as it's such a strong grower. Here in the UK that's not likely because it's not frost hardy. Exceptionally long-flowering, very drought resistant and loved by butterflies. *Lantana camara* is pictured.

12 *Lavandula*
When you see the parched lavender fields in the south of France you can tell immediately how tolerant lavender is of heat. Many varieties are easy to grow from seed and they mostly strike quickly and easily from cuttings. Pictured is *Lavandula angustifolia* 'SuperBlue'.

13 *Pelargonium*
Another plant hailing from southern Africa and also very satisfying to grow from seed. Many varieties (such as 'Sweet Mimosa', pictured) are easy to propagate from cuttings too.

14 *Salvia*
Many of the species, such as *Salvia microphylla*, originate from Central America, and many hybrids (such as those in the Mirage series) have been bred from them. They'll tolerate the most harsh conditions. This one pictured, 'Mirage Deep Purple', is tough.

15 *Salvia rosmarinus*
(syn. *Rosmarinus officinalis* Prostratus Group)
You'll see rosemary self-sown into terrace walls all over the Mediterranean, receiving little water or organic matter at its roots. That's how tough it is. I love it for pots.

16 *Sparrmannia africana*
A plant for massive impact in a pot. African hemp is not hardy, but it makes a great and tolerant houseplant if brought in before the frosts.

Shade-tolerant plants

Opposite *Nicotiana* 'Whisper Mixed', *Pelargonium tomentosum* and *Plectranthus ciliatus* 'Nico' all in the shade on the north side of the barn.

Summers may be getting hotter and drier, but most gardens also have an area of shade to contend with. At Perch Hill, we treasure these shadowy spots as they allow us to grow shade-tolerant plants in pots to bring colour, form and scent to what might otherwise be quite drab areas.

Behind the barn, tobacco plants fill the place with perfume as soon as the heat of the sun begins to fade in the evening. *Nicotiana* 'Whisper Mixed' is one of the strongest growers and we always have that here, but it's the towering *N. sylvestris* and powerfully incense-scented *N. alata* 'Grandiflora' we truly love. Mix them with the uniquely shade-tolerant *Pelargonium tomentosum* for shade pots that have never looked so good.

In terms of bulbs, we've had success with two glamorous plants that bring life to low light areas. The first is eucomis. These pineapple lilies, as they're known, seem to be happy in sun or light shade, are easy to grow in pots and are very striking. The second is the late-flowering *Lilium speciosum* var. *rubrum*. We've had that planted in the same pot now for well over ten years and have barely done anything for it. I keep my eye out for lily beetle, but this species seems to have much better resistance than the June-flowering lily forms (such as *L. regale*), which can be blighted by the scarlet beetle.

Best of the shade-tolerant plants throughout the year

Some people garden almost entirely in shade, but we all have at least a bit of it. We've tried and tested a large range of shade-tolerant plants over the years and these are our favourites.

1&3

1 *Athyrium niponicum* var. *pictum*
Commonly known as frosted or Japanese painted fern, this plant is so beautiful it deserves pride of place in a pot. You could plant with other things (such as browallia, pictured), but it can hold its own.

2 *Begonia*
Begonias are good for a classic splash of colour. We grow 'Glowing Embers' (pictured), which really looks after itself aside from an occasional water and feed (store tubers over winter so you can grow them again the following year). We also love the foliage begonia 'Gryphon' for its silver speckled leaves. It's not hardy, but it makes a superb winter houseplant if you bring it indoors.

3 *Browallia*
Browallias are in the nightshade (*Solanaceae*) family. *Browallia speciosa* 'Blue Bells' is an annual variety that I love, with handsome and long-flowering bells (pictured with *Athyrium niponicum* var. *pictum*).

4 *Brunnera*
With clear blue flowers like a forget-me-not and (with many varieties, such as 'Jack Frost', pictured) and quite elegant, marbled leaves, brunnera is a good backdrop to white tulips in the shade.

5 *Coleus*
An annual bedding plant, this comes in a huge range of appealing shapes and colours. It thrives in shade.

6 *Eucomis*
With pineapple-like flowers, handsome leaves and elegant, long-lasting seedheads, pineapple lilies are one of those plants that are sold as sun lovers, but we find they tolerate shade. *Eucomis comosa* 'Sparkling Burgundy' and *E.* 'Leia' (pictured) are both wonderful.

7 *Gaura lindheimeri* (syn. *Oenothera lindheimeri*)
This is most commonly recommended for sun, but does fine in shade. You won't get as many flowers, but still enough to look good. Airy, loose and excellent for sombre spots. Pictured here is 'Sparkle White' in foreground and 'The Bride' behind.

8 *Heuchera*
We have lots of these in pots by our back door. Evergreen through the winter, they're invaluable for colour. New shades, leaf patterns and even shapes are being bred all the time. We rather love the copper-coloured ones (like 'Peach Flambé'), the crimsons ('Sugar Berry', in the Little Cutie series, pictured) and the acid-greens ('Citronelle'). The one problem with heucheras is they are prone to vine weevil, particularly when grown in pots (see p225).

9 *Hosta*
Small or large, these make excellent pot plants for shade. 'Sum and Substance' is striking, pictured here with *Eucomis bicolor* and *Cheilanthes lanosa* (known as the hairy lip fern). Cover the pot rim with Vaseline or encircle the pot with copper tape to help keep slugs and snails at bay.

10 *Hydrangea*
The classic shade-loving *Hydrangea petiolaris* is quite a vigorous climber. For pots, I'm fond of the pretty and compact *H. paniculata* 'Little Lime' (pictured).

11 *Lilium*
Our favourite lilies for shade are *Lilium speciosum* var. *rubrum* (pictured), *L. s.* var. *album* and *L. s.* 'Uchida'.

12 *Lophospermum erubescens*
There aren't many plants that happily grow in shade that give you flower as well as glamour, but lophospermums (commonly mistaken for asarinas) do both. I love them for their large snapdragon-like flowers on long, cascading vines. They look great billowing down to the ground from a hanging basket.

13 *Nicotiana*
Part of the nightshade (*Solanaceae*) family, these are unusual amongst annuals in that they can take sun or shade, except for *N. altata* 'Grandiflora', which likes dappled shade or shade only.

14 *Pelargonium tomentosum*
A peppermint-scented, downy, silver-leaved pelargonium that thrives in shade. It's not hardy, so it comes inside for the winter and luckily makes an excellent houseplant.

15 *Plectranthus ciliatus*
This New Zealand native loves dry shade and is good as ground cover. It needs to come inside for the winter and makes a welcome houseplant.

Dahlias

Opposite *Dahlia* 'Dreamy Nights' with *Verbena* 'Sissinghurst' and *V.* 'Showboat Dark Violet'. The pots are surrounded by *Tagetes* 'Cinnabar', *Persicaria orientalis* and *V. rigida*.

If you like your pots as spectacular and flower-filled as they can be, and you love colour, dahlias should be at the top of your growing list. It's now that they reach their peak and they carry on looking good until it gets properly cold and wet at the end of autumn. For this time of year, there's no competition.

Dahlias have reigned supreme in the garden here since I discovered the chocolate-crimson 'Rip City' in Monet's Garden at Giverny 25 years ago. 'Rip City' is too tall and top-heavy for pots, but it was the plant that set me on the path to dahlia obsession and holds a special place in my heart.

I'm always on the look out for new and interesting forms and we've trialled hundreds of varieties here. I've seen many more over the years during my annual visits to breeders and dahlia suppliers, both here in Britain and in the Netherlands. More recently, social media has become another invaluable resource, a great place to spot the exciting new plants emerging from the USA and New Zealand.

Pot-compatible forms have become our main priority in the trials here over the last five years and an important driver in the selection process for the new dahlias we've worked with breeders to create. There are dahlias suitable for every part of the garden (apart from shade), but to work well, even in a large pot, it's important they are quite contained in size. We're usually looking for a dahlia that reaches 60–90cm (2–3ft), and have cast the net very wide. There is the odd giant such as 'Black Jack' (pictured on p414) – which has handsome foliage and dark, strong stems, and I think looks good in a pot despite its height – but generally speaking, being under a metre is desirable.

There are, of course, compact varieties bred for window boxes and smaller containers, but on the whole we've found these lack grace. They are often so covered in flowers that the petals of one bloom almost touch those of its neighbour – it looks too much. We grow a few of these, such as 'Dreamy Nights', 'Top Mix Salmon' and 'Dalaya Devi' (pictured on p9).

I can't write about dahlias without underlining the fact that, for pots, they have to be one of the most sustainable and least time-consuming things you can grow. Dahlias are tender perennials, easy to store from one year to the next, so you don't need to buy them fresh every spring. In a pot, they are more vulnerable to frost than when growing in the ground, so you will need to lift the tubers once the tops of the plants are singed and blackened by frost, or just before (see p401). Then you simply store them somewhere cool and dry through the winter before bringing them out the following March for replanting.

Originally from Central America, dahlias love sun. We find, planted in a fertile, moisture-retentive potting compost (equal parts loam from mole hills, if you can find them, well-rotted organic farmyard manure and peat-free or homemade compost), they put up with heat better than many container plants. They don't like prolonged drought, but they will revive, it just slows flower production. And they're a cinch to propagate. You can buy one tuber and, by division or from cuttings, quickly turn it into five plants. Even as a beginner, I can almost guarantee you'll succeed if you have a go in April (see p177).

Left *Dahlia* 'Blue Bayou' being visited by a red admiral butterfly. Right *Dahlia* 'Waltzing Matilda' with common carder bees.

Dahlias are also one of the key food sources for our precious pollinators late in the growing year. If you grow the forms where you can see into the centre of the flower – those in the Single-flowered, Collarette and Anemone-flowered groups (see p296) – you'll find that dahlias are a hugely valuable nectar and pollen source from late summer to winter. Along with ivy, they're one the favourite feeding grounds of bees and butterflies when most of our wildflowers have finished flowering. From carefully watching the pollinator visits, we find 'Blue Bayou' and 'Abigail', as well as 'Lou Farman' and 'Sarah Raven', the best for butterflies, particularly red admirals, which forage late in the year. 'Waltzing Mathilda' is great for bees, followed close behind by 'Josie', 'Totally Tangerine' and 'Bishop's Children'. But honestly, every one of these open-flowered forms excels.

Combine all of these characteristics and dahlias have to be the indisputable queens of any sunny pot garden in late summer and autumn. For showiness, reliability, length of flowering and number of flowers balanced against cost and time, there just isn't a family that can compete. As long as you have even one small corner with some sun, you've got to grow them!

Pot designs with dahlias

In terms of pot design, we tend to combine our dahlias with one of three things: half-hardy annuals like cosmos, tender perennial climbers or salvias.

You need a good gang of late-flowering half-hardy annuals that coincide perfectly with dahlias in their flowering season. One combination that is hard to beat is *Cosmos bipinnatus* 'Apricotta' with the similarly coloured *Dahlia* 'Kelsey Annie Joy', plus a loose and beautiful cloud of frothy annual grass like *Panicum* 'Frosted Explosion' growing in between. And then there's D. 'Bishop of Auckland' with C. b. 'Rubenza'. That also makes a great pairing. It works to swap the grass for a amaranthus to play the role of the Filler. This crew also reach their peak late in the year and their soft texture and cascading form helps to counteract any rigidity you might get from the perky uprightness of the dahlias.

Sticking with cosmos, but the tuberous kind, we underplant dahlia 'Waltzing Mathilda' with the velvet-brown chocolate cosmos (*C. atrosanguineus*). Also the blush-brown chocolate cosmos 'Pink Flamingo' with the crazy dahlia 'Frizzle Sizzle'.

One of our most successful pot themes is dahlias and tender perennial climbers. Above and through every pot of dahlias in the Dutch Yard you'll find either an ipomoea or a thunbergia. We have them climbing up silver birch frames and cascading down to soften pot edges. It's hard to conceive of a better pairing.

Last but not least, good from now and getting better as most other flowers start to fade, are the salvias. The pairing possibilities here are endless, but one of our long-standing favourite combinations for whopper troughs is *Dahlia* 'Totally Tangerine' with *Salvia* 'Amistad' (pictured on p42): the saturated orange and blue respectively create the perfect contrast, made all the better by scattering seedlings of the grass *Panicum* 'Sparkling Fountain' in between. That's almost the perfect example of not just Bride (dahlia), Bridesmaid (toffee-coloured grass) and Gatecrasher (salvia), but also Thriller (dahlia), Filler (grass) and Pillar (salvia) – see p38 and p43 for more on these design tools. We have now reproduced it in smaller pots with the more compact dahlia 'Josie', the salvia 'Lake Onega' (which is just like 'Amistad' but half the height) and the frothy perennial grass *Eragrostis spectabilis*. That's a triumph too!

Previous page The Dutch Yard with dahlias, grasses and tender perennial climbers filling our view to the east.
Opposite One of my favourite whopper pots for summer and autumn: *Dahlia* 'Waltzing Mathilda' and *Thunbergia alata* 'African Sunset' climbing over a silver birch frame.
Below *Dahlia* 'Schipper's Bronze' with *Cuphea subuligera* and *Pennisetum* 'Vertigo'.

Dahlia Classification

There are 15 classifications in total, but I've listed the ones we use the most in pots. The forms and shapes really do vary, and there's certainly a dahlia for every taste.

Anemone-flowered

These are the ones that look like they have a flower within a flower. Surprisingly, they're good for pollinators – each of the mini-tubular florets at the centre of the flower is full of nectar. The dahlias are usually compact enough to make fantastic container plants. For pots, we grow lots including 'Abigail', 'Sarah Raven' and 'Rosie Raven'.

Ball and Pompon

The neat and tidy dahlias in these groups used to be hated for their perceived uptightness and drumstick formality, but they have an unusually good vase life for dahlias and are increasingly popular with florists. We grow a few here for

Below A single dahlia stem in each vase shows the range of flower forms.

pots including 'Vino', 'Brown Sugar' and 'Small World'. Great for contrast with the large-flowered varieties.

Paeony-flowered and Single-flowered

These two groups are very well known, with many developed from the historical 'Bishop of Llandaff'. They are all singles or semi-doubles, making them excellent for pollinators, and many have dark, chocolate-coloured foliage, which gives them good presence in a pot. Favourites for containers are 'Bishop of Auckland', 'Lou Farman' and the mix of colours in the seed-grown strain 'Bishop's Children'. We also love the super single, star-shaped 'Honka' varieties for pots, especially 'Honka Fragile', which is white with a faint red edge.

Decorative

These dahlias tend to be the ones with the largest flowers and most petals, which are usually broad but pointed at the tip. Most are too tall and chunky for pots, but we grow a few that work well including 'Molly Raven' and 'Labyrinth' – this one is on the verge of being too flower-heavy for a pot, but is so beautiful it's worth the extra staking needed. The so-called 'dinner plate' dahlias are in this group, but they don't suit pots.

Cactus and Semi-cactus

These classic, spiky-flowered varieties have the strongest architectural presence as a cut flower, with needle-shaped petals pointing this way and that. Even though very tall, I love 'Black Jack' for pots, as well as 'Josudi Mercury' for its spiky pompoms in a wonderful burnt coral.

Collarette

A single row of petals with a row of secondary petaloids at the centre of the flower. One of my favourite soft and warm palette dahlias, 'Kelsey Annie Joy', is in this group.

Miscellaneous

This seems to be where varieties that are hard to classify get put. A hotch-potch of different, but usually newish varieties. A good choice for pots is 'Waltzing Mathilda'.

Best of the dahlias

As with any showy flower, I recommend separating dahlias by colour and keeping palettes 1 and 2 away from palettes 3 and 4 (see p26–33). There are some bridge points between the two pairs: 'Molly Raven', 'Night Silence' and 'Sarah Raven' almost fit into the first group, but – to my eyes – they go best in the second. We don't grow many soft-coloured dahlias and even fewer whites, and only the most unusual shapes and colours made it into this list.

Dark and Rich / Boiled-sweet Brilliant

1 *Dahlia* 'Abigail' (Anemone-flowered)
'Abigail' is like the ever-popular 'Blue Bayou', but a little smaller so perfect for pots. Hugely floriferous. It's named after our head buyer who loves dahlias and particularly the anemone, pollinator-friendly varieties. H: 90cm (3ft).

2 *D.* 'Adam's Choice' (Anemone-flowered)
Named after my husband, this one is a truly lovely shade of toffee apple crossed with a gingernut biscuit. It's brand new – he spotted it on a visit to a breeder and we both fell in love with it! For its first year at Perch Hill we planted it with the green-tasseled *Amaranthus caudatus* 'Viridis' to make the perfect pollinator- and bird-friendly pot for summer and autumn. The dahlia feeds the bees, the amaranth the birds. H: 75cm (2½ft).

3 *D.* 'Bishop's Children' (Single-flowered)
Seed-grown and at its best with the compact, self-seeding *Verbena rigida*, both in a pot and a vase. These two are also brilliant for birds and bees. 'Bishop's Children' has dark-coloured foliage, which looks great in a pot. H: 90cm (3ft).

4 *D.* 'Bishop of Auckland' (Single-flowered)
One of the first dahlias we grew and much loved for its simple, single, pollinator-friendly flowers in chocolate crimson. H: 90cm (3ft).

5 *D.* 'Black Jack' (Semi-cactus)
With ebony stems and crimson-washed leaves, this makes a wonderful foliage plant for summer and, late to flower, it becomes more and more splendid as its huge, spiky petalled flowers open into their full velvet glory. H: 1.5m (5ft).

6 *D.* 'Brown Sugar' (Ball)
We're always on the look out for unusual coloured, pot-friendly forms and this shot to the top of our must-grow list when we trialled it. It has neat, but not too neat ball shaped flowers in flame to burnt sugar tones. Intensely coloured and glorious. H: 1m (3ft).

7 *D.* 'Dahlegria Tricolore' (Single-flowered)
This one falls between palettes 1 and 2: it opens a bright pink then moves to a coral as the flowers develop and fade. Bred for pots, it has simple flowers with crimson-washed leaves. Hugely flowery. H: 60cm (2ft).

8 *D.* 'Dalaya Devi'
(Miscellaneous)
One of the few more compact varieties we grow, this one truly excels with nothing about it unbalanced or over the top. With crimson, plush-textured flowers, it's perfect for planting with something equally strong-growing and prolific, such as *Petunia* 'Tidal Wave Red Velour' or *Cuphea* × *purpurea* 'Firefly'. H: 60cm (2ft).

9 *D.* 'Dalaya Meena Sanya'
(Miscellaneous)
More purple than its crimson brother 'Dalaya Devi', this has similarly been bred for pots and is flowery for months on end. Hard to beat if you want a compact form. H: 60cm (2ft).

10 *D.* 'Dreamy Nights'
(Miscellaneous)
Intensely purple, rosette-like flowers with bronze (or rather almost black) leaves. We grow this in pots for edible flowers as it is very floriferous, covered from top to toe in blooms from early July until November. Also pictured on p288. H: 50cm (20in).

11 *D.* 'Frizzle Sizzle'
(Fimbriated)
A unique, almost clown-like dahlia – like a dahlia in cosmos disguise. It is compact and super pretty, but strong and punchy looking with it. H: 80cm (2½ft).

12 *D.* 'Josie'
(Anemone-flowered)
One shade brighter than 'Totally Tangerine' and a bit more petite. This is another dahlia we spotted in a trial, selecting it for its brilliant flowers, pollinator value and, most of all, its elegance and pot-compatible size. We named it Josie after our head gardener as she loves pot gardening and dahlias equally amongst all things horticultural. H: 75cm (2½ft).

13 *D.* 'Josudi Mercury'
(Semi-cactus)
New to our trial in summer 2022, I fell for this straight away. It has the most perfect spiky cactus flowers which are unusually small, slightly bigger than a golf ball, in coral washed with wine red. It grows to over a metre, so a little tall for pots, but the flowers are such an ideal mini-size, it's worth the extra staking. H: 1.2m (4ft).

14 *D.* 'Lou Farman' (Single-flowered)
While on the hunt for a pinkish 'Waltzing Mathilda' that is good for pollinators, we found this dahlia amidst a huge crowd of others in a breeder's field in 2018. We named it after my business co-founder and great friend. It has large, single, butterfly-like flowers and is a little on the tall side for a pot, but is easy to support as it has skinny, elegant growth and light leaves and stems. H: 90cm (3ft).

15 *D.* 'Rosie Raven' (Anemone-flowered)
This one is also new and named after my eldest daughter. It extends the Anemone-flowered group with its dark blackcurrant colouring. Truly this is as opulent a colour and texture as you'll find – each petal and the nectaries at the centre of the flower look as if they have been cut from silk velvet. H: 75cm (2½ft).

16 *D.* 'Roxy' (Single-flowered)
Brilliant magenta-pink single flowers with so-called bronze (though in fact almost black) leaves. Famously good for pots and very floriferous. It has been around for years, tried and tested. H: 50cm (20in).

17 *D.* 'Samourai' (Semi-cactus)
A crazy, sea-anemone-like dahlia, with tentacles pointing all over the place in crimson-purple and white. This is compact enough to be good for a pot and very floriferous. It's good with a similar-scale cosmos, such as the semi-double 'Fizzy Rose Picotee'. H: 1m (3ft).

18 *D.* 'Schipper's Bronze' (Single-flowered)
Utterly marvellous in a container. The colour of rusty tin with a bit of conker brown mixed in; some flowers are a more muted apricot. Dark foliage. H: 75cm (2½ft).

19 *D.* 'Schipper's Choice' (Single-flowered)
Hot off the press, a saturated, yet bright pink single dahlia with large flowers. Keep an eye out for it as the breeder is still building up tuber stocks. It has been 'adopted' by my Dutch friend and colleague Dicky Schipper, who has been on many visits to trial fields with me over the years. We tend to love the same things, including this. H: 75cm (2½ft).

20 *D.* 'Totally Tangerine' (Anemone-flowered)
One of my absolute favourites and usually the first to appear amongst this selection. It will need staking, but flowers non-stop. Mix it with the deep blue *Salvia* 'Amistad' or 'Lake Onega' for a strong colour contrast, together with *Panicum* 'Sparkling Fountain' to add a light and airy filler. These will look good for a five-month stretch. H: 60cm (2ft).

21 *D.* 'Vino' (Pompon)
In a dark wine red, this makes a lovely combination with dahlia 'Waltzing Mathilda' and, as a filler, *Thunbergia alata* 'African Sunset'. H: 1m (3ft).

22 *D.* 'Waltzing Mathilda' (Miscellaneous)
A long-standing favourite for pots at Perch Hill, this is one we have known and grown for years and it still sits in our top ten. Super busy with bees as soon as the sun comes out. H: 75cm (2½ft).

Soft and Warm / Soft and Cool

1 *Dahlia* 'Evanah' (Decorative)
For a truly cupcake-sweet mix to make you smile, grow 'Evanah' and 'Small World' (p307) in the same or adjacent pots. Fill the gaps with a compact white cosmos (try 'Sonata White') to create a cumulonimbus of froth below. H: 1m (3ft).

2 *D.* 'Happy Days Cream White' (Single-flowered)
It's rare for us to find a cream or white dahlia that is a suitable size for a pot, good for pollinators and pretty with it, and that's why I fell on this one in our trials. The Happy Days series was bred for pots and the varieties are compact, but not too much so. H: 45cm (1½ft).

3 *D.* 'Happy Single Kiss' (Single-flowered)
Compact with lovely buff apricot flowers with dark centres that match the stems and the foliage. These were bred for pots and are ideal if planted with something to soften and loosen the pot combination, such as *Thunbergia alata* 'African Sunset' grown to trail without a climbing frame. H: 60cm (2ft).

4 *D.* 'Heroine' (Single-flowered)
A new, large-flowered, single, mid-pink dahlia with a plum petal base. It really stood out in our summer 2022 trial for its compact habit and handkerchief-like flowers. We've moved it from the garden to pots and predict it will fare very well. H: 60cm (2ft).

5 *D.* 'Kelsey Annie Joy' (Collarette)
Not a strong grower or tuber maker, so breeders are not so keen on this one, but I adore its flowers, which look like a child's drawing. It's also the loveliest mix of apricot to crème brûlée shades. It thrives in a pot and mustn't be allowed to disappear! H: 75cm (2½ft).

6 *D.* 'Molly Raven' (Decorative)
Our pot plant supremo! Named after my youngest daughter, this is a must-have for a whopper pot combination: flowery, glamorous and reliable. It looks good with any of the tender perennial climbers and maybe *Hibiscus acetosella* 'Mahogany Splendor' (pictured on p14). It's on the tall side, but still works well in a pot. H: 1.2m (4ft).

7 *D.* 'Mystic Dreamer' (Single-flowered)
Available more widely as rooted cuttings than tubers (it is not a strong tuber former), this is one of the few mauves we grow for pots. We partner it with scabious and verbenas in matching colours in our long-standing Butterfly Pink Pot Collection (pictured on p294). Bees and butterflies love this mix of nectar-rich flowers. H: 50cm (20in).

8 *D.* 'Night Silence' (Decorative)
Newly bred and making it straight into our top ten list, this has a unique matt quality to its flowers that makes it super classy. It's also hugely floriferous and cuts well. Wine red with a more muted, faded petal edge. Superb. H: 90cm (3ft).

9 *D.* 'Sarah Raven' (Anemone-flowered)
Beautiful bicoloured flowers with terracotta outer petals and an oxblood-red heart. It also has a better-than-average vase life and superb straight stems that make it perfect for cutting. We've noticed it has pollen-dusted petals for the whole of summer and autumn with apparently a very copious production of pollen (protein) as well as nectar (carbohydrate) for pollinators. H: 90cm (3ft).

10 *D.* 'Small World' (Pompon)
The epitome of a drumstick dahlia with perfect globe flowers in the softest pink to white atop long, strong stems. This is great planted in contrast to other showy, soft-coloured forms. H: 1m (3ft).

11 *D.* 'Top Mix Salmon' (Single-flowered)
I spotted this at the dwarf end of a trial field in the Netherlands – it's an area I normally stride past, but I was drawn to the soft, muted tone of its flowers. Grown not on its own, but combined with loose and lovely things such as petite grasses and trailers such as calibrachoas, this is ideal for a large, low table centre pot and will flower all through summer and autumn. H: 40cm (16in).

August

August is, simply and enjoyably, a continuation of the garden jobs and duties from the last couple of months, as well as helping to keep the pots looking good for as long as possible.

Now that droughts tend to be a more common occurrence, watering and harvested rainwater (if it hasn't run out) are absolutely key at this time of year. Feeding also moves up a notch to keep everything in good heart. In July, we aim to feed pots once a fortnight, whereas now this moves to once a week. Deadheading or picking flowers is another important theme. If you're going away, don't feel guilty about stripping the garden of every bud and flower amongst your dahlias and annuals in pots before you leave. That will keep them going. While you're away, if longer than a week, ask a friend to both water and pick. Remember the saying: the generous gardener has the most flowers. That's true in August more than any month. In a dry spell, and with flowers unpicked or deadheaded, you'll otherwise return to find your pots in a sorry state. So trade some watering for flowers!

As the month goes on, we shift into major propagation mode, making our way through our tender perennial plants from one end of the garden to the other, with osteospermums, argyranthemums, arctotis, salvias and pelargoniums all pillaged for cuttings that gradually fill the polytunnel benches. That's our main occupation this month.

One small job: if you have any hyacinth bulbs stored from last year, put them in a paper bag and pop them into the bottom of the fridge. Leave them there for a month, chilling, before planting into bowls and storing in the cold and dark (see p343). They should be in flower by Christmas and you won't need to buy more expensive forced and prepared bulbs.

Opposite Deadheading flowers in pots in the Dutch Yard. We try to do this weekly from now on to maximise flowering.
Right Deadheaded dahlia flowers decorating the compost bays.

Below Taking pelargonium cuttings
as insurance against any losses
over winter.

Bulb Designs for Pots

August tends to be a quiet month in the
garden, with much less to do than September,
so it's the ideal moment to get going with pot
designs for spring. I have a list of the different
groupings of pots in the different areas of the
garden and I work my way down it, thinking of
exciting new combinations for each grouping,
using perhaps some new tulips we discovered
the previous year and mixing them with our
tried and tested favourites.

With spring pots, designs really focus on
the narcissi and tulips, with some pot toppers
to go with them. This keeps combinations
simple, as you don't really have to think about
form. Work out first what you want as your
Bride – the main diva in the mix – and from
there it's easy to select the Bridesmaid, as
ideally this will be a colour that matches, but
in a slightly less showy, smaller form. Then
pick the colour contrasting Gatecrasher (see
more on this in the design chapter on p38).

It's a good idea to get any bulb orders in
while you still have the pick of bulb suppliers'

stock. Ordering online means you can be pretty certain the bulbs will have been stored in the right conditions and will be sent out to you at just the right time. Garden centres are fine, but take care to check bulbs have no mould and ideally no shoots (certainly at this time of year) – you're looking for a good firm texture.

Taking Tender Perennial Cuttings

We find that it's in late summer into autumn that we have the highest success rate with rooting tender perennial plants including salvias, heliotropes and pelargoniums. Many of these originate in the southern hemisphere, so it's now that their ancestry and genetics tell them it's spring. We can root pelargoniums pretty well in spring too, but salvias definitely give us better results if propagated now.

Pelargoniums can be stored on a window ledge in the house and they'll look elegant until you give them a haircut before the new season's growth spurt in early spring. Keep them dry and cool while indoors, watering no more than once a month.

- Cut a short piece of stem from the main plant ensuring it is from the current year's growth. Choose a non-flowering stem that has a soft tip but has hardened at the end.
- Trim to just below a leaf node (joint), so the cutting is 5–6cm (2in) long. Short cuttings root better than long ones. Just below a

leaf node is where there is the highest concentration of natural rooting hormone. We don't use rooting hormone powder as we find a high percentage of our cuttings root consistently and quickly without it.

- Strip off all leaves except the top pair. Remove the stem tip. It's at the top that the growth hormone concentrates, so by pinching it out, apical dominance is removed to encourage root formation.
- Fill small pots with a mix of one part fine grit to two parts compost. Insert the cuttings around the edge of the pot, spaced about 4–5cm (2in) apart so their leaves don't touch. By placing them round the edge, not in the centre, you encourage quicker root formation, as the new roots quickly hit the side of the pot, break and branch into more lateral rootlets.
- Water the compost well. Place the pot in a greenhouse with shading if it gets too hot. Only water when the compost is dry. Avoid water touching the leaves if you can.
- Cuttings often root in 3–4 weeks. Check for roots showing in the drainage holes and, once formed, pot each cutting on into its own pot.
- If any of the cuttings show the slightest signs of botrytis (browning of the cutting or visible mould), take them out as this will quickly spread to the others.
- Store them under cover through the winter, for planting out next spring.

September

September is the moment our annual climbers pick up the colour baton. It's these quick-growing and densely flowery triffids we rely on this month and beyond. Dahlias are magnificent in September and are often pot partners with the climbers, but as night temperatures fall, their colours start to fade. In contrast, the asarina, cobaea, ipomoea and thunbergia are reaching their peak, covered with flowers right to the tip of their frames and throughout their cascading vines.

The climbers we grow are mostly tender perennials, but they're treated as annuals (one-year performers) because of their lack of frost resistance. Their perennial nature means they have a slightly slower growth pattern compared with true annuals, so most don't flower until late summer or autumn (to give them a head start, we sow them in February, see p84). Once they come into bloom, though, there's nothing to compete with them from now until our first hard frost in November or December.

The joy of these climbers is partly down to the architecture of their frames. I love the look of our woven towers, so much more elegant than a clutch of shiny bamboo canes. They look fantastic from the moment they're created in spring and right through summer, and they look even better now swathed with foliage and flowers, their spires standing tall in our pot landscape. We have pots with frames throughout the garden and, if you come to visit in September, they are one of the most prominent highlights. The question we are most frequently asked is, how do you make them? And it's simple to explain (see p202 and p229).

I had been growing this group of short-lived climbers for several years before it occurred to me that without a frame to climb over, the same plants could well make beautiful curtains and hanging swags from balconies, tall pots or baskets. And they do. Now we grow the more vigorous ones (such as cobaea and some ipomoeas) as Spillers (cascading down) as well as Pillars (standing tall) – see p43 for more on these two terms. They're invaluable plants for softening the edges of large pots and disguising walls, fences or a trellis, growing up one side of a frame and cascading down the other in a flowery waterfall. So, September is the month for vertical pot gardening in both directions. I also think of it as the month for perfume.

Like March, this is a month when the beginning feels utterly different from the end. Night humidity is increasing and light levels decreasing steeply as the days go by. And, just like March, this is when scent is most important in the garden. It seems to me like the perfumes are contained in the air's moisture creating a balloon of fragrance, so we need to make sure we have plants to fill that balloon.

I will never forget visiting Monet's Garden at Giverny in late September, over 20 years ago. Jonathan Buckley (the photographer I worked with then and still do now) and I were allowed in at dawn to photograph the sunrise. We were intending to shoot the dahlias for our book, *The Bold and Brilliant Garden*, but as we walked through the top terrace we got distracted.

It wasn't the dahlias that bowled us over, but the brilliant pink and purple *Phlox paniculata* having its last floriferous flush. And it wasn't so much the look of it as its scent. As we walked towards each clump, the fragrance hit us – hugely powerful, as strong as incense in a Catholic church and just as delicious. If we kept walking a few paces beyond that particular patch, the change was equally abrupt – out of the fragrant cloud we came. It was as memorable as only scents can be and it's been one of my ambitions to recreate this in our September garden.

That said, we don't use perennial phlox as our perfumeries in pots. They demand a lot of water and most are better growing – as in Monet's Garden – in the borders. Instead, we use plenty of fragrant plants ideal for pots (see p319).

Between the climbers and the perfume providers, September is full of pot possibilities. The year has not come to an end.

Scented plants

Opposite An all-purple, scented pot filled with *Phlox* '21st Century Blue' and *Heliotropium arborescens* 'Midnight Sky'.

There are so many plants we could turn to for sources of wafting fragrance from pots at this time of year – we aim for a good range of easy-to-grow varieties.

Heliotropes are at their best in September and I love them for their scent. They have an unusual fragrance, sweet and vanilla-like with a hint of cooked cherries thrown in. The rare *Heliotropium arborescens* 'Reva' reigns supreme here. This is tall and elegant (not dumpy like many of the more widely available forms) and has mauve flowers and bright green leaves. 'Reva' is easy to propagate from cuttings, is reliably perennial (if given frost protection) and has good resistance to botrytis and other fungal diseases, which this family can be prone to. 'Midnight Sky' is another good one, with more saturated purple flowers and, again, good disease resistance.

We mix our heliotropes (so-called cherry pies) with other similarly coloured things such as lavender, *Osteospermum* 'Erato Blue' (not perfumed) and the scented-leaf *Pelargonium* 'Attar of Roses'. Or we alternate 'Midnight Sky' and 'Reva' in their own pots down the centre of a table (pictured on p321). We've also found pairing these two with a nemesia creates a wonderful succession of colour and scent. In its own pots, *Nemesia* 'Wisley Vanilla' can be added to give scent and flowers from May, when it first opens. The heliotropes pick up from midsummer and, a little later, the nemesia hopefully makes a comeback (if cut back in July, it usually gives a second flush in August and September), so you then get both flowering away at the same time.

Buddlejas bred for containers are another late summer must-have for scent. We've been trialling compact forms in the Buzz series and Dreaming series, and love them all. We started with 'Buzz Lavender' and have since moved on to 'Dreaming White' and 'Buzz Wine'. They all have a good arching, curving stem habit that makes them brilliant for pots in combinations or solo. We find that if we deadhead these through the summer, they're still flowering now.

If we're lucky (as these are tricky to coax into flower), we have some pots of tuberose in pride of place. We plant the tubers in late June and we give them basal heat and keep them in the greenhouse where it's warm and bright. And I love the easy-to-grow mignonette (*Reseda odorata*), which was popular with the Victorians for scenting greenhouses and orangeries with its catch-on-the-wind spicy fragrance. Too few of us grow this now. Sow the seed in April or May for September flowers. If you love the idea of fragrant clouds around plants, then you can't be without *Nicotiana alata* 'Grandiflora' – that's the strongest scented tobacco plant we grow and, as long as this is sited in dappled shade, it should still be flowering away now.

Those are our top plants for drifting scent through the September garden, but there are also plants that need a squeeze to their leaves to release their perfume, and these are just as valuable. Many are growing at full tilt now.

I love the evergreen lemon myrtle (*Backhousia citriodora*), for its super strong citrus scent. This is one step better than lemon verbena, but the two are equally delicious in a tisane. Many of the scented-leaf pelargoniums are stellar in this department too. Leading the pack for me are the minty *P. tomentosum*, the lemony ones such as 'Queen of the Lemons' and *P. crispum* 'Cy's Sunburst', and the rosy 'Attar of Roses'.

Last but absolutely not least is the edible crew: basil, mint and tomatoes. For basil, I'd recommend *Ocimum* 'African Blue' – it has amethyst-ebony stems and purple flowers and, unusually, its high point is September. It's substantially hardier than any other basil we've trialled and flowers (if we bring it into the greenhouse) almost until Christmas. It's an elegant pot plant on its own and a great filler with potted dahlias. Any of the mints are fantastic for scent, but I particularly love eau de cologne mint (*Mentha × piperita* f. *citrata*) – it's the one used in the perfume industry rather than as a culinary herb.

For tomatoes, I'd recommend 'Red Alert' or 'Tumbling Tom' for pots, as well as the most elegant of all, 'Micro Cherry'. The combination of its tiny, jewel-like fruits, finely cut fragrant leaves and compact, but tumbling habit make it the queen of tomatoes for containers. Give it some space – at least a 2-litre pot – and quite a bit of TLC (regular feeding and watering). These tomatoes might not throw their fragrance, but if you pinch out an axillary bud as you pass, they still deliver.

Best of the scented plants throughout the year

These are our favourite pot-compatible, scented plants throughout the year. There are many other options for fragrant plants in pots, such as tulips ('Ballerina', 'Wyndham', 'Request'), nemesias or chocolate cosmos, but the ones in this list seem to have the power to cast their perfume.

1 *Buddleja*
The ones in the Buzz series and Dreaming series have done well in our trials and are a pot-compatible size. They give a sweet honey scent for summer and into autumn. 'Buzz Indigo' is pictured.

2 *Citrus*
There are so many different types of citrus plant that give you lovely, scented pots through winter indoors. The blossom is, of course, fantastic, as is the spring fruit. We are just building a new greenhouse at Perch Hill and are going to fill it with citrus for winter into spring. We're then going to move the pots outside onto a brick apron as soon as the frosts are over.

3 *Clematis*
Some clematis are super fragrant and can be compact enough to work in a large container. I love clematis spilling out of tall, narrow-necked, Cretan-style oil jars, the type you see at Sissinghurst Castle. For white, scented plants in summer, we grow *Clematis* 'Sweet Scentsation' (pictured) and, in a whopper pot, *C. terniflora* var. *mandshurica*, which smells of marzipan and thrives in sun or dappled shade, flowering from midsummer to autumn.

4 *Daphne*
The more compact varieties work well in pots. *Daphne* × *transatlantica* 'Eternal Fragrance' or 'Pink Fragrance' just carry on producing flowers for months, not weeks, from spring until autumn. Also fantastic is the pale and mid-pink *D. odora* 'Aureomarginata' (pictured).

5 *Dianthus*
There are lots of dianthus that give you a decent display in a set of table-centre pots with fragrant flowers in summer (try the Cocktail series or 'Pink Kisses', pictured), but the rather ramshackle and untidy 'Mrs Sinkins' is, I think, the best of them all. It has an intense and delicious clove-like fragrance and grows well in a pot.

6 *Erysimum*
There's almost no better perfume than wallflowers in spring. There are many new compact varieties, but for strength of fragrance I'd recommend the old-fashioned seed-grown varieties such as *Erysimum cheiri* 'Fire King' or 'Blood Red', as well as 'Spring Breeze Sunset' (pictured). It's worth knowing there are a few that have no perfume.

7 *Heliotropium*
Heliotropium arborescens 'Reva'
(pictured) and 'Midnight Sky'
win hands down, certainly
better than 'Dwarf Marine'
in our view. Ideal for striking
September containers.

8 *Hyacinthus*
All hyacinths are at their best
in pots in early spring. Blue
hyacinths have the strongest
fragrance (see p67).

9 *Jasminum*
Jasminum polyanthum, the
classic, white-flowered
jasmine, needs to be kept in a
greenhouse, protected from
frosts, so it's not for everyone.
But if you have a greenhouse,
it will fill the whole space
with fragrance for much of
spring. *J. officinale* 'Clotted
Cream', with its soft yellow
flowers, is hardy, so ideal for
pots being left outside.

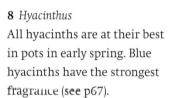

10 *Lilium*
It's the classic oriental hybrid lilies such as 'Casa Blanca' and 'Stargazer' (pictured) along with the *Lilium regale* varieties that have the most powerful and heady scent. They are all a little top-heavy and tall in a pot, so will almost certainly need support. They are low maintenance and grow happily in pots, but be vigilant in looking for lily beetles and don't let them get too hot – in the wild, most lilies grow in dappled shade.

11 *Lobularia maritima*
Sweet alyssum varieties such as 'Snow Princess' and those in the Stream series (such as 'Summer Stream', pictured) smell like honey, particularly so when it's warm. So we line up pots of these on our zinc-topped table in May and June – the zinc radiates the sun's heat and makes them smell even stronger. This is a wasteland and seaside plant and very drought tolerant; it thrives in poor soil.

12 *Lonicera*
Lonicera periclymenum 'Chic et Choc' (pictured) and 'Rhubarb and Custard' are compact varieties of honeysuckle, perfect for large, deep pots.

13 *Narcissus*
You want the Tazetta and Jonquilla types for the most reliable fragrance (see p105). We love 'Actaea' in the Poeticus group, but it's not the showiest for pots. And of course, *N. papyraceus* (the paperwhite daffodil), together with 'Cragford' and 'Avalanche' if you want indoor perfume for the winter months. This spring we also trialled three new varieties in pots: 'Lieke', 'Moonlight Sensation' and 'Starlight Sensation' (pictured with *Viola* 'Beaconsfield'). All three were exceptional – deliciously and powerfully fragrant, hugely long-flowering and the two Sensation varieties were exceptionally multiheaded, with up to eight flowerheads on one stem. Small, delicate and exquisite with it for April and May are 'Segovia' and 'Xit'.

14 *Nicotiana*
The two perfumed tobacco plants we grow for pots are *Nicotiana sylvestris* 'Only The Lonely' (pictured) and *N. alata* 'Grandiflora'. It's handy that they both thrive in shade.

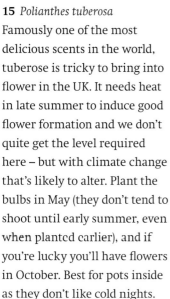

15 *Polianthes tuberosa*
Famously one of the most delicious scents in the world, tuberose is tricky to bring into flower in the UK. It needs heat in late summer to induce good flower formation and we don't quite get the level required here – but with climate change that's likely to alter. Plant the bulbs in May (they don't tend to shoot until early summer, even when planted earlier), and if you're lucky you'll have flowers in October. Best for pots inside as they don't like cold nights.

16 *Reseda odorata*
Mignonette is not a looker, but I love it for its olive-green, copper and ochre tones and gentle, yet wafting vanilla-like scent. It was apparently popular with the Victorians and was planted in orangeries for its scent and essential oil. It is still used commonly in the perfume industry. It's a hardy annual and very easy to grow. Sow in early spring, plant out in pots in April, and it will flower from May right through summer.

17 *Rhododendron*
Rhododendron 'Fragrantissimum' (pictured) reminds me so much of my childhood – we used to have a large pot of it and the even larger 'Polar Bear'. Both had huge white bells and an incredibly powerful perfume in late spring. This needs a greenhouse though, and only flowers for about a month, so it's a luxury.

18 *Rosa*
We have found most roses advertised for pots tend to struggle with fungal diseases (black spot and mildew), and take a lot of watering and feeding to look good. There are a few exceptions, such as the fragrant shrub rose 'Little White Pet' (pictured), with its buttonhole flowers in pink and white.

19 *Sarcococca*
Sweet box, as it's known, is a shade-tolerant evergreen. Our favourite here is *Sarcococca hookeriana* var. *digyna* 'Purple Stem'. It's a bit big for a pot, growing to 1.5m (5ft), but hugely worthwhile and can be clipped after flowering. It spreads slowly and only needs potting once every three years. This flowers through most of winter.

20 *Trachelospermum jasminoides*

Star jasmine does a bit better in the ground than a pot, but it can be grown successfully in a container with regular watering or an irrigation system. Ideal for rambling slowly along fences from a big pot in a courtyard. An evergreen, it has intense jasmine-scented lookalike flowers in July and August. Surprisingly, this thrives in shade as well as sun, with the foliage turning bright red in winter shade, adding to its interest.

Annual climbers

Opposite A pair of dolly tubs positioned either side of the entrance to the Perennial Cutting Garden with *Maurandya scandens* 'Violet' (syn. *Asarina scandens* 'Violet'), *Thunbergia alata* 'Alba' and *Glandularia* 'Aztec Silver Magic'. Next page The Oast Garden in September. *Dahlia* 'Bishop's Children' fills all our whopper pots, while the castor oil plant, *Ricinus communis*, surrounds it in the borders. *Petunia* 'Tidal Wave Purple' and *Cobaea scandens* tumble and climb from the former water troughs on the balcony above.

Tender perennial and annual climbers are the stars of the show for September, the providers of architecture and vertical emphasis for our pots – we'd have a lesser garden without them.

In my top ten plants, I'd have to include *Cobaea scandens*, the cup and saucer vine, and I would recommend this for all but the tiniest garden. It comes in purple and white and is my go-to for vases from September to December. I have a particular soft spot for the standard purple form, which is even more vigorous than the white-flowered one (*C. scandens* f. *alba*), so much so that it's hard to believe it will be okay in a pot, but we find it is fine in a large container. Almost every year we plant it on the balcony outside the Oast House in a 2m (6½ft) long, 60cm (2ft) deep water trough, and it thrives. From here, we allow it to trail down almost to the ground.

We also use cobaea over what we consider to be an ugly wall on either side of the main chimney breast of the farmhouse. The wall is covered in quite coarse render, too expensive to replace, so instead we have two deep farm buckets at either end with one cobaea plant in each. They're topped with a silver birch teepee to help start them off, then we give them simple wires between eyes spaced at 45cm (18in) all the way up on both sides of the chimney. The plants thrive in their deep buckets and are only cut down by hard frosts in this sheltered spot, usually around Christmas. As an added bonus, cobaea (as it is without suckers) does not take its toll on the wall. All in all, there are few better romping screens to cover ugly features!

There's one important thing to know about cobaea, though: it needs to reach around two-metres tall before it starts to flower, so sowing early is key. Sown in March or April, it gets to this height just in time to be clobbered by the autumn frost. Sown in January or February, along with your sweet peas, and you'll have a plant nearly a metre tall, climbing on a teepee, by the end of May. Plant these out once the spring frosts have passed, and they will start flowering in August or September.

Next in terms of vigour comes the whole ipomoea, commonly known as morning glory, brigade. I remember seeing an entire field filled with a purple ipomoea in Ischia, the island off Naples in Italy. Just a few plants had colonised over an acre, growing like triffids, with no frost to contend with. These tender perennials behave as annuals in the UK, because the frost cuts them down in autumn. But if grown in pots that are portable – and you have the space inside in a greenhouse or conservatory – they will keep growing and flowering happily all through the start of winter and then, after a brief pause, continue the following summer.

The *Ipomoea* genus is large and varied, and we grow several types for our pots. The first are the classic trumpet-flowered, morning glories, like the ones I saw in Ischia. Most need strong light levels to do really well, but we find the purple-flowered *I. purpurea* 'Grandpa Ott' is the stand out, because its flowers don't die by noon (the flowers of many, including the beautiful but frustrating *I. tricolor* 'Heavenly Blue', die after a few hours).

Then there are a couple of elegant flowering forms. I'm mad about the delicate, highly cut leaves of *I. quamoclit*, which we

Below *Rhodochiton atrosanguineus* with *Thunbergia alata* 'African Sunset', a much-planted pot duo at Perch Hill.

use as a lacy spiller from window boxes or as an ethereal climber over a silver birch teepee. We bring this into the greenhouse to give us flowers to decorate with fairy lights for Christmas – it loves that extra bit of late-season shelter.

More well-known and widely grown is *I. lobata*, commonly called Spanish flag. This is a strong grower, easy and reliable. I love its vigour in contrast to the delicacy of its yellow- and orange-hooded flowers.

The last lot are popular in France and used there in huge urban bedding schemes – these are the foliage, heart- or hand-shaped *Ipomoea batatas* varieties. We grow lots of the ebony-leaved 'SolarTower Black' with compact dahlias and salvias (see p354) and other late-season plants – there are few better things for trailing over the edges of large pots which need softening. There are various acid-green ones too, if you want something zesty to break up the darkness of crimson and near-black dahlias. They look good for the whole of autumn and cut well, lasting two weeks or more in a vase.

I also have to rave about the whole *Thunbergia* genus. There has been a huge amount of development and breeding in the last five years or so. The standard varieties of *T. alata* have long been available in either bright yellow or orange with a dark well at the centre of the flower. These are good, but in my view, there are others now which are more exciting. The great planstwoman, Derry Watkins, introduced me to *T. a.* 'African Sunset' about 15 years ago and I've grown it every year since. I love the way it changes colour from coral-mahogany when it first opens to soft apricot after a couple of weeks – this makes it super versatile in terms of which palette you can use it in.

Having loved 'African Sunset', we have since trialled many others including whites ('Alba', pictured on p328), pinks (try 'Rose Sensation' in the Arizona series) and various tones of orange from terracotta ('SunEyes Orange') down to the plushest mahogany ('Sunny Susy Brownie', my new favourite).

It's worth mentioning one final group of plants here: the exceptional petunias in the Tidal Wave series. These are so vigorous that, given a frame, they will climb as well as trail. With a bit of support, 'Tidal Wave Red Velour', 'Tidal Wave Silver' and 'Tidal Wave Purple' (pictured on p330 growing on the balcony of the Oast House) will push themselves upwards.

Best of the annual climbers

The majority of these climbers are tender perennials in their native habitats, but here in the UK, we tend to treat them like annuals.

1 *Cardiospermum halicacabum*
I've seen love-in-a-puff growing wild in America, clambering over fences and into trees. It's the only true annual in this list. I love this plant from the moment I sow its jet-black seeds with their perfect white hearts (hence its Latin name, which means heart seed) to its last moment in autumn when its seedcases hang like puffed up green balloons. To be honest, it isn't a prolific grower here and really needs a more mild autumn, but it's great in amongst our tomato vines in the greenhouse. It makes the tomatoes look even lovelier and its flowers also help draw in pollinators to fertilise them.

2 *Cobaea scandens*
The common name, cup-and-saucer vine, gives it all away – the flowers really do look like mini-teacups sitting on saucers, and very lovely for that. The flowers are large compared to all the other climbers here, the size of an espresso cup. *Cobaea scandens* (pictured) is vigorous: its green buds open to green-washed purple flowers that deepen in colour as they age. The calyx is pretty even without the petals and goes on to form chunky, passion-fruit-like seedheads. The leaves and growth tips are all washed with purple. The less vigorous *C. scandens* f. *alba* also has green buds, but these open to pure white flowers.

3 *Ipomoea batatas*
The true sweet potato, this is an easy-to-grow, robust, tender perennial climber, grown for its ornamental leaves not flowers. I've seen this grown inside, around the huge windows of a flat in Paris, and it looked magnificent, trained on tacks as a kind of window fringe. Very happy, vigorous and long performing in a garden pot too. 'Marguerite' (pictured) has vibrant, acid-green, heart-shaped leaves. 'Sweet Caroline Light Green' has more hand-like leaves in the same vivid colour. 'SolarTower Black' (pictured on p354) is a near-black crimson with heart-shaped leaves. And 'Blackie' is the same colour but, again, its leaves are more like a hand.

4 *Ipomoea lobata*
The so-called Spanish flag, named for its red and yellow bands of colour – red at the top of each group of flowers, moving to soft yellow at the base. It's pretty vigorous, but needs shelter from the wind to flourish.

5 *Ipomoea purpurea* 'Grandpa Ott'
The best performer in all our trials of the morning glories. It grows well and flowers for much more of the day than 'Heavenly Blue'.

6 *Ipomoea quamoclit*
Beautiful, fine, lacey leaves that are almost as lovely as the flowers themselves, which are very like jasmine flowers but in a brilliant scarlet.

7 *Maurandya and Lophospermum*
Sometimes mistakenly confused with European *Asarina*, these are known as Mexican snapdragon vines: their flowers look like snapdragon flowers scattered up and down a vine, though in some cases the bells are larger. In our pastel plantings we use the pink species form *Lophospermum erubescens*, as well as the white 'Bridal Bouquet', and the mauve *Maurandya scandens* 'Mystic Rose'. For our more saturated palettes we go for the amethyst-purple *M. s.* 'Violet' (pictured). These plants are also happy in shade and are great in hanging baskets.

8 *Phaseolus coccineus*
It's good to have an edible flower, vegetable and pretty climber all in one, and runner beans are just that. They're ideal for a small garden and happy in a pot growing over a teepee climbing frame. We love the coral-coloured 'Sunset' (similar to 'Aurora'), pictured.

You can also grow red-flowered 'Polestar', white-flowered 'White Lady' or the red and white 'Painted Lady'.

9 *Rhodochiton atrosanguineus*
Not a vigorous grower, but the purple bell vine is a beautiful and delicate climber. Its hanging bells come complete with a clapper at their heart.

10 *Thunbergia alata*
For rich and bright shades, look to the Arizona series. 'Rose Sensation' is a lovely strong to mid-pink, 'Dark Red' is very similar. In the SunEyes series, there's the gentle lemon-yellow 'Lemon Star', fruity 'Orange', the warm, faded ochre of 'Terracotta' and the brilliant tangerine 'Superstar Orange'. 'Sunny Susy Brownie' (pictured) is also a favourite of mine in deep mahogany crimson. For a similar mahogany but with a with a stripe of apricot on the outer edge of each petal, try 'Tangerine Slice A-Peel'. These are all grown from cuttings not seed. If you need a pastel shade, 'African Sunset' (pictured on p332) is the one we've grown here for longest, from seed. *T. alata* 'Alba' (pictured on p328) has the classic white flowers with black centres.

Next page A huge pot at the centre of the Perennial Cutting Garden filled with the stellar *Salvia* 'Lake Onega'. Thunbergias climb up and over the metal arches down the central path, looking good very late in the year.

September

The number of jobs starts to pick up again once summer is over. Autumn sowing of hardy annuals begins in earnest now and the season of bulb planting launches again.

If you want your dahlias and pelargoniums to keep looking good for as long as possible, keep deadheading. As rainfall increases, you'll need to up the regularity of this – flowers go over faster in the wind and rain.

Watering can usually stop this month and feeding can tail off too, except for dahlias. Keep feeding them if you want flowers into October. Pots filled with certain tender perennials – thunbergia, rhodochiton, as well as heliotropes and petunias – will also need feeding. They can come into the greenhouse once frosts threaten and, with a bit of shelter, they can flower until Christmas, so it's worth continuing feeding for a late-season boost. We have experimented with doubling the concentration of feed at this stage in the year and compared this to feeding twice a week. We found the strength of the feed can draw moisture from the plant roots and have the opposite of the desired effect, so it's better to feed twice weekly.

In September we start to plan and sow our pot toppers for planting in October or early November to bring us cheer in winter and spring. We want the seed-grown pot toppers to be ready for planting out when we create our pot lasagnes in about four to six weeks. That's also the time we change our summer and autumn table centre pots, replacing them with plants that will look good for the next season.

Potting on Cuttings

Cuttings that were taken over the summer and left to root in the polytunnel or greenhouse need to be potted on into their own individual pots now.

Just upturn the pot, give it a sharp tap and the whole lot should fall out: compost, roots and all in a block. Gently prize each rooted cutting apart. As with pricking out, aim to handle the new plants by their leaves, not stem or roots. Move each rooted cutting into its own 1-litre pot full of peat-free compost. Water, then place back onto a heated bench, mat or propagator if you have one.

Sowing Pot Toppers

My favourite pot toppers are the ones that look (and taste) good from winter into spring (see p118). Planting our pot toppers mainly happens in October (see p381), but we get going with the ones we grow from seed now, so we have established plants ready for winter.

Violas and *Visnaga daucoides* (syn. *Ammi visnaga*) can be sown in September into seed trays and transplanted to their final pots in October. Violas have tiny seeds and we don't want huge numbers, so we sow them into a half-sized seed tray split in two by a cane to prevent us getting carried away (see p86). For pot gardening you want a good range, but not

Below Planting anemone corms.
The corms (still in their net bag)
are soaked for a couple of hours to
plump them up before planting.

large numbers of any one. For cerinthe, hardy
salad leaves, hardy herbs (like parsley) and
hardy greens (like kale), we sow into modules
or Jiffy-7s (see p172) and similarly plant these
out in October.

When planted above bulbs, the bulb foliage
will choke smaller salad leaves in the end, but
we'll have had four or five months of harvest
before that happens.

....

Planting Early Bulbs

Planting certain bulbs in early autumn enables
us to have flowers early in the new year, and
I'm all for that. We plant our anemones now
for that reason, as well as hyacinths, muscari
and some narcissi by the end of the month.
All these bulbs require and benefit from a
more complex root structure than a tulip, so
planting them now gives them time to build
those roots. These are planted and then put
somewhere cool but covered in a polytunnel
or cold frame. A garden shed (with some light)
would be fine too. We don't plant tulips into
pots until November and that's also when we
construct most of our bulb lasagnes.

Anemone coronaria
There is a newly bred lot of anemones
coming from Israel (where they grow wild),
in a good range of colours and some hugely
tall and impressive ones from Italy (Biancheri
Creazioni is the famous breeder there).

I love 'Jerusalem Blue', with its big, purple-blue
flowers that have a soft, plush texture, as well
as 'Galilee Giant'. We've also been growing an
elegant double called 'Fullstar Red'. The great
thing about anemones, compared to many
bulbs, is that one corm produces countless
flowers over several months, from the end of
winter and all through spring.

We mainly grow these in pots under cover
to bring us cheer in February and we collect
them on a table outside once they're in flower,
if no harsh weather is forecast. If frost is in
the offing, we bring them under cover again.

- Soak corms in a bowl of water for a couple of hours so they plump up.
- Plant individual corms into 1-litre pots of peat-free compost, about 5cm (2in) deep and about 10cm (4in) apart. They have knobbly bulbs so you can't really tell which end is which, but they don't mind which way you plant them. Some varieties are more conical and go pointy end down.
- Water them well on planting and then leave them be.
- Store in a greenhouse or cold frame until February, when they should start to flower.
- If you want to mass a few together in a window box or larger container, wait until the leaves are growing well and then transplant them to their final pot.
- Check occasionally that the soil is not bone dry, but don't overwater. They'll rot if too wet, but need moist soil.

Forcing hyacinths

For hyacinths in time for Christmas and also all through January and February, get going with them now (see p67 for hyacinth varieties). You can buy unprepared bulbs (ones that haven't been pre-chilled) and prepared bulbs that have been chilled. If you have unprepared bulbs, pop them in a paper bag and into the bottom of the fridge for four weeks. Then treat both types of bulbs the same.

Plant a handful in a pot or a bowl, with added drainage, every fortnight until around mid-October.

They need to be grown in a well-drained but moist environment with a soil structure that is strong enough to anchor them. That's often the problem with cheap, shop-bought forced bulbs: they are planted in peat-based compost, which when it dries out becomes as light as dust and can't hold the elongating stem and top-heavy flowerhead. At Perch Hill, we use molehills – they give us the perfect, crumbly, fine soil. With no access to molehills, use John Innes No. 3 or a specially formulated peat-free bulb compost. To this, add some grit. To a bucket of molehill soil, add just under half a bucket of grit. If you're using John Innes, use a ratio of 1 part grit to 3 parts compost.

Add 2.5cm (1in) of pure grit in the bottom of every pot, then add a shallow layer of the compost and grit mix. Then add the bulbs with the pointy tip just below the soil surface. Fill in around those with the compost mix.

Once planted, leave them somewhere dark and cold – a temperature of 5–10°C (41–50°F) is ideal – for 10 weeks before bringing them out into warmth and light. When the sprouts are up to a good 2–3cm (1in), bring the pots in somewhere warm (above 15°C/59°F) and they should be in flower within three to four weeks.

The cold fools them into thinking its winter, stimulating a biochemical response inside the bulb to make it start flowering. The cool and dark gives the root time to develop before the warmth and light pulls the flower and leaves from the bulb.

To stop the stems and leaves flopping about, create a nest of twigs to support them, or a smaller version of a pot ring (see p229).

One note of caution: hyacinth bulbs can irritate the skin, so wear gloves.

Forcing amaryllis

One amaryllis bulb looks good, but three or five look even better, though their bulbs are a bit pricey.

These South American natives do not require a cold spell as the hyacinths do, so if you plant amaryllis towards the end of September, they will be in flower in eight to ten weeks and should then go on looking good for the same length of time. (See p393 for amaryllis varieties.)

- Before planting, hydrate the desiccated roots by soaking them in tepid tap water overnight. Rest the base of the bulb on the rim of an appropriately sized jam jar or glass so that all the roots (but not the bulb base), can sit in the water below (pictured opposite).
- Amaryllis like a tight-fitting pot, with about 2.5cm (1in) between the bulb and the side of the pot. The pot size will depend on the age and size of the bulb you're planting, but as a rough idea, for one bulb you'll need a 15–20cm (6–8in) diameter container with a depth of at least 30cm (12in). This will allow plenty of room for good root growth. If you plant several, leave just 3-4cm (1½in) between each bulb.
- The bulbs have a tendency to rot, so drainage is vital. Put a handful of crocks in the bottom of your pot to help with this.
- You can use potting compost, but they like their soil fertile, so a mix of 1 part well-rotted manure, 1 part grit or sand, and 2 parts leaf mould is even better.
- In the wild, they root quite superficially, with about one third of their huge bulbs poking out of the soil. This allows heavy rain to flow away from the crown of the bulb easily and lessens the likelihood of rot. You should plant them like this in a pot. It's important that the shoulder of the bulb sits a third above the surface of the compost. It's the apex of the bulb (where the leaves emerge) that is the most vulnerable to rot and where water can seep in and decay the heart, so this part mustn't sit wet on watering. It might look odd, with the bulb perched high, but that's how it should be.
- Planted so high, the whole thing is in danger of becoming top-heavy and toppling over as it grows. They grow to at least 45cm (18in), depending on the size of the bulb and variety, so they will need some support. You can just tap a cane in and tie the stem to that as soon as it gets to a decent height. But if you've planted more than one bulb, it's good to go one step further. Poke in a bunch of twigs (ideally ones that look good at this time of year, such as silver birch, dogwood, hazel or alder) around the edge and a few branches in between, taking care not to pierce a bulb as you go. You can weave them into a basket or small pot ring (see p229 and pictured on

p392). A twiggy nest also looks good and provides support.

- These are hot-country tender plants and they love the warmth. Place them in a light and well-ventilated spot, free from draughts, somewhere that's about 20°C (68°F). A shelf above a radiator is ideal.
- Keep the compost moist until a shoot appears and then water more frequently, about twice a week. Water from the top using tepid tap water, not from the bottom, and once the water has drained through into the saucer, tip it away. Don't overwater.
- Feeding is essential. You can add a complete slow-release fertiliser to the potting medium when you plant or use a liquid fertiliser twice a month when in flower. This ensures you have an even bigger, better bulb for next year.
- When every flower on one stalk is over, cut it off to just above the bulb nose. With a large bulb, there should be at least one or two more flowering stems to come. After flowering is completely over, continue to feed the plant (once every 6 weeks) and water it until the leaves begin to yellow.
- Cut the leaves back to about 6cm (2½in). Keep the bulbs somewhere dark and cool, allowing a dormant period of 10 weeks.
- After the dormant period, repot in fresh compost. Start watering again 8–10 weeks before you want them to bloom.

October

The Dutch Yard is jam-packed with pots still brimming with flowers and colour at the start of October. But this month, like February and March, is so variable in Sussex: one year it's sunny and even warm for weeks at a stretch, while the next it can be solidly wet, with equinoctial gales. Great swathes of the garden can be entirely flattened in a couple of days.

We still have large pots with our handmade birch and willow climbing frames out in the garden, the tall climbers now decorating them like lace, but sadly the structures can be broken in substantial winds, so these are gradually taken down and the pots gathered up so they can be planted with bulbs. And, as the weather cools, some of the potted plants get brought under cover, into the greenhouse and cold frames.

As the weeks go by, our remaining pots increasingly take centre stage. We collect them from the outer reaches of the garden and bring them into the courtyard and place them along paths around our front and back doors, and we create groups of small pots to raise up on our outdoor tables and our wellhead.

The whole tuberous (rather than annual) cosmos posse, including the chocolate-scented, almost-black *Cosmos atrosanguineus*, as well as its even longer-flowering pink cousin *C. peucedanifolius* 'Flamingo' (pictured on p352), are major favourites for the table outside the barn, which is a prominent part of our view directly south from the barn's huge windows. These both flower for several more weeks and, with stem ends seared in just-boiled water, they also provide beautiful and delicate-looking cut flowers for vases indoors.

As well as the table pots, we have several large edible plants that look good late in the year, offering structure amongst the lower-scale pots. There is our beloved kale 'Redbor' and more compact 'Curly Scarlet', which we love for pots at almost any time of year. And one of our most recent trials was of ten different fig trees all in pots (pictured on p222). While I admit we didn't get much fruit from them in their first year, I loved the way they looked in the middle of autumn, their great, hand-like leaves turning ochre, but not yet falling. They give a lush, generous scale and are a real October high point. *Ficus carica* 'Little Miss Figgy' has been bred to be compact and suitable for containers, but we found even the whopper classic, 'Brown Turkey', is good and handsome in a pot. With its roots restricted, it even gave us some fruit. That's the rule with figs: contain their roots and they'll fruit more generously.

We have lots of potted chillies at the start of the month, and I love them for their flavour and heat, but also for their autumn colour. We find *Capsicum annuum* 'Pearls', with its spinning-top-shaped fruit, one of the hardiest and we grow it not just to spice up food, but for its abundant elegance in a pot.

Previous page *Rhodochiton atrosanguineus* growing over a silver birch teepee with salvias around the base including *Salvia* 'Blue Note' and *S*. 'Dyson's Gem'.
Below The chilli pepper *Capsicum annuum* 'Pearls'.
Opposite Kale 'Curly Scarlet' growing in a pot on our veg bank, surrounded by *Dahlia* 'Bishop's Children' and nasturtiums.
Next page Climbers over the arches in the Perennial Cutting Garden including *Thunbergia alata* 'Sunny Susy Brownie' and *Cobaea scandens*, with *Dahlia* 'Dreamy Nights' in pots lining the path.

It needs to be moved into the greenhouse once night-time temperatures fall below 8°C (46°F), but the timing of that drop in temperature varies wildly here. We start to keep an obsessive eye on the weather forecast so we don't miss the turning point and fail to bring tender plants under cover, but we want them to look good outside for as long as we can push it.

I adore pomegranates in every possible way: I love the fruit, cut or whole, the juice, the tree itself, the plant's brilliant orange blossom and the fiery colour the leaves turn in the autumn. I have a dwarf form in a pot called *Punica granatum* var. *nana* and it's my pride and joy. As with the chillies, we need to keep an eagle eye on the weather so it's not left out when it gets too cold, though pomegranates are in fact hardier than one might imagine. Down the road, in a sheltered yard in the gardens of Great Dixter, there is a handsome, mature tree that has survived many years. It's beautiful, but I also adore my baby tree: it starts to form fruit every autumn, but at a bead-like size, they tend to drop off as the nights get cold.

I'd consider lemon verbena to be part of the edibles club for October. It flowers in July and August, its delicate white sprays forming a halo above its brilliant, zesty green leaves, which together with the airy seedheads, remain late into the year. As soon as you get a couple of cold nights in succession, the leaves yellow and drop, but if the pot is in the sheltered Dutch Yard or Rose Garden, this often isn't until November.

There are certain plants we cut back in August, giving them a good haircut to reduce their growth by about a third. These are often flowering away now, fit to burst. Our erigeron is pumping out flowers again, so we run a few pots down the centre of one of our outdoor dining tables. Even though garden lunches, let alone dinners, are no longer tempting, these look good in pride of place. We also have plenty of trailing verbenas in almost any colour you want, *Nemesia* 'Wisley Vanilla' and *Euphorbia hypericifolia* 'Diamond Frost', as well as the intense and beautiful, blue pimpernel, *Anagallis monellii*. These all give us strong and reliable tabletop pots in autumn.

Last but not least, I come to our number one October pot troupe: salvias. The late and long flowerers with a compact but elegant growing habit are, to me, the queens of the October pot garden, still flowery and impressive.

Salvias

Opposite Our whopper terracotta pots in the Dutch Yard with *Ipomoea batatas* 'SolarTower Black', *Nemesia* 'Boysenberry' (Fairy Kisses series) and *Salvia* 'Lake Garda'.

If I walk around my own or any other garden in October, the plants that shine out, covered in jewel-like flowers from ground to sky, are salvias. And even this late in the year they're buzzing with pollinators of all shapes and sizes. If they're not deadheaded and allowed to run to seed, you'll find the finches and tits paying regular visits to feast on the seeds too. We have long grown, and loved, *Salvia microphylla* and *S. greggii* forms amongst a range of smaller salvias for pots. Put together the brilliant pink *S. m.* 'Cerro Potosí' (named after the mountain in Mexico where plant hunter Jamie Compton found it), the vibrant red *S.* 'Jezebel' and the plum-purple *S.* 'Nachtvlinder' (which means 'night butterfly' in Dutch) and you have a pot that looks like a chest of jewels and flowers until November here with minimal TLC (pictured on p268).

Josie Lewis, our head gardener, and I both read that there was some evidence that underplanting with salvias helps to keep the roses free of fungal disease, including both black spot and powdery mildew. In 2017 we trialled this theory and carpeted our Rose Garden with small-leaved and relatively compact salvias as companion plants. We soon realised it worked, but we also noticed how long these plants flowered, even after the perpetual roses had given up for the year. That's when we started using them in our pots. They give huge value in terms of longevity and colour, on and on they go into late autumn, later than any other family of plants. There isn't a year that goes by when we don't use the three salvias I mentioned above, plus their pastel-coloured equivalents, such as *S.* 'Tutti Frutti', *S.* 'Peach Parfait' and *S. greggii* 'Stormy Pink'.

The *S. patens* varieties such as 'Cambridge Blue' and 'Guanajuato' are not as hardy as the stellar *S. microphylla* and *S. greggii* performers and, though velvety and jewel-like in their colour and texture, and also lovely in pots alone or in combinations, they start to look tired at this time of year.

Culinary sage, which flowers a bit and is very handsome in a pot, is not nearly as showy as these generously flowering forms.

There are also some excellent salvias that are just a bit too big for the average pot. One of my favourite garden varieties, *S. involucrata* 'Hadspen', is too tall for a pot, and *S.* 'Amistad' (pictured on p42) is a tad on the giant side, although we do grow them very successfully in our very long, very deep water troughs.

There isn't really a salvia I don't like and, luckily for us pot gardeners, there is an ever-increasing range that are perfectly suited to containers of a modest size. Top of the class for me are a whole new generation, recently bred in the Netherlands. They are in the Salgoon series (also called the Lake series), with most named after an international lake. We trialled nine varieties here recently and I fell in love with almost every one. They were stellar, performing despite a summer of extreme drought and heat, beautiful and healthy throughout, with soft-textured flowers in pure, saturated colours. They're around a third the size of 'Amistad', yet still graceful and elegant, without a hint of the stunted feel you sometimes get with small varieties of plants born to be tall. Our favourite was the twin to 'Amistad'

Below Salvias 'Kisses and Wishes', 'Lake Onega' and 'Blue Suede Shoes'.

in colour and texture, 'Lake Onega'. The even deeper purple 'Lake Baikal' was close behind in the intensity and duration of its performance, while the brilliant, plush magenta 'Strawberry Lake' and 'Lake Garda' were both superb.

In terms of design, I recommend planting these salvias with one of the tender perennial climbers that also perform well and flower at the same time from midsummer to late autumn. Varieties of the sweet potato vine, *Ipomea batatas*, are ideal, with their strong, bold leaves. You'll see lots of these planted with salvias at Perch Hill, still looking marvellous until at least the end of the month. The purple bell vine, *Rhodochiton atrosanguineus*, is also a perfect companion. For salvias in softer colours, we use *Thunbergia alata* 'African Sunset'.

All the salvias in the 'best of' list are easy, drought-tolerant plants on the edge of being hardy. In pots, they are more vulnerable to frost and winter cold than in the ground, so we do bring them in and store them frost-free over the coldest months. Most of the varieties have turned out to be easy to propagate bar the Salgoon/Lake series, which, certainly in the cold winter of 2022–2023, were tricky to keep going. We lost most of our plants and would take more care protecting them in future.

If I only had room for one troupe for my summer and autumn pots, dahlias, tender perennial climbers and compact salvias would each be front-runners. No pot garden should be without at least a few of all three in my view. You'd just be missing out!

Best of the salvias

Most of the salvias I recommend for pots are around a metre in height or less. 'Amante' and 'Amistad' are glamorous and velvety beauties, and we occasionally use Salvia curviflora in pots with dahlias, but these three are on the tall side for most containers.

Rich and Bright

These are a selection of jewel-like salvias, covering colours from palettes 1 and 2 (see p26 and p28).

1 *Salvia* 'Blue Note'
A classic and now widely available variety that has sapphire-blue flowers – lots and lots of them. This is just the right size for a medium pot and is near the top of my list.

2 *S.* 'Dyson's Crimson'
Compact, small-leaved and highly aromatic, this is one we first chose for underplanting our roses. It's tricky to find, so if you do grow it, it's important to look after your plants and take cuttings from one year to the next.

3 *S. greggii* Mirage series
'Mirage Deep Purple' is the amethyst-coloured brother to 'Blue Note', both are hugely reliable with a five- or six-month flowering season. The harder to find 'Dyson's Gem' is almost identical in colour, habit and scale. 'Mirage Neon Rose' (pictured) has fuchsia to coral flowers that have a large bottom lip. It's covered densely with flowers all summer and autumn.

4 *S.* 'Jezebel'
This has zingy red flowers that stand out strongly from darker red calyces and stems.

5 *S.* Lips series
I sometimes spend Christmas in London and always have a beady eye on other people's gardens as I walk around. I've spotted the following three salvias flowering happily

right through the winter, admittedly in the ground rather than a pot, but they just seem to flower without a break. 'Amethyst Lips' is purple and white, 'Cherry Lips' (pictured) is deep pink and white, and 'Hot Lips' is red and white. 'Hot Lips' was the first one in this crew to be released and it's the one I'm least keen on – the contrast of red and white is a little too strong for me, but it is an incredible doer.

6 *S. microphylla* 'Cerro Potosí'
Brilliant pink, with larger flowers than most and exceptionally long-flowering, 'Cerro Potosí' is one we've grown at Perch Hill for over ten years and it's still in our top five salvias, despite lots of newcomers.

7 *S.* 'Nachtvlinder'
One of our favourites at Perch Hill, with soft, velvety flowers in the deepest plum purple. Its flowers are small, but there are so many of them.

8 *S.* Rockin' series
Another new series that's hugely long-flowering. 'Blue Suede Shoes' (pictured) is bright blue with bright green serrated leaves forming a good contrast. 'Fuchsia' is a stunning colour, but not as strong growing as the blue form.

9 *S.* 'Royal Bumble'
Similar in tone to 'Jezebel', but a deeper red. Both flower for similar lengths of time and have similar branching, flowery habits.

10 *S.* Salgoon series
A brand-new series (also known as the Lake series) bred for pot growing. These varieties are just the right size, less than half the height of 'Amistad' and 'Amante', but with similar tubular-shaped flowers. They come in different sizes to suit different containers, from tall to compact. 'Lake Garda' is a brilliant pink, long-flowering and only 40cm (16in). 'Lake Onega' matches 'Amistad' in colour and is beautiful with it. 'Strawberry Lake' (pictured) is another pink, one tone softer than 'Lake Garda' and seems to be a little hardier. These have become our top-ranking favourite at Perch Hill. Many salvias are brilliant for pots, these are truly exceptional for length of season and size of flowers.

11 *S. splendens* × *darcyi* 'Roman Red'
I love to have this at our doorstep in summer and autumn. It is as covered in flowers when we bring it under cover in late autumn as it is when we plant it.

12 *S.* Wishes series
As its name implies, 'Ember's Wish' is like orange and red burning embers. 'Love and Wishes' (pictured) is one of my favourites: it's slightly taller and looser in habit than most of the others here, with plush-textured flowers in a delicious wine purple. Very similar and almost interchangeable with 'Salmia Dark Purple'.

Soft and Pale

This selection covers cool and warm pastel colours from palettes 3 and 4 (see p30 and p32). These all grow less than a metre tall.

1 *Salvia greggii* 'Icing Sugar'
This has a dense covering of mid-pink flowers that look as though they've been dusted with icing. It glistens and sparkles, in a good way.

2 *S. greggii* 'Mirage Cream'
This one is in the excellent Mirage series and its flower colour is like a very milky latte. It's similar to 'Peach Parfait', but it is quite short at around 35cm (14in).

3 *S. greggii* 'Stormy Pink'
The softest pink of any we've trialled – a true sugared almond colour – and one of the tallest of the pale-flowered forms. This is similar to 'Krystle Pink' in its hue. 'Mirage Soft Pink' is also similar, if one tone cooler and a bit shorter.

4 *S. × jamensis* 'Sierra San Antonio'
A rather lovely peach melba colour, which goes well with soft-coloured dahlias such as 'Kelsey Annie Joy' and 'Happy Single Date', as well as being a good match for *Thunbergia alata* 'African Sunset' as a frilly skirt in pots.

5 *S. × jamensis* 'Trebah'
It's useful to grow a pure white, or almost white, salvia as it mixes so well with other soft-coloured, pastel-toned plants. This has just a touch of pink through it.

6 *S.* 'Kisses and Wishes'
This is in the great Wishes series and has larger flowers than the other varieties in this palette. It's more upright, too, with less bushy growth. One of my favourites.

7 *S.* 'Tutti Frutti'
There's a beautiful contrast between the plum calyx and mid- to soft-pink flowers.

Best of the long and late performers

As well as salvias, tender perennial climbers and dahlias, there are some invaluable plants that keep our pot garden looking good throughout October. Small containers of trailing verbenas, arctotis, bidens and the good old, reliable argyranthemum look as good as the day they came into flower in June. After 30 years of trialling, here are the long performers I recommend.

1 *Anagallis monellii*
Blue pimpernel looks as fresh as a daisy late in the year. The cultivated form has larger, more saucer-like flowers than the wild one, which you'll see dotting wasteland and sand dunes in the Mediterranean. This makes it even more striking and showy, but no less reliable or drought tolerant. It's the blue cousin of our glamorous British wildflower, scarlet pimpernel (*Anagallis arvensis*). These plants flower for at least three months solid and, with many varieties, you can almost double that.

2 *Arctotis*
I've long loved these late summer and autumn performers. With their silvery, felted leaves and large flowers, they're striking, but they're also useful – brilliant in both heat and drought, needing minimal TLC. *A. × hybrida* 'Flame' is a beautiful warm terracotta and 'Wine' (pictured) is a lovely smoky pink with a dash of deep red.

3 *Argyranthemum*
Some of these can be on the dull side, making overly neat domes of single daisy flowers that have a slightly plastic look about them, but there are some great exceptions. The Grandaisy series, including 'Grandaisy Deep Red' (pictured), with its classic Catherine-wheel-style flowers, is a winner, as are the semi-doubles and doubles such as 'Madeira Crested Merlot'. It's late in the season when these truly come into their own.

4 *Bidens*
There seem to be quite a lot of daises in this late-performing club and here is another one. It comes in a wonderful intense selection of mahogany, oranges and yellows. I remember a dire wet day in November when we were running a course on colour in the garden – it felt rather ironic, the lack of it. We had several pots of bidens, which we promptly brought in and put in pride of place. It's remarkable for its late colour, flowering well after almost everything else in the garden. I love the saturated-coloured ones, like 'Spicy Margarita' and 'Hot and Spicy' (pictured).

5 *Brachyscome*
There are lots of these in blue and white, my favourite being the intense 'Blue Star'. I see these flowering away in Hastings, the seaside town near us on the Sussex coast, where even blasted by salt winds they flower all summer and autumn, still blooming on Christmas Day in sheltered yards.

6 *Chaenostoma*
Commonly known as bacopa, this is not generally thought of as the most glamourous family of plants, with mini, trailing vines of small flowers in pastel colours (the white, *Chaenostoma cordatum* 'Snowflake', is the most widely seen), but my neighbour in London has this in a window box on a deep ledge and I now take it seriously, as I see it flowering twelve months

of the year. We use it in a large, low pot on a table in the middle of our lawn. It's paired with *Dichondra argentea* 'Silver Falls' and *Festuca glauca*. This is as low maintenance as it gets!

7 *Cobaea scandens*
We go on picking from our cup and saucer vines until December in mild years. They're guaranteed late-season performers. The purple form seems hardier and more robust than the white *C. scandens* f. *alba* (pictured). See p334 for more on cobaea.

8 *Dianthus* 'Green trick'
This dianthus is a great foliage accompaniment to any of these late-season pot plants. It's an unusual plant with fresh green drumstick pompoms that aren't true flowers. That means it's

sterile, so it just goes on and on. It's pictured here with *Erigeron karvinskianus*.

9 *Erigeron karvinskianus*
No garden should be without this excellent daisy-flowered plant, which flowers on and off from April and prolifically sets seed. It's a very low maintenance, able to grow from cracks in walls and paths.

10 *Fuchsia*
Fuchsia microphylla forms with delicate flowers and leaves are late-season stalwarts, which can keep flowering right through the winter if brought into the greenhouse out of the worst of the wet and cold. *F.* 'Dying Embers' (pictured) is a favourite, with hanging bells that have an aubergine-coloured corolla and dusky red sepals. Lovely!

11 *Hydrangea*
Hydrangea paniculata 'Little Lime' (pictured) still looks good now and I love the larger *H. macrophylla* 'Wedding Gown' for this time of year. Its flowers are lacy and elegant, starting off ivory, turning greenish and finally flushing with a deep red that turns almost slate grey by this stage in the year. This needs a large pot.

12 *Ipomoea*
Ipomoea lobata is starting to struggle with the rain now, but the foliage forms (*I. batatas* 'SolarTower Black', for example, pictured) carry on looking perky until the first hard frost. There's nothing better in pots with salvias this late in the year.

13 *Osteospermum*
African daisies are not just drought tolerant, but also good for flowering until they hit frost. I love their firework flowers in the richer shades. New ones appear every year, such as the compact winner 'Purple Sun' (pair it with a foliage plant like *Coleus* 'FlameThrower Salsa Roja', pictured). We try not to get too hung up on one variety, as they come and go a bit, but truly, every one we've tried has been good value.

14 *Pelargonium*
It's often the ivy-leaved forms such as 'April Hamilton' and 'Surcouf' (pictured) which carry on flowering outdoors right up until the first frost. They'll need to be brought indoors once the cold weather sets in, but then they make great houseplants. The scented-leaf *P. tomentosum* and *P. quercifolium* also look good through autumn and winter under cover.

15 *Penstemon*
The varieties in the Pensham series have done particularly well in our trials, with the mid-pink 'Just Jayne' the longest performing of all. My parents grew 'Garnet' (syn. 'Andenken an Friedrich Hahn') sixty years ago in their garden and we still have this one in pots here (pictured), flowering until very late.

16 *Rhodochiton atrosanguineus*
The purple bell vine is slow to get going and reaches its best moment in August or September, even from a February sowing, but then flowers well, with great elegance, until cut down by a hard frost. This is one of the few things I love growing in a hanging basket, its delicate vines beautifully cascading lightly from a height.

17 *Rudbeckia*
I love a pot full of the short-lived perennial varieties, such as *Rudbeckia hirta* 'Sahara' (pictured), with its semi-double flowers in a palette of colours, from milky coffee and soft lime to mahogany and crimson. Famously late flowering.

18 *Scaevola*
Scaevola are invaluable at this time, their trailing curtains growing down the sides of their pots and sprawling outwards at ground level. I'm so impressed by this family, particularly late in the year. We find the mauve-blue forms of the popular fan flower (such as 'Dream Blue', pictured) look good for longest, with new buds still forming well into November. This is a classic Spiller for

a pot (see p43). Plant on its own or mix with a compact dahlia such as 'Abigail'.

19 *Thunbergia*
Another in the climber brigade. They're all still looking good, including the one we use the most, *Thunbergia alata* 'African Sunset' (pictured) and 'Orange Diverse', the longest performing in our most recent trial, flowering four weeks beyond the others until almost Christmas.

20 *Verbena*
Verbenas are great late in the year. I wrote about the pink 'Sissinghurst' in July (see p236), but you can pick almost any. The tender perennial Endurascape series has been developed for road and roundabout landscaping and bred to be low-maintenance, high performance. And there's also the seed-grown *Verbena rigida*, or the compact *V. bonariensis* 'Lollipop', as well as *V.* 'Showboat Crimson Velvet' (pictured). When they do eventually finish flowering, the birds love to feast on the seed.

Plants for pollinators throughout the year

There are some fantastic plants that are busy with bees and butterflies for all months of the year, but crucially at times when there's generally a dearth of pollinator food – early and late in the year. This is the list of exceptional, pollinator-friendly plants that we always try to include in our pot garden.

1 *Agastache*
All hyssops are great for pollinators and most flower long and late. Favourites with us for pots are *Agastache pallidiflora* 'Rose Mint' and *A. aurantiaca*, but there are so many good ones, almost any will do!

2 *Allium tuberosum*
All alliums are fantastic for pollinators, but the majority are a bit too large for pots and they have messy looking leaves that make them far from ideal for containers, but we find garlic chives a great exception. It flowers long and late. If you cut it back after its first early summer flowering, you'll get another flush to keep you going until mid-autumn at least. Whenever I walk past our pots, they're humming with bees.

3 *Antirrhinum*
Good old traditional snapdragons are often busy with bees in our garden. As long-flowering tender perennials, they are definitely pot-worthy and I love growing a mix of colours from the same palette in one large container. Alternatively, go for one colour with a splash of a contrasting hue and follow the Bride, Bridesmaid, Gatecrasher rule (see p38). The deep crimson 'Opus Red Beauty' is pictured.

4 *Borago*
Borage is excellent for pollinators early or late in the year. It is a hardy annual which, if sown inside in February, can be in flower by April; and if sown in July, flowers from September right through to winter. Its foliage looks less scraggy if it avoids the summer heat, making it

extra pot-worthy. All parts of the plant are edible, with the flowers often used to decorate ice cubes and drinks.

5 *Buddleja*
The butterfly bush *Buddleja davidii* is an obvious option for pollinators, but is too large and thuggish for pots. More compact forms (still perfumed, drought tolerant and needing minimal TLC) are now available and we grow 'Hot Raspberry', 'Buzz White', 'Buzz Wine' and 'Buzz Indigo' (pictured), as well as one in the Dreaming series ('Dreaming Lavender') that has been growing happily in a large pot for over five years. Highly recommend.

6 *Caryopteris*
Pollinators can be short of food late in the year when most of our wild and garden

flowers are over, so anything guaranteed to be a rich nectar source at that time has enhanced value. That's true of caryopteris. I love the contrast between its silvery leaves and blue flowers, made all the richer in new forms such as *C. × clandonensis* 'First Choice' (pictured), which is also compact and neat for pots.

7 *Cerinthe major* 'Purpurascens'
We try to do a second, and even third, sowing of cerinthe for late-season pots. It's such an easy and elegant plant (though needs a bit of staking) and, as a hardy annual, will put up with some winter cold. Its common name is honeywort and it is indeed stacked with nectar at the apex of each of its purple bells.

8 *Cosmos*

I think cosmos has pretty much everything going for it: it's an easy-to-grow half-hardy annual, it's cut-and-come-again (so great for vases), it's stacked with pollen, and it flowers long and hard all through summer and much of autumn. The cut flower varieties such as 'Purity' and 'Dazzler' are on the tall side for pots, so we grow 'Rubenza', 'Sonata White' (pictured), 'Apricotta', 'Xanthos' and 'Xsenia'. They are all under a metre tall so only need light (if any) support.

9 *Dahlia*

The Single, Collarette and Anemone-flowered varieties win the pollinator's vote. 'Sarah Raven' has the most abundant pollen of any amongst our 100 or so varieties, dripping with it when the sun is shining. Pictured here is 'Bishop of York'.

10 *Digitalis*

The standard white and pastel coloured foxgloves (such as *Digitalis purpurea* 'Sutton's Apricot') are great for pots during the May gap, but they're tall, so the pot needs to be substantial. Even better for containers are the compact and newly bred *D. × valinii* 'Foxlight Ruby Glow' (pictured) and the glamorous *D. lanata*

'Café Crème', *D. parviflora* 'Milk Chocolate' and *D. ferruginea*, which has copper spires that look like they've been carved from wood. As soon as the sun's out, these are heaving with bees working the spire from the bottom up.

11 *Echinacea*
There's been much breeding of these short-lived perennials and there are plenty suitable for containers. We love 'Green Envy' and 'Sombrero Hot Coral', which both seem to live for two to three years and then fade. For truly perennial pots, there are the classics such as 'Magnus' (pictured).

12 *Fritillaria*
Turn a *Fritillaria imperialis* (pictured) flower upside down and look right into the apex of the flower and there you'll see great droplets of nectar. I love each and every one in a pot and, as long as you give them moist soil in dappled shade, they'll grow happily from one year to the next. Keep your eyes peeled for lily beetle and remove them – fritillaries are cousins of lilies and can be the first spring host for these pests.

13 *Helianthus*
You'll see bees rolling around in the pollen of sunflowers, literally coating themselves in gold. Most varieties are full of protein-rich seeds and so they are ideal for birds too. They tend to be a bit tall and towering for pots, but we grow the annual varieties *Helianthus annuus* 'Sonja', 'Ms Mars' (pictured) and 'Micro Sun' for pots, which all come in under 90cm (3ft).

14 *Heliotropium*
Not only are heliotropes deliciously scented, but they are also a big favourite with butterflies and bees. The one we grow most for pots is 'Reva' (pictured), a much stronger, taller and flowerier option than 'Marine', which is most commonly found in garden centres.

15 *Iris*
Transient in their flowering, irises don't usually make the grade for pots, but you can forgive them their fleetingness for their exceptional beauty and texture and their early flowers, when there's so little around. That's why we grow rafts of *Iris reticulata* (such as 'Alida', pictured) and *I. histrioides*, which flower in February. Another one we adore here for a wet habitat is the water iris 'Black Gamecock', which likes its roots covered in up to 5cm (2in) of water. We have this planted in an old tin bath and, when watering the other pots, we refresh it every few days.

16 *Lavandula*

There isn't a lavender that butterflies and bees don't love. We've got a pot lavender trial in progress as I write this book, with lots of the more compact varieties such as 'Hidcote' and 'Miss Muffett' (pictured), planted up and doing well. But you can go tall, too, to give your pots an upper storey: try French lavenders, *Lavandula dentata* or the super showy *L. stoechas* forms.

17 *Papaver*

Papaver rhoeas 'Amazing Grey' (pictured) is a new form that is ethereal in its beauty, and we love the biennial Iceland poppy *P. nudicaule* for early spring pots that start off in the greenhouse. They are so generous with pollen that you can sit and watch several bees at a time in the flowers.

18 *Primula*

Flowering from February, sometimes even earlier, the polyanthus crew are invaluable for pollinators in the first few months of the year when the queen bumble bees are emerging from hibernation. The polyanthus 'Stella Lilac' (pictured) is a favourite for pots, but there are so many to choose from (see p59). They thrive in dappled shade.

19 *Rudbeckia*

As well as offering fantastic late-season colour, rudbeckias are also a great source of both pollen and nectar, and the birds love their seeds. For pots, I particularly love *Rudbeckia hirta* 'Cherry Brandy', which is easy to grow from seed.

20 *Salvia*

Select any of the more compact salvias for great colour combinations in pots for summer and autumn (see p355) or go for one of the whoppers such as 'Amistad' (pictured) as the crowning glory of a truly enormous pot.

21 *Scabiosa*

Famously good for butterflies and bees, scabiosa excels, though some types are longer flowering than others. *Scabiosa columbaria* 'Flutter Rose Pink' goes on and on through summer and autumn and, compact, is ideal for a pot, as is *S. atropurpurea* 'Blue Cushion' (pictured).

22 *Tagetes*

We mainly grow *Tagetes patula* 'Burning Embers', 'Bo Jangle' (pictured) and 'Konstance' for our pots. The first and second are single-flowered French marigolds, the third a double; all are constantly busy with butterflies and bees. As half-hardy annuals, they flower from June to November in a mild autumn. We grow them (like salvias) as companion plants. They help to control aphid infestations (great with tomatoes in a greenhouse) and their flowers are edible.

23 *Tithonia*

With their spectacular plateau-like orange flowers, Mexican sunflowers are much-loved by butterflies as they provide steady landing and feeding pads. On the tall side, growing to 1.8m (6ft), these will need staking in a pot, but mixed with dahlias they give wonderful late summer and autumn colour. Or grow the shorter *Tithonia rotundifolia* 'Fiesta del Sol' (pictured), which is about 1m (3ft).

24 *Verbena*

The whole verbena clan are fantastic plants for wildlife. Their flowers are stacked with nectar and their seeds are favourites for many birds including goldfinches. *Verbena bonariensis* 'Lollipop' grows to under a metre, making it ideal for an upper storey in a pot. And we grow lots of the compact and hugely floriferous *V. rigida*. These are first-year-flowering perennials that are easy to grow from seed.

October

October is a busy month in the pot garden, with the emphasis shifting from revelling in how your pots are looking and keeping them going for as long as you can, to making preparations for next year. Even deadheading is tailing off as autumn truly sets in, while watering can almost always come to an end. Feeding becomes less important too, as pot combinations tire and the flowering season of even dahlias begins to wrap up.

Bulb planting is our major October task, as well as planting pot toppers over the bulbs to give their roots a chance to get down and grow before the true winter freeze. A pot topper is as it sounds, the plant that forms the surface layer in a winter container through which bulbs are planted below.

October is also the time to dig up plants and bulbs from the garden for our pots, either to force under cover or simply to have raised on our outdoor tables and doorsteps for winter flowers. Perennials such as hellebores, primroses, polyanthus and clumps of aconites and snowdrops are all ideal in this role. Dig up small clumps, particularly from hidden areas where you won't miss them, and pot them into handsome terracotta or zinc containers.

For the early-flowering varieties of hellebore, such as *Helleborus* × *ballardiae* 'Maestro' and *H.* × *b.* 'Merlin', as well as one or two plants you might want to bring inside for Christmas, such as *H. niger*, you need to cut back the leaves now, as you pot them. Cutting off all the leaves limits the spread of the fungal infection black spot, one of the few afflictions with which hellebores suffer. Be careful not to damage any emerging flower buds as you cut the leaves off. Pot them up into compost enriched with well-rotted farmyard manure or homemade compost, water and firm them in well.

Planting Bulbs in Pots

As with the rest of autumn, this is another big month of bulb planting. We wait until November and December to plant our tulips in pots as late planting seems to really help prevent tulip fire (blight). But any hyacinths or narcissi that are not already in their containers need to be planted now, as well as any smaller-scale bulbs such as muscari, crocus and iris. We use lots of the last two here as pot toppers over bulb lasagnes, and lots of all three for our smaller pots and window boxes.

- Fill pots ¾ full with peat-free compost.
- Cram the bulbs into the pot so that they are almost, but not quite, touching. To get something looking spectacular, we plant at twice the density we would in the garden, so rather than twice the width of the bulb, space them out at just one width of the bulb. And if we have plenty, we plant in at least a double layer.
- These bulbs all need a spell in the cold (at a temperature below 10°C/50°F) for

Previous page Dismantling pots of half-hardy annuals (including *Panicum* 'Frosted Explosion') to make room for bulb lasagnes.

Opposite Planting a bulb lasagne in a black plastic inner pot, with *Viola* 'Tiger Eye Red' as a pot topper forming the final layer.

12–15 weeks. Put them in a cold frame, or if you don't have one, just leave them outside. They need this cold phase to develop their root systems before the demands of flowering.

- Check them every couple of weeks to see if they're starting to sprout. When you see they are sprouting, move them somewhere warmer (into a greenhouse) if you want to force them on for earlier flowering, or just leave them where they are for flowering slightly later.

Planting Pot Toppers

We used to leave the tops of all our pots bare, but then it occurred to us, we don't need to look at a sea of brown compost from October to April, we could just grow *more* plants. So now I've tried to train myself into seeing soil/compost as an opportunity – if I spot a patch of brown, I think, why aren't we growing things to enjoy in that space from autumn to spring? See p118 for my favourite pot toppers.

Now is the moment to start planting these toppers over all your bulbs except tulips. It's too early to plant tulips, so make sure you reserve some plants for your tulip pots and lasagnes in November.

If you have perennials such as hellebores, cardoons and heucheras, as well as biennials such as wallflowers and the black-leaved cow parsley, *Anthriscus sylvestris* 'Ravenswing', in your garden, you can dig a few plants up and transplant to pots around this time of year.

You might also have seedlings from plants like violas sown in September (see p341), these need to be planted out now too.

How to plant pot toppers

- Finish your medium and large pots off with a top layer of 10cm (4in) of multipurpose, peat-free compost. This stops weed seed germination, which sometimes happens with manure. Fill to the final level, which should be 3–4cm (1–1½in) below the pot rim.
- Plant pot topper seedlings/plants into this, just as you would into the soil in the ground.
- If you can move the pots, rock them a little to settle the compost, but if too big, this is not essential.
- Once your planting is done, water in well. Add labels to the pot edge.

November
& December

It's changeover time again for all our main pots at Perch Hill. Depending on the weather, autumn may go on for a few weeks yet, but inevitably the dahlia and climber combinations start to look past their best and will need to be taken apart in the first weeks of winter. In the garden borders we mulch the dahlia crowns deeply and leave them where they are. With the protection of the compost, we find they almost always survive, but in a pot the cold can get at all sides and the tubers are more vulnerable to frost. The potted tubers need to come in and be dried and wrapped before being stored until spring.

Pelargoniums aren't safe outside in pots either, so some come into the house and onto our window ledges and the rest are stored in the polytunnel or greenhouse. There are certain varieties of pelargonium that keep flowering until Christmas and can take centre stage in the house – I have a great fondness for these. Chunky, strong and a favourite here for winter is the ever-flowering 'Aurora'. I often have a large pot of that in pride of place in our bedroom for uplifting winter cheer. The ivy-leaved pelargoniums, such as 'Surcouf', 'April Hamilton' and 'Tommy' are also reliable late performers, so they come in to trail over deep window ledges or from the tiers of one of our plant theatres. And I love the long- and late-flowering 'Kewensis', with its open, starry, coral-red flowers, which cut well too.

On a table in my work room I have a few truly bright ones, like 'Kewensis', set against varieties such as 'Tommy' (with plush, almost black flowers), 'Chocolate Peppermint'

Previous page A basket of forced, fragrant paperwhite narcissus.

(with crimson-centred, green-scented leaves) or the delicate, ferny, *P. denticulatum* 'Filicifolium'. I also like combining these with large pots of the shade-tolerant *P. tomentosum* and the elegant *Begonia* 'Gryphon', which has beautiful marbled foliage. Both make the best winter houseplants, even in a dark corner, and are guaranteed to go on looking good inside all winter with minimal TLC.

We have established 'houseplant watering Friday': a fixed day is the best way to remember to water indoor plants every week, though with pelargoniums now moving into dormancy, you only need to water every other week and, even then, just a minimal amount.

Jewel-like nerines join the pelargoniums in the house. We did a trial of nerines that are good for pots and found that a new generation, such as *Nerine bowdenii* 'Mister John' and 'Mister Nick', came out on top for showiness and length of indoor flowering. Unlike the more traditional varieties, these have been bred to be quick to flower within a couple of years of propagation. They need a little support from a few silver birch twigs to keep them looking their best, but they are heat and drought tolerant, so ideal for bringing inside over winter. When the flowers go over and they start to die back in the run up to Christmas, they go under the bench in the greenhouse until they start to shoot in late spring. We then bring them out and – along with everything else – give them an occasional watering.

I also love the dry shade plant, *Plectranthus ciliatus* 'Nico', which comes in for protection from the frost. Its dark green leaves with jewel-like purple on the reverse are almost indestructible. And I have to mention the vast, hand-like leaves of *Geranium maderense* (giant herb Robert). This is not in flower now (it flowers in May and June), but it is still hugely handsome and statuesque for the winter.

We have a few whopper pots with giant tender plants that need to come in now too. My favourite is *Sparrmannia africana* (African hemp). I remember seeing these used as Christmas trees in the window of homeware store The Conran Shop 20-odd years ago and I thought it was such a stylish idea. The huge, bright green, lily-pad leaves hold well into the new year if you can keep the plants frost-free, and they give a great sense of green abundance – so much more elegant than any rubbery houseplant in my view. We bring at least one large pot of this in to join *Fuchsia paniculata*, which is giant by now. Propagated in the spring, this fuchsia reaches 1.5m (5ft) if you let it. By the start of winter its flowers are replaced by slate-blue berries in upright, grape-like clusters. I love it.

Smaller in scale and so more manageable are a couple of other fuchsias. One is 'Dying Embers' (about 1m/3ft tall), the other the delicate and miniature *Fuchsia microphylla* subsp. *hemsleyana* 'Silver Lining'. Both seem to flower endlessly, even in winter. These can come outside onto window ledges or stand in sunny doorsteps, but you need to be ready to bring them in if severely cold weather is forecast. And for those who love bold and architectural plants, the succulent *Echeveria lilacina* is a winner and can slot into even the smallest space – it takes no looking after, just make sure it gets sun. I love this threaded with strings of mini-lights to brighten a side table.

You need a large room or space in a porch, greenhouse or conservatory to store many of these plants and keep them safe, but they make for glamorous interiors. We have a collection in our kitchen/living room which makes it feel full of life right through winter. That's important to me.

Below The ever-flowering *Pelargonium* 'Aurora'.
Next page A collection of jewel-coloured pelargoniums – invaluable for life-enhancing winter pots inside.

Opposite Pots of the Christmas
rose, *Helleborus niger*, which is so
nice as a temporary resident inside.

For colour, flowers and fragrance, forced bulbs in pots bring
extra pizzazz inside at this time of year and until the spring.
Paperwhite daffodils are the quickest and easiest to force into
flower from November and their perfume is marvellous. That's
my view. Josie (our head gardener) hates the scent – apparently
how one perceives their fragrance is genetic. Fragrance aside,
I like paperwhites to look simple in a terracotta or zinc pot,
five or seven bulbs to a pot, with a carpet of moss and some
supporting twigs to give them instant presence in a room.
These can be joined by the first of the forced hyacinths and
amaryllis in the weeks building up to Christmas.

Rather than having a pot exodus, with everything coming
under cover, it's important to have a few things which carry
on outdoors and can be brought into prominent places for
winter cheer and interest on doorsteps, balconies and in sunny
yards. That's where truly hardy plants come in. There are a few
evergreens that we use to give some bones to our pot display.
I'm not so keen on dwarf conifers (my father had a passion for
these in the 1970s, and I wasn't sure then and remain unsure
now), and I think box balls are a bit unimaginative. Instead,
I love potted rosemary for its relaxed shapes, scent and the
fact that we can also use it in the kitchen. *Salvia rosmarinus*
Prostratus Group (syn. *Rosmarinus officinalis*) is a winner for a
pot and we combine it with potted sarcococca and compact
crimson-leaved pittosporums. We've just trialled *Pittosporum
tenuifolium* 'Breebay' and loved it, both for winter form and for
picking the odd sprig for a vase. It's another evergreen that
needs almost zero maintenance.

For hardy flower-givers, there are of course early-flowering
hellebores. We grow *Helleborus* × *ballardiae* 'Maestro', a deeply
glamorous plant with slate-grey-blue flowers that become slate-
grey-burgundy as they develop. This flowers from November
until the spring. I'm equally keen on *H.* × *sahinii* 'Winterbells',
which is widely sold in Scandinavia as a houseplant, but is
happier outside and its green clusters of bells are invaluable
for winter beauty and food for late-season pollinators.

The so-called Christmas rose, *H. niger*, flowers naturally now
too, with 'Potter's Wheel' a good, large-flowered variety and
'Snowdrift' a new semi-double with an extra ruffle of petals
(like a Collarette dahlia) at the centre of pure white flowers.
We have a few of these in pots for winter on the doorstep.

They can come inside for a week or so, but need the outdoor cold to maximise their length of flowering.

Add to these some early potted snowdrops such as *Galanthus elwesii*, which can be easily forced for December, and a smattering of the small-flowered violas and polyanthus (such as *Primula* 'Lilac Lace'), and you can collect together a good petite outdoor windowsill collection.

Flowers and colour for your winter pots might be a bit sparse out of the main growing season, but if you have a few reliable plants up your sleeve, it's still a realistic aim.

Bulbs for forcing

At this time of year, it's all about decorating our home with pots, and this becomes increasingly important as Christmas approaches. The simplest way to do this is with forced or naturally early-flowering bulbs. Forcing means you trick the plant into thinking it's been through winter by giving it a period of out-of-season cold. It is then induced to flower a few weeks earlier than its natural flowering time. You can buy so-called 'prepared' bulbs where this cold treatment has already been done, or you can do it yourself by putting the bulbs in the bottom of the fridge for about a month before planting.

We have a succession of plants to take us through the winter from November until March. The easiest to start with are paperwhite daffodils (see p401). Unlike other narcissi, they don't require chilling to promote flower production, so they're the best to kick off with.

Then we move onto hyacinths (see p67 and p343). These take us from Christmas into the new year. By this stage, other daffodils can be easily forced (such as 'Tête-à-tête', 'Cragford' and 'Avalanche') and we mass them with early crocus, miniature iris and muscari on plant theatres and tables, indoors and out. If a very cold night is forecast, we cover them with fleece or bring them in overnight.

And finally we have amaryllis (see p344 and p393), which we store from one year to the next so that the bulbs slowly increase in size. With every year of growing and storing, you add to the girth of the bulb and, with that, the number of flower stems and the number of flowers at the top of each stem. Year on year, these become more and more impressive. It's worth the effort, so don't be tempted to chuck them.

Amaryllis

Opposite *Hippeastrum* 'Nymph', which is even better planted three bulbs to a pot. This pot flowered for a three-month stretch.

The bulb most relevant to pot growing in the weeks building up to Christmas is hippeastrum, more widely known as amaryllis. I'm never entirely sure that I'd be as keen on these if they flowered at any other time of year, but the fact that they are easily induced to flower for winter and early spring sways me – as does the extraordinary length of flowering of some varieties.

Those of you that like the petite, dainty and delicate just aren't going to be fans of amaryllis. Everything is big about them: their balloon-like bulbs, their chunky, hollow stems and their tuba-like flowers, which stand tall and proud.

What we've found from our trials is that the doubles flower for almost twice as long as the single forms (which is common with other plants, such as tulips). With tulips, it's because the nectaries have been bred into second petaloids and so the flowers don't draw in pollinators and are never pollinated. They keep flowering on and on in the hope that an insect will fertilise the flowers and their reproduction job will be done, but this crucial step never occurs.

I imagine it's the same for amaryllis – and it makes for supremely impressive and worthwhile plants. We had a pot of three 'Nymph' bulbs (which has white petals softly marked with pink) last winter and it flowered for three months. My favourite spot for this is in our guest room where the curvy fullness of these flowers matches the floral wallpaper. It would be hard to beat at any time of year, but the fact that this is in winter, bowls over whoever sees it.

To keep them flowering well, keep them out of direct sunlight once in flower, and try to keep them slightly cool. Then as each flower fades, cut it off individually, leaving the others to bloom. See p344 for forcing amaryllis and instructions for storing the bulbs.

Best of the amaryllis

You'll see from my selection that I'm not keen on the classic scarlet reds you see on the high street in the build up to Christmas. And the peach amaryllis are fine in spring, but jar for me in December, so these are omitted too. The deep, dark reds, whites and greens are more my thing – much classier in my view.

1 *Hippeastrum* 'Alfresco'
Lovely double white petals with a green wash. Elegant and slightly scented.

2 *H.* 'Emerald'
One of finest of all varieties with the most natural-looking flowers in green, with just faint markings of crimson. This is the most fleeting in its flowering.

3 *H.* 'Green Magic'
Truly beautiful and magnificent, this is probably my all-round favourite. It has huge flowers and lots of them, but in the most subtle green that's washed lightly with wine red.

4 *H.* 'Lemon Lime'
A gentle eau de nil green-grey rather than a bright lime, despite the name. I fell on this when I first saw it filling a vast greenhouse in the Netherlands. It was so distinct and stood out a mile away for its classy, subtle colours. I still love it.

5 *H.* 'Lemon Star'
This has pure white petals with a pretty lime-green throat. It's what I think of as a bit of a classic.

6 *H.* 'Mandela'
Various varieties of very dark burgundy amaryllis have come onto the market since I started growing them about 30 years ago. This relatively new one is superb, with crimson buds followed by the plushest flowers you'll find. Perfect for Christmas. It's slightly shorter and less top-heavy than some of the others, so only needs very minimal (if any) support.

7 *H.* 'Marilyn'
A double white, with shorter stems than most. I used to think this was a disadvantage, but in fact I find it useful as it doesn't need staking like many of the rest.

8 *H.* 'Nymph'
The flowers have an ivory base with green and red stipples and stripes, but only lightly and prettily. Outstandingly long-flowering in our trials.

9 *H. papilio*
Indeed, like a tropical butterfly, as its name implies. This has a green base with light wine-red stipples, with the same delicious mix of colours as 'Tosca', but more green, less crimson and so lighter with it.

10 *H.* 'Picotee'
A pure, fresh white with just the lightest red eyeliner edge to each petal and a slight sparkle, which to me suits Christmas perfectly.

11 *H.* 'Tosca'
One of my favourites. It has a deep red throat fading out beautifully as it reaches the green petal edge. Impressive.

November & December

The year might be drawing to a close, but it's not yet time to hang up your trowel in the pot garden. One of the main jobs of the whole year – planting tulips – happens now.

I've always recommended planting tulips late in the year, but with increasingly wet springs encouraging the fungal disease tulip fire (blight), it's more important than ever. A good frost or two is an important part of protecting them from blight and, often for us, the frosts don't set in until November and December. Tulip fire's spores are wiped out in the soil if it gets properly cold, but it's worth going for a belt and braces approach: wash your pots with a natural disinfectant such as Citrox before planting. This kills any spores that might be carried over from one season to the next.

At this time of year, we also keep planting pots and bowls of hyacinths to take us through the grey months of January and February (see p343). We plant them into bowls of bulb fibre, the bulb nose just below the compost surface, and stash them somewhere dark and cool. You'll be grateful come the new year.

Planting Tulips in Bulb Lasagnes

For dense and flowery pots of tulips, I plant them in what the Dutch call a 'bulb lasagne', layering them up one on top of the other. The emergent shoots of the lower level just bend around anything they hit sitting over their heads and keep on growing.

In our large long toms and Danish terracotta pots, I plant 15 bulbs in each layer, so there are 45 bulbs in a triple decker. If you choose the right mixture of tulips, you'll get the correct heights of stem to work well together and flowers that come all at the same time.

I often add a final fourth layer of iris or crocus, just poking them in beneath the compost surface. *Iris reticulata* is a wonderful way to start the whole procession off in February, just when we need a little cheer, and the elongated foliage that comes later makes a good foil for the tulip's flowers.

Previous page left Pots of
Agapanthus 'Midnight Blue'
in our open-fronted barn in
winter. This variety can take
cold but not wet and cold.
By protecting them from rain,
they have thrived through
severe winters for 20 years.
Previous page right
Planting *Iris reticulata*
bulbs to form the final layer
of a bulb lasagne.

Below Measuring the
layers while planting a
tulip bulb lasagne.

- If you're planting a mix of bulbs, the largest and latest flowering bulb goes in deepest, moving to the smallest and earliest in the top layer. The larger the bulb, the more starch it has for the longer journey into the light, when the leaves start to photosynthesise and make their own food.
- If you're planting just tulips to flower at the same time, mix them up together in a bucket and plant randomly.
- Plant the bulbs slightly further apart than you would if you were planting them in a single layer. Around 2–3cm (1in) apart.

- Plant the bottom layer at a depth of 30cm (12in) and the middle at 20cm (8in). The top layer of bulbs should be planted 10cm (4in) below the compost's surface.

Once all the layers are planted, we have experimented with many different ways to prevent squirrels or rats devouring the bulbs or digging them up to store them. You can firmly attach chicken wire over the top of the pot. That works but doesn't look great. We have also tried chilli powder – and chilli flakes – spread densely over the compost surface and,

Below Rose prunings resting
over a pot of bulbs to help keep
marauding rodents at bay.

sadly, this is not guaranteed squirrel proof.
But we have found this combined with
properly spiky twigs and branches of things
like holly, dried sea holly flowers and, maybe
best of all, very thorny rose prunings, works
well. It also looks okay – natural twigs are a bit
easier on the eye than wire.

We have also found that adding pot toppers
helps to deter rodents from having a bulb feast.
Wallflowers are effective, as is *Ammi visnaga*,
cerinthe and violas. It's getting late to put these
out (particularly in the north, where frosts
are likely to have started) but if the pot topper

plants have been potted on to prevent them
becoming pot-bound, it's good to add these now
in the final layer (see p381 for instructions on
planting and p118 for some options).

Lifting Dahlias

If you have dahlias in pots, the tubers need to
be brought in for the winter.

- After the first hard, leaf-blackening frost
  in November or December, cut the plants
  back to 10cm (4in).
- Dig them up or knock them out of the pot.
- Dry off the tubers indoors for 1–2 weeks.
  Do this by standing them upside down to
  drain the stems. We put ours in crates in
  the polytunnel.
- Remove any remaining loose soil and then
  pack the tubers into boxes of dry compost.
- Store so that they are frost-free in a shed
  or under the bench in the greenhouse.
  You can keep them in a cellar or cold room
  indoors but avoid warmth or they may rot.

Forcing Paperwhite Narcissi

For the earliest winter flowers, paperwhites
are your best bet. This whole crew originate
from a species *Narcissus papyraceus*, wild in
the Mediterranean and Middle East, but not
reliably hardy. Many varieties are available

Opposite Paperwhites as a table
centrepiece supported with
silver birch. I hang baubles from
the twigs as we get closer to
Christmas. Kept cool, this looks
good for over a month.

Next page Snow covering
everything, including
our long tom pots, in the
Perennial Cutting Garden.

and are easy to force into flower indoors. The bulbs begin to grow as soon as they are planted, with flowers appearing in about a month. They thrive in a moist, fertile potting mix. Cool temperatures between 10–18°C (50–65°F) and indirect light will help to prolong the bloom time.

Plants can be balanced on stones, gravel or shingle with a bit of water at the container base. But my favourite way to grow them – and make the most impact – is in a layered wedding cake, with one pot on top of another.

- You need two pots of different sizes. The first should be as large a pot or bowl as you can fit in the middle of your table to form the base of the arrangement, with a smaller one for stacking on top. You can add a third if you have space. Narcissi bulbs are large, with an extensive root structure, so deep pots are ideal.
- You can plant the bulbs initially in plastic pots and then move them into your final pot as they come into flower or do them straight into their final planting pot.
- Plant the bulbs about 2–3cm (1in) apart into bulb fibre. You can also use loam-based compost, lightened with some grit. Plant the bulbs just below the soil surface.
- Most varieties take 16–18 weeks from planting to flowering, but not paperwhites. These are super speedy and need only 4–6. And they don't require a period in the dark either, which makes them doubly easy.

- Keep the compost moist but not dripping wet.
- Once they shoot, with leaves up to 20–25cm (8–10in), bring them into the warm.
- If they're still in plastic pots, transfer them into your final pots. Pack the flowering bulbs in as thickly as you can.
- Poke in a handful of silver birch or hazel twigs in every pot layer to support them, spacing them at about 10cm (4in) around the outside of each pot, making sure you've pushed them right to the bottom.
- Bend the twigs at right angles, 15–20cm (6–8in) from the compost surface. Then start twisting and weaving each onto its neighbour, doing so horizontally. When you arrive back at where you started, bend back over to secure the end of the last bit of twig. This looks lovely and staves off collapse, keeping the whole thing looking good for longer.
- As a final touch, drape the twigs with silver and clear glass baubles and surround the whole thing with a halo of candles on the table.
- Once it's all over, bear in mind that the paperwhites are not hardy (go for N. 'Avalanche' and 'Geranium' if you're looking for a hardy one), so once they've finished flowering, leave them in their pots for next year, or dry them off and repot them again next autumn.

Index

Page numbers in **bold** indicate
a main entry; numbers in *italic*
refer to the illustrations

A

aconites 379
Agapanthus 13, *174*, 175–6, *210–11*,
   278, *398*
   A. 'Midnight Star' *230*, 239, 278, *278*
Agastache 278, 372, *372*
   A. aurantiaca 372
   A. × *hybrida* 'Arizona Sandstone'
   278, *279*
   A. pallidiflora 'Rose Mint' 372
Allium karataviense 188, 190
   A. tuberosum 372, *373*
alyssum *see Lobularia maritima*
Amaranthus caudatus 'Viridis' 298
amaryllis *see Hippeastrum*
Amelanchier 104, *122–3*
   A. × *lamarckii* 'Robin Hill' 41
Anagallis arvensis 364
   A. monellii 16, 353, 364, *365*
Anemone 342, *342*
   A. blanda 'White Splendour' 70–1, *70*
   A. coronaria 55, *61*, 342–3
   A.c. 'Fullstar Red' 342
   A.c. 'Galilee Giant' 342
   A.c. 'Jerusalem Blue' 342
Angelonia angustifolia 'Archangel
   Dark Rose' 20, *21*
annuals 127, 174–5, 200–1, 206,
   229, 231
Anthriscus 'Ravenswing' 118, *118*, 381
   A. sylvestris 118, *118*
Antirrhinum (snapdragon) 43, 82,
   83, 85, 125, *129*, 197, 271, 372
   A. majus 236
   A. m. 'Appleblossom' 85, 232
   A. m. 'Chantilly Light Salmon' 236
   A. m. 'Giant White' 85, 232
   A. m. 'Liberty Classic Crimson' 85
   A. m. 'Opus Red Beauty' 372, *373*
   A. m. 'Sonnet Crimson' *237*
   A. m. 'Sonnet Orange Scarlet' *45*, *237*
   A. m. 'Sonnet Purple' *237*
   A. m. 'Sonnet Burgundy' *45*
aphids 126, 267, 377

Arctotis 180, 277, 309, 364
   A. × *hybrida* 'Flame' 364
   A. × *h.* 'Wine' 364, *365*
Argyranthemum 277, 278, 309, 364
   A. 'Grandaisy Deep Red' 249,
   364, *365*
   A. 'Grandaisy Red' *6*, 273, 278, *279*
   A. 'Lolly' *352*
   A. 'Madeira Crested Merlot' 364
   A. 'Madeira Red' *6*
Armeria pseudarmeria 'Ballerina Red'
   134
Asarina 313, 336
Asparagus setaceus 185
Athyrium niponicum var. *pictum* 284, *284*
aubrieta 277
auricula *see Primula auricula*

B

Backhousia citriodora 320, *321*
bacopa *see Chaenostoma*
basil 320
bay trees 47
bees 55, 95, 139, 291
Begonia 284
   B. 'Glowing Embers' 284, *285*
   B. 'Gryphon' 284, 384
Bidens 277, 364
   B. 'Hot and Spicy' 364, *365*
   B. 'Spicy Margarita' 364
biennials 206, 225, 228
black spot 379
Borago 372, *373*
botrytis 87, 311, 319
box balls 389
Brachyscome 366, *366*
   B. 'Blue Star' 366
Briza 174
Browallia 284
   B. speciosa 'Blue Bells' 284, *284*
Brunnera 40, 284
   B. 'Jack Frost' 284, *285*
Buddleja davidii 13, 175, 277, 319,
   372, *373*

B. d. 'Buzz Hot Raspberry' *237*
B. d. 'Buzz Indigo' 322, *322*, 372, *373*
B. d. 'Buzz Lavender' 43, *238*, 239, 319
B. d. 'Buzz White' 372
B. d. 'Buzz Wine' 278, *279*, 319, 372
B. d. 'Dreaming Lavender' 372
B. d. 'Dreaming White' 319
B. d. 'Hot Raspberry' 372
bulbs: buying 310–11
   designing pots 15–16, 310–11
   dismantling pots 175, 197–8
   dwarf bulbs 118
   forcing 343–5, *345*, 390, 401–3
   planting 130, 342, 379–81
butterflies 139, 212, 236, 291

C

Calceolaria 'Kentish Hero' *44*, *312*
Calendula 126
   C. officinalis 'Indian Prince' 175,
   208, *209*, 212
Calibrachoa 39, 43, 205, *210–11*,
   231, 258, **260–1**, *263*
   C. 'Appleblossom' 263, *263*
   C. 'Black Cherry' 260
   C. 'Cabaret Red' 261
   C. 'Double Can-Can Wine Red' *44*, 260
   C. 'Double Dark Lavender' 263
   C. 'Double Ruby' 261, *261*
   C. 'Double White Improved' 263
   C. 'Doublette Love Swept' 261
   C. 'Million Bells Crackling Fire' 260
   C. 'Million Bells Red' 260–1
   C. 'Million Bells Terracotta' 261, *261*
   C. 'Orange Punch' 260, *261*
   C. Superbells 'Double Ruby' 256
   C. Superbells Unique 'Tropical
   Sunrise' *5*, *216*
Capsicum annuum 'Pearls'
   348–53, *348*
Cardiospermum halicacabum 334, *334*
cardoons 32, 381
Caryopteris 372–3

C. × *clandonensis* 'First Choice' 373, *373*

Cerinthe 39, 97, 126, 342, 401
    C. major 'Purpurascens' *34*, 90, 118, *119*, 175, 208–12, *209*, 373, *373*

Chaenostoma (bacopa) *238*, 366, *366*
    C. cordatum 'Snowflake' 366

chard, rainbow 120

Chasmanthium latifolium 43

Cheilanthes lanosa 286, 287

chervil 119, *119*

chillies 348–53, *348*

Chimonanthus praecox 257

choisya 142

Citrus 322, *323*

Clematis 238, 322
    C. 'Alionushka' 238
    C. 'Blue River' 238
    C. × *durandii* 238
    C. 'Madame Julia Correvon' *254–5*
    C. 'Prince Charles' 238
    C. 'Sweet Sensation' 322, *323*
    C. terniflora var. *mandshurica* 322

Cleome 'Señorita Rosalita' 20, *21*

climbers 13, 43, 127, 201, 229, 295, 313–14, **328–37**

Cobaea 125, 173, 201, 229, 313, 314
    C. scandens 83, 84–5, *85*, 329, *330–1*, 334, *335*, *350–1*, 366
    C. s. f. *alba* 329, 334, 366, *367*

Coleus 284, *285*
    C. argentatus 'Silver Shield' *238*
    C. 'FlameThrower Salsa Roja' *259*, 368, *369*

comfrey 225, *226*, 227

compost 84, 86, 126, 198

conifers, dwarf 389

Cosmos 171, 172, 231–2, 236, 273, 347, 374
    C. 'Apricot Lemonade' 232
    C. atrosanguineus 16, 291, 347
    C. bipinnatus 'Apricotta' *128*, 232, 291, 374
    C. b. 'Rubenza' *128*, 232, 291, 374
    C. b. 'Sonata Carmine' *128*, 232
    C. b. 'Sonata White' *22*, 23, 128, 231, 304, 374, *374*
    C. b. 'Velouette' *233*
    C. 'Dazzler' 374
    C. 'Fizzy Rose Picotee' 302
    C. peucedanifolius 'Flamingo' 347, *352*

C. 'Pink Flamingo' 291

C. 'Pink Popsocks' 232

C. 'Purity' 374

C. 'Sensation Pinkie' 232

C. 'Xanthos' 374

C. 'Xsenia' 232, 374

Crocus 13, 55, 89, 379, 390, 399
    C. chrysanthus 'Ladykiller' 54
    C. c. 'Snow Bunting' 54
    C. minimus 'Spring Beauty' *46*, 54
    C. s. subsp. *atticus* 'Firefly' 54, *54*, 118
    C. tommasinianus 54

Cuphea subuligera 44, 249, *295*
    C. 'Torpedo' *8*

cutting gardens 174

cutting patch pots 208–12

cuttings 125, 171, 311
    dahlias *176*, 177
    Pelargonium 87, 242
    planting 200–1
    potting on 341
    Salvia 87

Cyclamen 53, 55, 89
    C. coum *46*, *391*

Cymbalaria muralis 277

Cynara cardunculus 118, *119*

D

daffodil *see Narcissus*

Dahlia 12, 13, 15, 39, 125, 128–9, 171, *176*, 177, 180, 197, 198, 200, 201, 202, 225, 229, 231, *234–5*, 271, *272*, **288–307**, *309*, 313, 341, 383, 401
    D. 'Abigail' 20, *21*, 291, 296, 298, *298*, 370
    D. 'Adam's Choice' 298, *299*
    D. 'Bishop of Auckland' 291, 297, 298, *299*
    D. 'Bishop of Llandaff' 297
    D. 'Bishop of York' 374, *374*
    D. 'Bishop's Children' 128, 236, 291, 297, 298, *299*, *330–1*, *349*
    D. 'Black Jack' 19, 289, 297, 298, *299*, *414*
    D. 'Blue Bayou' *290*, 291, 298
    D. 'Brown Sugar' 297, 298, *299*
    D. 'Dahlegria Tricolore' 298, *299*
    D. 'Dalaya Devi' *8*, 23, *23*, 82, 205, 289, 300, *300*

D. 'Dreamy Nights' 205, *288*, 289, 300, *300*, *350–1*

D. 'Evanah' 304, *304*

D. 'Frizzle Sizzle' 291, 301, *301*

D. 'Happy Days Cream White' 304, *304*

D. 'Happy Single Kiss' 304, *305*

D. 'Heroine' 304, *305*

D. 'Honka Fragile' 297

D. 'Josie' 205, 291, 295, 301, *301*, *316–17*

D. 'Josudi Mercury' 297, 301, *301*

D. 'Kelsey Annie Joy' 291, 297, 304, *305*

D. 'Labyrinth' 297

D. 'Lou Farman' 291, 297, 302, *303*

D. 'Meena Sanya' 300, *300*

D. 'Molly Raven' *14*, 297, 304, *305*

D. 'Mystic Dreamer' *5*, *306*, 307

D. 'Night Silence' *306*, 307

D. 'Rip City' 289

D. 'Rosie Raven' 296, 302, *303*

D. 'Roxy' 302, *303*

D. 'Samourai' 302, *303*

D. 'Sarah Raven' 291, 296, *306*, 307, 374

D. 'Schipper's Bronze' *295*, 302, *303*

D. 'Schipper's Choice' 302, *303*

D. 'Small World' 297, 304, 307, *307*

D. 'Top Mix Salmon' 289, 307, *307*

D. 'Totally Tangerine' *42*, 205, 291, 295, 301, 302, *303*

D. 'Vino' 297, 302, *303*

D. 'Waltzing Matilda' *45*, *290*, 291, *294*, 297, 302, *303*

Daphne 322
    D. odora 'Aureomarginata' 322, *323*
    D. × *transatlantica* 'Eternal Fragrance' 322
    D. × *t.* 'Pink Fragrance' 322

deadheading 225, 228, *228*, *308*, 309, 379

Dianthus 322
    D. 'Green Trick' 366, *367*
    D. 'Mrs Sinkins' 322
    D. 'Pink Kisses' 322, *323*

Diascia 278
    D. barberae 216
    D. b. 'Blackthorn Apricot' 216
    D. 'Little Tango' 218, *219*
    D. personata 215–16, *272*, 278, *279*

Dichondra argentea 'Silver Falls' 366, 181

Digitalis (foxglove) 41, 225, 228, 265, 374–5
  D. ferruginea 375
  D. lanata 'Café Crème' 374–5
  D. parviflora 'Milk Chocolate' 375
  D. purpurea 'Sutton's Apricot' 374
  D. × valinii 'Foxlight Ruby Glow' 374, *374*
dismantling pots 175
dividing plants 175–7
dome supports 229
drought-tolerant plants **276–81**
dwarf bulbs 118

E
Echeveria 278
  E. elegans 278, *279*
  E. lilacina 385
Echinacea 375
  E. 'Green Envy' 375
  E. 'Magnus' *374*, 375
  E. 'Sombrero Hot Coral' 375
Eragrostis spectabilis 295
Erigeron 82, 126, 200, 265, 277, 353
  E. karvinskianus 19, *42*, 85, 184, *186–7, 204*, 206, 278, *279*, 366, *367*
Eryngium giganteum 'Silver Ghost' 220, *220*
Erysimum (wallflower) 38, 43, 97, 119, 133, 139, *145*, 225, 228, 265, 322, 381, 401
  E. cheiri 'Blood Red' 139, 322
  E. c. 'Fire King' 139, 322
  E. c. 'Spring Breeze Sunset' 322, *323*
  E. 'Sugar Rush Purple Bicolour' 4, 119, *119*
Eucomis 283, 284
  E. bicolor *286*, 287
  E. comosa 'Sparkling Burgundy' 284, *352*
  E. 'Leia' 284, *285*
Euphorbia 142
  E. 'Breathless Blush' 180
  E. characias subsp. *wulfenii* 'John Tomlinson' *96*
  E. hypericifolia 'Diamond Frost' 19, 180, *180*, 200, 353
  E. oblongata 175, 208, *209*, 212

F
fertilisers 225, 227, 265–7, 309, 341
Festuca glauca 366

Ficus carica 'Brown Turkey' 348
  F. c. 'Little Miss Figgy' 348
figs 198, *222–3*, 348
fleece, horticultural 87
Foeniculum vulgare 119
  F. v. 'Giant Bronze' 119, *119*
forcing bulbs 343–5, *345*, 390, 401–3
form, designing pots 43–5
foxglove *see Digitalis*
Fritillaria 89, **90–4**, *92–3*, 134, 198
  F. 'Early Sensation' 91, *95*
  F. 'Helena' 91
  F. imperialis 91, *374*, 375
  F. i. 'Sunset' 91, *91*
  F. meleagris 55, 91, *95*
  F. persica 91
  F. raddeana 94, 95
frost protection 87, 201
Fuchsia 265
  F. 'Dying Embers' *352*, 366, 385
  F. microphylla 366, *367*
  F. m. subsp. *hemsleyana* 'Silver Lining' 385
  F. paniculata 385
  F. triphylla 'Eruption' *259*
fungal diseases 355, 399

G
Galanthus (snowdrop) 55, 89, 379
  G. elwesii 54, 390
  G. nivalis 'S. Arnott' *46*, 53
Gaura 277
  G. lindheimeri 278, *279*, 284, *285*
  G. l. 'The Bride' 278, 284, *285*
  G. l. 'Sparkle White' 278, 284, *285*
  G. l. 'Whiskers Deep Rose' 278, *279*
Gazania 180, 271, *272*, 277, 281
  G. 'Daybreak Bright Orange' *280*, 281, *316–17*
Geranium maderense 384
Gerbera 13, 234–5, 271, *272*
  G. 'Sweet Sunset' *316–17*
Gladiolus murielae 277, *280*, 281
Glandularia 'Aztec Silver Magic' 44, *328*
Gloriosa superba 'Tomas de Bruyne' 273
Gypsophila 83
  G. elegans 'Kermesina' 208

H
half-hardy annuals 127, 133, 171, 200–1, 229, 231

hardy annuals 171, 174–5, 206, 341
Helianthus (sunflower) 126, 171, 172, 173, 375
  H. annuus 'Micro Sun' 173, 375
  H. a. 'Ms Mars' 173, *374*, 375
  H. a. 'Sonja' 375
Helichrysum petiolare 'Silver' 44
Heliophila coronopifolia 208, *209*
Heliotropium (heliotrope) 311, 319, 341, 375
  H. arborescens 'Dwarf Marine' 324
  H. a. 'Marine' *23*, 375
  H. a. 'Midnight Sky' *238, 239, 318*, 319, *321*, 324
  H. a. 'Reva' *315*, 319, *321*, 324, *324*, 375, *375*
Helleborus 55, 89, 133, 203, 379, 381
  H. × ballardiae 'Maestro' 379, 389
  H. × b. 'Merlin' 379
  H. niger 203, 379, *388*, 389–90
  H. n. 'Potter's Wheel' 389
  H. n. 'Snowdrift' 389
  H. × sahinii 'Winterbells' 389
herbs 119, 342
Heuchera 120, 175, 203, 225, 287, 381
  H. 'Citronelle' 287
  H. 'Crème Brûlée' 120
  H. 'Peach Flambé' 120, 287
  H. sanguinea 'Splendens' *25*
  H. 'Sugar Berry' *286*, 287
  H. 'Wild Rose' 120, *120, 182–3*
× *Heucherella* 120
  × *H.* 'Sweet Tea' 120
Hibiscus acetosella 'Mahogany Splendor' *14*, 43, 44, 127, 304
Hippeastrum (amaryllis) 344–5, *345*, 389, 390, **392–7**
  H. 'Alfresco' 394, *394*
  H. 'Emerald' 55, 394, *395*
  H. 'Green Magic' 55, 394, *395*
  H. 'Lemon Lime' 394, *395*
  H. 'Lemon Star' 394, *395*
  H. 'Mandela' 394, *395*
  H. 'Marilyn' *396*, 397
  H. 'Nymph' 55, *392*, 393, 397, *397*
  H. papilio 397, *397*
  H. 'Picotee' 397, *397*
  H. 'Tosca' 397, *397*
honesty 97, *140*
honeysuckle *see Lonicera*
Hosta 287
  H. 'Sum and Substance' *286*, 287

Hyacinthus (hyacinth) 53, 55, **66–79**, 133, 175, 309, 324, *324*, 342, 343–4, 379, 389, 390, 399
  H. orientalis 'Aida' 74, *74*
  H. o. 'Aiolos' 76
  H. o. 'Anastasia' 68, 74, *74*
  H. o. 'Anna Marie' 78, *79*
  H. o. 'Annabelle' 78, *79*
  H. o. 'Blue Star' 74, *75*
  H. o. 'Carnegie' 76, *76*
  H. o. 'China Pink' 78, *79*
  H. o. 'City of Bradford' 78, *78*
  H. o. 'City of Harlem' 76, *76*
  H. o. 'Dark Dimension' 74, *75*
  H. o. 'Delft Blue' 70, 74, *75*, 78
  H. o. 'Eros' 72, *73*
  H. o. 'L'Innocence' *70*, 71, 76, *76*
  H. o. 'Jan Bos' 72–3, *73*
  H. o. 'Miss Saigon' 72, *72*
  H. o. 'Multiflora White' 76, *77*
  H. o. 'Peter Stuyvesant' 74, *75*
  H. o. 'Pink Festival' *68*, 73, *73*
  H. o. 'Purple Sensation' *50–1*, 72, *73*, 78
  H. o. 'Purple Star' *70*, 74, *75*
  H. o. 'Sky Jacket' 78, *78*
  H. o. 'Splendid Cornelia' 78, *79*
  H. o. 'White Pearl' 76, *391*
  H. o. 'Woodstock' *66*, 68, *69*, 72, *73*
  H. o. 'Yellowstone' 76
Hydrangea 13
  H. macrophylla 'Wedding Gown' 368
  H. paniculata 'Limelight' 238–9
  H. p. 'Little Lime' *238*, 239, *286*, 287, 368, *368*
  H. petiolaris 287

I
Iceland poppy *see Papaver nudicaule*
Ipomoea 15, 265, 295, 313, 314, 332–3
  I. batatas 333, 334, 357
  I. b. 'Blackie' 334
  I. b. 'Marguerite' 334, *335*
  I. b. 'SolarTower Black' 82, 333, 334, *354*, 368
  I. b. 'Sweet Caroline Light Green' 334
  I. lobata 127, *272*, 333, 335, *335*, 368, *368*
  I. purpurea 'Grandpa Ott' 332, 335, *335*
  I. quamoclit 332–3, 336, *336*
  I. tricolor 'Heavenly Blue' 332, 335
Iris 13, 55, 89, 375, 379, 390

  I. 'Black Gamecock' 375
  I. histrioides 53, 375
  I. reticulata 53, 90, 118, 375, 399
  I. r. 'Alida' 53, *54*, 375, *375*
  I. r. 'Harmony' *52*, 53, *54*
  I. r. 'Purple Hill' 53
irrigation 265
Isotoma axillaris 'Gemini Blue' 44

J
Jasminum officinale 'Clotted Cream' 324
  J. polyanthum 324, *324*
Jiffy-7's 126, 172–3, *172*

K
kale 120, *120*, 348, *349*

L
Lantana 281
  L. camara 280, 281
Lathyrus odoratus 'Anniversary' 212
  L. o. 'Blue Velvet' 212
  L. o. 'Earl Grey' 212, *213*
  L. o. 'Matucana' 212, 265
  L. o. 'Nimbus' 212, *213*
  see also sweet peas
Lavandula (lavender) 198, 281, 319, 376
  L. angustifolia 'SuperBlue' 278, *279*, *280*, 281
  L. dentata 23, 376
  L. 'Hidcote' 376
  L. 'Miss Muffett' 376, *376*
  L. stoechas 376
lemon verbena 353
Leucojum aestivum 40
Lilium (lily) 129, *286*, 287, 325
  L. 'Casa Blanca' 325
  L. regale 283, 325
  L. speciosum var. *album* 287
  L. s. var. *rubrum* 129, 273, 283, 287
  L. s. 'Uchida' 129, 287
  L. 'Stargazer' *324*, 325
lily beetle 95, 267, 283, 325, 375
Linaria 83, 126, 174, 206–7, 265
  L. maroccana 'Little Sweeties Mix' 206, *209*
Lobularia maritima (alyssum) 325
  L. m. 'Lavender Stream' 184
  L. m. 'Snow Princess' 184, *184*, 325
  L. m. 'Summer Stream' *324*, 325

Lonicera (honeysuckle) 13, 175
  L. periclymenum 'Chic et Choc' *237*, 238, *324*, 325
  L. p. 'Rhubarb and Custard' 238, 325
Lophospermum 336
  L. erubescens 286, 287, 336
  L. e. 'Bridal Bouquet' 336
Lotus berthelotii 45, 200

M
Macleaya 254–5
Malus 'Comtesse de Paris' 139
  M. 'Evereste' 139
  M. × *robusta* 'Red Sentinel' 139
Maurandya 336
  M. scandens 'Mystic Rose' 336
  M. s. 'Violet' *328*, 336, *337*
Mentha × *piperita* f. *citrata* 320
mice 84
mildew 267
mint 320
mizuna 'Red Knight' 120, *121*
modular trays 126, 172–3
Muscari 92–3, 134, 138, 189, 198, 342, 379, 390
  M. armeniacum 'Siberian Tiger' *4*, *107*, 138
  M. a. 'Valerie Finnis' *138*
  M. aucheri 'Blue Magic' *138*
  M. 'Baby's Breath' 113
  M. 'Big Smile' *138*
  M. 'Esther' 138
  M. 'Helena' 138
  M. 'Pink Sunrise' *135*, 138, *138*
mustards 120

N
Narcissus 13, 38, 89, **104–17**, 133, 175, 198, 310, 342, 379, *382*
  N. 'Actaea' 325
  N. 'Arctic Bells' 107
  N. 'Avalanche' 130, 390, 403
  N. 'Baby Boomer' 107, 116, *116*
  N. bulbocodium 107
  N. b. 'Golden Bells' 107, 116, *116*
  N. 'Canaliculatus' *105*, 107, 110, *111*
  N. 'Cragford' *52*, 53, 130, 325, 390
  N. 'Elka' 106, 110, *111*
  N. 'Falconet' 116, *116*
  N. 'Frosty Snow' *104*, 107, 114
  N. 'Geranium' 403
  N. 'Grand Soleil d'Or' 53, 107, 116, *117*

N. 'Hawera' 107, 110, *111*
N. 'Inbal' *108–9*
N. 'Katie Heath' 107, *108–9*, 110, *111*
N. 'Kokopelli' 107, *108–9*, 116, *117*
N. 'Lemon Drops' 107, *108–9*, 112, *112*
N. 'Lieke' 325
N. 'Martinette' *108–9*
N. 'Minnow' 4, 107, *107*, 112, *112*
N. 'Moonlight Sensation' 325
N. 'More and More' 117, *117*
N. papyraceus 325, 401–3
N. 'Pink Charm' 106, *108–9*, 112, *112*
N. 'Prinses Amalia' *4, 107*, 112, *112*
N. 'Prom Dance' *108–9*
N. 'Quail' 117, *117*
N. 'Sailboat' *40, 94, 95, 107, 112*, 113
N. 'Segovia' 106, 113, *113*, 325
N. 'Silver Chimes' *41, 107*, 113, *113*
N. 'Sir Winston Churchill' 106, 113, *113*
N. 'Stainless' 106, *108–9*, 114, *114*
N. 'Starlight Sensation' 114, *114*, 325, *325*
N. 'Tête-à-Tête' 107, 117, *117*, 390
N. 'Thalia' *41, 107*, 114, *115*
N. 'White Petticoat' 107, 114, *115*
N. 'W.P. Milner' *52*
N. 'Xit' *17, 41, 106, 108–9*, 114, *115*, 325
N. 'Ziva' 114, *115*
Nasturtium 265, *349*
Nemesia 13, 180, 197, 205, *210–11*, **214–21**, *234–5*, 265
N. 'Blue Lagoon' 220, *220*
N. 'Blueberry Ice' 221, *221*
N. 'Boysenberry' 218, *218, 354*
N. fruticans 218
N. f. 'Framboise' *5, 216*, 218
N. f. 'Mirabelle' *217*, 218
N. f. 'Myrtille' 218, *219*
N. f. 'Wisley Vanilla' 218, 319, 353
N. 'Karoo Dark Blue' 218, *219*
N. 'Lady Anne' 219, *219*
N. 'Lady Lisa' *20, 21, 214*, 215, 216, 219
N. 'Lady Ruby' 219
N. 'Nesia Burgundy' 220, *220*
N. 'Nesia Tropical' 220
N. 'Nesia Tutti Frutti' 220
N. 'Papaya' 221, *221*
N. 'Sunsatia Plus Papaya' *5, 216*

Nerine 384
N. bowdenii 'Mister John' 384
N. b. 'Mister Nick' 384
nettles 227
Nicotiana (tobacco plant) 283, *286*, 287
N. alata 'Grandiflora' 41, 283, 287, 320, 325
N. sylvestris 283
N. s. 'Only the Lonely' 41, 127, 325, *325*
N. 'Whisper Mixed' *282*, 283
nitrogen 227

O
Ocimum 'African Blue' 320
Onopordum acanthium 32
Osteospermum 39, 180, 197, 277, 309, 368
O. '3D Banana Shake' *276*
O. 'Akila White Purple Eye' *22, 23, 230*
O. 'Erato Blue' 319
O. 'Erato Compact Blue' *276*
O. 'Orsett' 246, *246*
O. 'Purple Sun' *276*, 368, *369*
O. 'Serenity Red' *276*
O. 'Serenity Rose Magic' *276*

P
Panicum 128
P. capillare 'Sparkling Fountain' 38, 295, 302
P. 'Frosted Explosion' *42, 43, 127*, 291
pansy see Viola
Papaver nudicaule (Iceland poppy) 55, 225, 228, 265, 376
P. rhoeas 'Amazing Grey' 126, 172, 376, *376*
paperwhite daffodil 53, 114, 130, 325, 389, 390, 401–3, *402*
parsley 119
Pelargonium 12, 38, 82, 87, 181–4, 197, 198, 205, 207, 228, 231, **240–53**, **256–63**, 267, 271, 273, 277, 281, 309, *310*, 311, 320, 368, 383–4, *386–7*
P. 'Aldwyck' 244, *244*
P. 'Appleblossom Rosebud' 250
P. 'April Hamilton' 246, *247*, 368, 383
P. 'Ardens' 244, *245*
P. 'Ashby' 181, *185*, 244, *245*
P. 'Attar of Roses' 200, *222–3, 238*, 239, 252, *252*, 319, 320

P. 'Aurora' 19, 181, *240*, 244, *245*, 383, *385*
P. 'Barbe-Bleu' 246, *247*
P. 'Chocolate Peppermint' 181, 200, *240*, 242, *252*, 253, 383–4
P. 'Clorinda' 244, *245*
P. 'Cola Bottles' *315*
P. crispum 'Cy's Sunburst' 253, 320
P. 'Decora Red' 249
P. 'Deerwood Lavender Lass' 200, 250, *250*
P. denticulatum 'Filicifolium' 384
P. 'Designer White' 250, *250*
P. 'Dragon's Breath' 247, *247*
P. 'Filicifolium' 242, 253, *253*
P. fulgidum 244
P. graveolens 253, *253*
P. 'Horizon Appleblossom' 250, *250*
P. 'Kewensis' 383
P. 'Lara Starshine' 248, 249, *352*
P. lobatum 244
P. 'Lord Bute' *240*, 248, 249
P. 'Marion Saunders' 246, *246*
P. 'Mystery' *240*, 248, 249
P. 'Orange Fizz' 253, *253*
P. 'Orsett' 181
P. 'Pink Aurore' *18*, 19, 246
P. 'Pink Capricorn' 248, 249
P. 'Prince of Orange' *222–3*, 251, *251*
P. 'Queen of the Lemons' 320
P. quercifolium 253, *253*, 368
P. 'Regalia Chocolate' 244
P. 'Shrubland Rose' 19, 248, 249, 273
P. sidoides 249, *249*
P. 'Supreme White' 251
P. 'Surcouf' *240*, 246, *256*, 368, *369*, 383
P. 'Sweet Mimosa' *222–3*, 251, *251*, 280, 281
P. tomentosum 253, *253, 282*, 283, 287, *287*, 320, 368, 384
P. 'Tommy' 181, *240*, 246, *246*, 253, 272, 383
P. 'Tornado Red' 249, *249*
P. 'Viletta White' 251, *251*
P. 'Ville de Paris Red' 249
Pennisetum 'Vertigo' *254–5*, 295
Penstemon 'Garnet' 220, *220*, 368, *369*
P. 'Just Jayne' 368
perennial pots 175
Persicaria orientalis 288

pests 126, 267
  see also aphids, vine weevils *etc*
Petchoa 258
  P. 'BeautiCal Bordeaux' *256*, 260
  P. 'BeautiCal Cinnamon' 258, *261*, 263
  P. 'BeautiCal French Vanilla' 258, 263, *263*
Petunia 39, 197, 205, 207, 231, **256–63**, 271, 273, 341
  P. × *atkinsiana* 'Blue Vein' 262
  P. × *a.* 'White' 262, *262*
  P. axillaris 257, 262, *262*
  P. 'Black Velvet' 260, *260*
  P. 'Easy Wave Burgundy Velour' *259*
  P. 'Lavender Sky' 257
  P. 'Lightning Sky' 257
  P. 'Priscilla' *262*, 263, *272*
  P. 'Sophistica Lime Green' 262, *262*
  P. 'Supertunia Latte' 262–3, *262*
  P. 'Tidal Wave Purple' 260, *261*, *330–1*, 333
  P. 'Tidal Wave Red Velour' 16, 23, *23*, 82, 127, *233*, *254–5*, 257, *259*, 260, 333
  P. 'Tidal Wave Silver' *20*, 127, 257, 263, 333
  P. 'Tumbelina Priscilla' 257
Phaseolus coccineus 336, *337*
  P. c. 'Aurora' 336
  P. c. 'Painted Lady' 336
  P. c. 'Polestar' 336
  P. c. 'Sunset' 336, *337*
  P. c. 'White Lady' 336
Phlox 128
  P. '21st Century Blue' *23*, *318*
  P. '21st Century Blue Star' *20*, 127
  P. '21st Century White' *22*, 23, *230*
  P. 'Crème Brûlée' 127
  P. paniculata 314
Phygelius 13
pinching out *125*, 174
Pittosporum 47
  P. tenuifolium 'Breebay' 389
plans, garden 81
plant lists 82
planting distances 82
Plectranthus 87
  P. ciliatus 180, 287, *287*
  P. c. 'Nico' *282*, 384
Polianthes tuberosa (tuberose) 320, 326, *327*
pollinators 55, 95, 97, 139, 291, **372–7**
polyanthus *see Primula*

pomegranates 273, *352*, 353
positioning pots 39–41
pot-bound plants 175–7
pot liners 198, *199*
pot rings 229
pot toppers **118–21**, 175, 198, 341–2, 379, 381, 401
potash 227
potting on cuttings 341
powdery mildew 267
pricking out 128, *129*, 171
Primula (primrose and polyanthus) 47–8, **58–65**, 128, 134, 172, 175, 203, 225, 376, 379
  P. auricula 62, 133, 203
  P. a. 'Black Jack' 134–8
  P. a. 'Lunar Eclipse' 134–8
  P. a. 'Purple Pip' 134–8
  P. 'Elizabeth Killelay' 62, *63*
  P. forbesii 62
  P. 'Francisca' 62, *63*, 203
  P. 'Garnet' 62, *62*
  P. 'Lilac Lace' 390
  P. malacoides 48, *58*, 62–3, *63*, 173
  P. 'Ooh La La Blood Orange' 63
  P. 'Ooh La La Pastel Pink' *50–1*, 63
  P. 'Snow White' *70*
  P. 'Stella Champagne' 48, 60, *64*, 65, *92–3*, 203
  P. 'Stella Lilac' 60, 65, 376, *376*
  P. 'Stella Neon Violet' 60, 65
  P. 'Stella Scarlet Pimpernel' 65
  P. 'Strong Beer' 65, *65*
  P. vulgaris 'Avondale' 65, *65*
Psammophiliella muralis 'Gypsy Deep Rose' 208, *209*
Punica granatum var. *nana* 352, 353
Puschkinia scilloides var. *libanotica* 113

R
rats 142–3, 400–1
replanting pots 198
Reseda odorata 320, 326, *326*
Rhodochiton 15, 265, 341
  R. atrosanguineus 14, 127, *272*, *312*, *332*, 336, *337*, *346*, 357, 370, *370*
Rhododendron 'Fragrantissimum' 326, *326*
  R. 'Polar Bear' 326
Ricinus communis 330–1
rocket 120
root trainers 83–4, 126

Rosa (rose) 41, 236, 355
  R. 'Little White Pet' 326, *326*
rosemary 47, 198, 389
rosemary beetle 267
Rudbeckia 38, 370, 376, *377*
  R. hirta 'Cherry Brandy' 376
  R. h. 'Sahara' 370, *370*

S
sage 356
salad leaves 120, 342
Salvia 12, 87, 126, 197, 207, 229, 266, 271, 273, 281, 291, 295, 309, 311, 353, **354–63**, 376
  S. 'Amante' 361
  S. 'Amethyst Lips' 358
  S. 'Amistad' *42*, 43, 295, 302, 356, 361, 376, *377*
  S. 'Blue Note' *280*, 281, *346*, 358, *358*
  S. 'Blue Suede Shoes' *356*, *360*, 361
  S. 'Cherry Lips' 358, *359*
  S. 'Dyson's Crimson' 358, *359*
  S. 'Ember's Wish' 361, *361*
  S. 'Fuchsia' 361
  S. greggii 171, 355
  S. g. 'Dyson's Gem' *346*, 358
  S. g. 'Icing Sugar' 362, *362*
  S. g. 'Krystle Pink' 362
  S. g. 'Mirage Cream' 362, *362*
  S. g. 'Mirage Deep Purple' 358
  S. g. 'Mirage Neon Rose' 358, *359*
  S. g. 'Mirage Soft Pink' 362
  S. g. 'Peach Parfait' 355, 362
  S. g. 'Stormy Pink' 355, 362, *363*
  S. 'Hot Lips' 358
  S. involucrata 'Hadspen' 356
  S. × *jamensis* 171
  S. × *j.* 'Sierra San Antonio' 362, *363*
  S. 'Jezebel' *254–5*, 355, 358, *359*, 361
  S. 'Kisses and Wishes' *356*, 362, *363*
  S. 'Lake Baikal' 357
  S. 'Lake Garda' *354*, 357, 361
  S. 'Lake Onega' *259*, *272*, 295, 302, *338–9*, *356*, 357, 361
  S. microphylla 171, 281, 355
  S. m. 'Cerro Potosí' *233*, 355, 358, *359*
  S. 'Nachtvlinder' 355, *360*, 361
  S. patens 355–6
  S. p. 'Cambridge Blue' 355
  S. p. 'Guanajuato' 355
  S. rosmarinus 'Benenden Blue' *178*
  S. 'Royal Bumble' *360*, 361

S. 'Salmia Dark Purple' 361
S. splendens × darcyi 'Roman Red' 361, *361*
S. 'Strawberry Lake' 357, *360*, 361
S. 'Tutti Frutti' 355, 362, *363*
S. viridis 'Blue' *209*, 230
Sambucus nigra 254–5
Sarcococca 326, *327*, 389
S. confusa 257
S. hookeriana var. digyna 'Purple Stem' 326, *327*
Saxifraga × arendsii 48
S. × a. 'Alpino Early Picotee' *50–1, 52*
S. atropurpurea 'Blue Cushion' 376, *377*
S. columbaria 'Flutter Rose Pink' 376
Scabiosa incisa 'Kudo Pink' *5*
Scaevola 370
S. 'Dream Blue' 370, *371*
scented plants **318–27**
Schizanthus 207
Scilla 89
S. mischtschenkoana *52*, 54
S. 'Pink Giant' 89, *94*, 95
seed trays 85, 86–7, *86*, 126, 127
seedlings 84–5, 171
buying 125, 171
pinching out 174
planting out 130–1, 200–1
pricking out 128, *129*, 171
seeds: sowing 83–7, 125, 126–8, 172–3, 225, 228
storing 126–7
shade-tolerant plants **282–7**
Silene latifolia 207
S. pendula 'Sibella Carmine' *206*, 207
S. p. 'Sibella Lilac' *206*, 207
S. p. 'Sibella White' *206*, 207
slugs 201
snails 201
snapdragons see Antirrhinum
snowdrop see Galanthus
sowing seeds 83–7, 125, 126–8, 172–3, 225, 228, 341–2
Sparrmannia africana 273, 281, *281*, 384–5
spinach 'Rubino' 120, *120*
squirrels 142–3, 400–1
storing seeds 126–7
sunflower see Helianthus
supports 202–3, *202*, 229, 313

sweet peas 15, 83–4, *83*, 125, 126, 130–1, *131*, 174, 212, 225, *272*

T
Tagetes 230, 271
T. 'Cinnabar' *288*
T. patula 'Bo Jangle' 376–7, *377*
T. p. 'Burning Embers' 376–7
T. p. 'Konstance' 376–7
teepees 202–3, *202*
thistle, giant 32
Thunbergia 15, 201, 229, 236, 265, 295, 313, 333, *338–9*, 341, 370, *371*
T. alata 200, 333, 336
T. a. 'African Sunset' 82, 127, *294*, 302, 304, *312, 332*, 333, 336, 357
T. a. 'Alba' *328*, 333, 336
T. a. 'Dark Red' 336
T. a. 'Lemon Star' 336
T. a. 'Orange' 333, 336
T. a. 'Orange Diverse' 370
T. a. 'Rose Sensation' 333, 336
T. a. 'Sunny Susy Brownie' 333, 336, *337, 350–1*
T. a. 'Superstar Orange' 336
T. a. 'Tangerine Slice A-Peel' 336
T. a. 'Terracotta' 336
Tithonia 377
T. rotundifolia 'Fiesta del Sol' 377, *377*
tobacco plant see Nicotiana
tomatoes 320, *321*, 377
top dressing pots 174, 175
Trachelospermum jasminoides 230, 327, *327*
tuberose see Polianthes tuberosa
tubers, dahlias 128–9, 177
tulip fire 399
Tulipa (tulips) *10–11*, 13, 38–9, 89, **96–103**, 105, 133, *136–7*, **140–69**, 171, 175, 179–80, 197–8, 310, 342, 393, 399–401, *399*
T. 'Abu Hassan' 150, *150*
T. acuminata *134*, 154, 155, 179, *182–3*
T. 'Amazing Parrot' *154*, 155
T. 'Amber Glow' *142*, 150
T. 'Angélique' 16, *17*, 164, 179
T. 'Antraciet' *4, 36–7*
T. 'Apricot Beauty' *160*, 161, 197
T. 'Apricot Copex' *34*, 161, *161*
T. 'Apricot Delight' 98, *98*

T. 'Apricot Emperor' 98
T. 'Apricot Foxx' *34*, 160, 161
T. 'Apricot Impression' 100, *100*
T. 'Apricot Pride' 98, *99*
T. 'Artist' 147, 158
T. 'Attila Graffiti' *154*, 155
T. 'Avignon' 162
T. bakeri 90
T. b. 'Lilac Wonder' 102
T. 'Ballade Silver' *40*
T. 'Ballerina' *34, 36–7*, 146, 154, 155
T. 'Bastia' 150, *151*
T. 'La Belle Epoque' *25*, 100, 147, 161, 162, *162*
T. 'Bellville' 150, *151*
T. 'Black Hero' *4*, 147, 150, *151*
T. 'Black Parrot' 150, *151*
T. 'Blue Heaven' *160*, 161
T. 'Blue Parrot' 167
T. 'Blumex Favourite' *178*, 179, 180
T. 'Blushing Lady' 146, 161, *161*
T. 'Boa Vista' 164, *164*
T. 'Brown Sugar' *41*, 147, 150, *151*
T. 'Brownie' *41*, 144, 150, *151*
T. 'Bruine Wimpel' 161
T. 'Burgundy' 153, *153*
T. 'Cairo' 152, *152*
T. 'Campbell' 155, *155*
T. 'Caviar' 146
T. 'Chato' 90, 98, *99*, 100, 146
T. 'China Pink' 157
T. 'China Town' 164, *164*
T. clusiana 'Lady Jane' 90, 102, *102*
T. c. 'Peppermintstick' 90
T. 'Concerto' 98, *99, 122–3*, 147
T. 'Continental' *142*
T. 'Copper Image' *34, 140*, 161, *161*, 163
T. 'Cornuta' *134*, 155, 179, *182–3*
T. 'Couleur Cardinal' 145
T. 'Crème Upstar' *140*, 163
T. 'Danceline' *25*
T. Darwin Hybrids 100, 146, 197
T. 'Doll's Minuet' 155, *155*
T. 'Dordogne' 162
T. 'Dream Touch' 152, *152*, 153, 179
T. 'Dreamer' *132*, 164, *165*
T. 'Estella Rijnveld' *156*, 157
T. 'Evergreen' 179
T. 'Exotic Emperor' *34, 40*, 41, 90, 98, *99*, 147, *148–9*, 167
T. 'Finola' 164, *165*

T. 'Flaming Club' *156*, 157
T. 'Flaming Parrot' *156*, 157, 179
T. 'Florosa' 164, *165*
T. 'Foxtrot' 164
T. 'Françoise' 148–9, 164, *165*
T. 'Gavota' *182–3*
T. 'Green King' 167, 179
T. 'Green Mile' 147, *156*, 157
T. 'Green Power' *166*, 167
T. 'Green Star' *166*, 167
T. 'Green Wave' *40*, *166*, 167, 168, 179, 197
T. 'Groenland' 147, 162, *166*, 167
T. 'Harbour Lights' 162, 164
T. 'Havran' *145*, 146, 152, *152*
T. 'Healthcare' 168
T. 'Helmar' *156*, 157, 179
T. 'Honky Tonk' *134*
T. humilis 'Little Beauty' 89, 102, *102*, 103
T. h. 'Odalisque' 89
T. h. 'Persian Pearl' 89, 102, *103*
T. 'Ice Stick' 15, *17*, 90, 97, 147
T. 'Ivory Floradale' 146
T. 'James Last' 167, *167*, 179
T. 'Lasergame' *40*
T. 'Lasting Love' *34*
T. linifolia 'Bronze Charm' 162, *162*
T. 'Louvre Orange' 147, 157, *157*
T. 'Mariette' *34*, 157, *157*
T. 'Menton' 161, 162, *162*
T. 'Merlot' 152, *152*
T. 'Mistress Grey' 167
T. 'Mistress Mystic' 145, *166*, 167, 197
T. 'Muriel' *24*
T. 'Mystic van Eijk' 100, *100*
T. 'Negrita' 146, 197
T. 'Negrita Parrot' *36–7*
T. 'Neper' 53
T. 'Nightrider' *24*, 158, *158*
T. 'Orange Emperor' 90, *96*, 98
T. 'Orange Favourite' *24*
T. 'Orange Marmalade' 145, 158, *158*
T. 'Orange Princess' *4*, 158, *159*
T. 'Orca' *88*, 90, *92–3*, 97, 100, *101*, 102, 121, *121*, 146, 158
T. 'Palmyra' *91*, 100, *101*, *142*
T. 'Pink Star' *140*, 162, *163*, 164
T. praestans 'Shogun' 90, 102, *103*
T. 'Pretty Woman' 19
T. 'Prinses Irene' *145*, 146, 158, *159*

T. 'Purissima' 15, *17*, *34*, *40*, 41, 90, 98, *99*, 147
T. 'Purple Dream' 153, *153*
T. 'Queen Ingrid' 69
T. 'Queen Jewel' 90, 100, *101*
T. 'Queen of Night' 41, *144*, 146, 152, *178*
T. 'Rems Favourite' 168, *168*
T. 'Request' 155
T. 'Ridgedale' *34*, 152, *153*, 163, 179
T. 'Rococo' 147, 158, *159*
T. 'Ronaldo' *52*, 102
T. 'Royal Acres' *4*, 158, *159*
T. 'Sanne' 162, *163*
T. 'Sarah Raven' *18*, 19, *34*, 146, 153, *153*
T. saxatilis 103, *103*
T. 'Silk Road' *140*, 163, *163*
T. 'Silver Cloud' 148–9, 168, *168*
T. 'Silver Parrot' *148–9*
T. 'Slawa' *134*, *144*, 153, *153*
T. 'Spring Green' 98, 145, 147, 168, *169*
T. 'Très Chic' 168
T. 'Tropical Lady' 168, *169*
T. turkestanica 89–90, 103, *103*, *122–3*
T. 'Unique de France' *34*
T. 'Vovos' *134*
T. 'Weber's Parrot' *40*
T. 'White Star' 168, *169*
T. 'White Touch' *25*, *40*, 168, *169*
T. 'White Triumphator' 168
T. 'White Valley' 98, 147

V
Verbena 13, 43, 127, *210–11*, 228, *234–5*, 236, *272*, 370, 377, *377*
V. bonariensis 'Lollipop' 370, 377
V. 'Homestead Purple' *352*
V. peruviana 'Endurascape White Blush' *5*
V. rigida 127, *228*, 236, *288*, 298, *352*, 370, 377
V. 'Showboat Crimson Velvet' 370, *371*
V. 'Showboat Dark Violet' *288*
V. 'Sissinghurst' 236, *237*, *288*, 370
V. 'Superbena Burgundy' *352*
Viburnum opulus 'Sterile' 239
vine weevil 203, 225, 287

Viola (pansy) 53–4, 89, 120, 128, 133, 134, *134*, 179–80, **188–95**, 265, 341, 381, 401
V. 'Beaconsfield' 325, *325*
V. 'Brush Strokes' 192, *192*
V. cornuta 'Antique Shades' 188, 189–90, 192, *193*
V. c. 'Sorbet Lemon Jump Up' 189
V. c. 'Sorbet Phantom' 54, 120, 189, 192, *194*
V. c. 'Sorbet Violet' 120
V. 'Green Goddess' 189, 190, 192, *193*
V. 'Irish Molly' 189, 192, *193*
V. 'Martin' *178*, 180, 192, *193*
V. 'Molly Sanderson' 189
V. 'Roscastle Black' 189
V. 'Tiger Eye Red' 54, 120, *121*, 189–90, 192, *194*, *380*
V. tricolor 120, 189
V. × wittrockiana 194
V. × w. 'Coolwave Raspberry' 194, *195*
V. × w. 'Frizzle Sizzle Burgundy' 195, *195*
V. × w. 'Frizzle Sizzle Lemonberry' *190*
V. × w. 'Matrix Sangria' 195, *195*
V. × w. 'Mystique Peach Shades' 189, 195, *195*
V. × w. 'Nature Antique Shades' *191*, 195, *195*
V. × w. 'Ruffles Dark Heart' *190*, 195
V. × w. 'Ruffles Soft Lavender' *190*, 195
V. × w. 'Ruffles Wine' *190*, 195
Visnaga daucoides 121, *121*, 341

W
wallflower *see Erysimum*
watering 86, 201, 225–7, 265–6, 309, 341, 384
whopper pots 198–9, 200
window boxes 133
wisteria *140*

Z
Zinnia 38, 125, 126, 171, 172, *172*, 225, 271

Acknowledgements

Opposite The towering *Dahlia* 'Black Jack', with deep red flowers and dark foliage, is a beautiful giant for a pot.

The making of this book has been hugely down to the support, dedication and creativity of two people: Josie Lewis and Jonathan Buckley. The three of us have been making and photographing pots at Perch Hill for a great many years and it has been a joy. A vast and heartfelt thank you to you both.

For your incredible hard work and cheerful help in making the garden and its pots look so good every month of the year, thank you again to Josie Lewis, and also to Rebecca Cocker, Colin Pilbeam, Jenny Huddart, Richard Lambden and Katie Schanche.

For horticultural fact-checking and advice, thanks go to four friends in the Netherlands: Dicky Schipper, Carien van Boxtel, Tony Lindhout and Rene Schrama. And in the UK, thanks to the botanist Jamie Compton. I know I'm as safe as I can be in the hands of Jamie and Zena (my editor).

For their general kindness and encouragement, thanks to Caroline Nevile and my agent Caroline Michel and her assistant Kieron Fairweather. At Bloomsbury, thanks go to Rowan Yapp, Lena Hall and Ellen Williams. Thanks to designer Glenn Howard for this, his third book in the *A Year Full of...* series. I think we've truly excelled ourselves this time.

For being encouraging readers along the way, thank you Anita Oakes, Josie Lewis and Kate Hubbard. And to the dynamic, sharp, quick and clever Zena Alkayat, who edited everything and managed the whole book-making process. Zena is a rare and brilliant jewel, and good fun and funny to work with, even when we're really up against it. Thank you again hugely Zena. We always get it done!

Finally, thanks to my husband Adam Nicolson, who is a generous critic but also the greatest enthusiast and fan of the garden as it changes from week to week. If he says a pot is looking good, I know we're spot on, and I rush to ring Jonathan to coax him down to Perch Hill with his camera.

Thank you so very much, all of you.

Most of the plants, bulbs, dahlias and seedlings, plus many of the pots included in this book are available from sarahraven.com